# 15 MINUTE
# GERMAN

from Stephanie + Julia

with lots of love + kisses + hugs :)

# 15 MINUTE
# GERMAN
## LEARN IN JUST 12 WEEKS

SYLVIA GOULDING

**DK**

London, New York, Munich, Melbourne,
and Delhi

**Senior Editor** Angeles Gavira
**Project Art Editor** Vanessa Marr
**DTP Designer** John Goldsmid
**Production Controller** Luca Frassinetti
**Publishing Manager** Liz Wheeler
**Managing Art Editor** Philip Ormerod
**Publishing Director** Jonathan Metcalf
**Art Director** Bryn Walls

Language content for Dorling Kindersley by
g-and-w publishing

Produced for Dorling Kindersley by
Schermuly Design Co.

First published in Great Britain in 2005 by
Dorling Kindersley Limited
80 Strand, London WC2R 0RL
Penguin Group (UK)

4 6 8 10 9 7 5
005-193209-May/2013

Copyright © 2005, 2013 Dorling Kindersley Limited
All rights reserved.

No part of this publication may be reproduced,
stored in a retrieval system, or transmitted,
in any form or by any means, electronic, mechanical,
photocopying, recording, or otherwise, without the
prior written permission of the copyright owners.

A CIP catalogue record is available for this book
from the British Library
ISBN 978-1-4093-3118-6

15 Minute German is available as a book on its own,
in an audio pack with two CDs, or as part of a
complete language pack.

Printed and bound in China by Leo Paper Products LTD.

Discover more at
**www.dk.com**

# CONTENTS

# How to use this book

This main part of the book is devoted to 12 themed chapters, broken down into five 15-minute daily lessons, the last of which is a revision lesson. So, in just 12 weeks you will have completed the course. A concluding reference section contains a menu guide and English-to-German and German-to-English dictionaries.

**Warm up**
Each day starts with a one-minute warm up that encourages you to recall vocabulary or phrases you have learned previously. The time in brackets indicates the amount of time you are expected to spend on each exercise.

**Instructions**
Each exercise is numbered and introduced by instructions that explain what to do. In some cases additional information is given about the language point being covered.

**Cultural/Conversational tip**
These panels provide additional insights into life in Germany and language usage.

**Text styles**
Distinctive text styles differentiate German and English, and the pronunciation guide (see right).

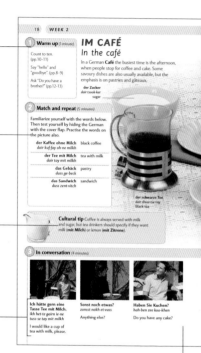

**In conversation**
Illustrated dialogues reflecting how vocabulary and phrases are used in everyday situations appear throughout the book.

**How to use the flap**
The book's cover flaps allow you to conceal the German so that you can test whether you have remembered correctly.

**Revision pages**
A recap of selected elements of previous lessons helps to reinforce your knowledge.

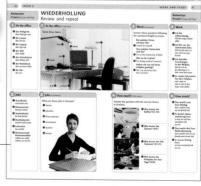

**Useful phrases**
Selected phrases relevant to the topic help you speak and understand.

**Useful phrases** (5 minutes)

Practise these phrases and then test yourself using the cover flap.

Ich hätte gern eine Tasse Kaffee, bitte.
*ikh het-te gairn ie-ne tuss-se kuf-fay, bit-te*

I'd like a cup of coffee, please.

Sonst noch etwas?
*zonsst nokh et-vuss*

Anything else?

Ja, ein Teilchen, bitte.
*yah, ine tile-khen, bit-te*

Yes, a Danish pastry, please.

Was macht das?
*vuss mukht duss*

How much is that?

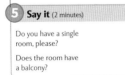

Danke. Was macht das?
*dun-ke, vuss mukht duss*

Thank you. How much is that?

Vier Euro, bitte.
*feer oy-roe, bit-te*

Four euros, please.

**Say it**
In these exercises you are asked to apply what you have learned using different vocabulary.

**5 Say it** (2 minutes)

Do you have a single room, please?

Does the room have a balcony?

## Pronunciation guide

Many German sounds will already be familiar to you, but a few require special attention. Take note of how these letters are pronounced:

**ch** pronounced from the back of the throat, as in the Scottish *loch*

**j** pronounced *y* as in *yes*

**r** rolled, produced from the back of the throat

**s** pronounced either *s* as in *see* or *z* as in *zoo*

**sch** pronounced *sh* as in *ship*

**ß** a special character that represents a double *ss*

**v** pronounced *f* as in *foot*

**w** pronounced *v* as in *van*

**z/tz** pronounced *ts* as in *pets*

German vowels can be tricky, with the same vowel having a number of different pronunciations. Watch out also for these combinations that may look like familiar English sounds, but are pronounced differently in German:

**au** as the English *now*

**ee** as the English *lay*

**ei** as the English *high*

**eu** as the English *boy*

**ie** as the English *see*

After each word or phrase you will find a pronunciation transcription. Read this, bearing in mind the tips above, and you will achieve a comprehensible result. But remember that the transcription can only ever be an approximation and that there is no real substitute for listening to and mimicking native speakers.

**Dictionary**
A mini-dictionary provides ready reference from English to German and German to English for 2,500 words.

**DICTIONARY**
English to German

**MENU GUIDE**

This guide lists the most common terms you may encounter on German menus or when shopping for food. If you can't find an exact phrase, try looking up its component parts.

**Menu guide**
Use this guide as a reference for food terminology and popular German dishes.

# GUTEN TAG
## *Hello*

### 1  Warm up (1 minute)

The Warm Up panel appears at the beginning of each topic. Use it to reinforce what you have already learned and to prepare yourself for moving ahead with the new subject.

In formal situations, Germans greet each other with a handshake. They are addressed with title **Herr** (*for men*) and **Frau** (*for women*) and last name. Nowadays the title **Fräulein** (*Miss*) is rarely used for adult women. Young people may greet each other with a kiss on each cheek.

**Hallo!**
*hal-loe*
Hi!

### 2  Words to remember (2 minutes)

Learn these expressions. Conceal the German with the cover flap and test yourself.

| | |
|---|---|
| **Guten Tag.** <br> *goo-ten tahk* | Good day/ <br> Hello. |
| **Guten Abend/Nacht.** <br> *goo-ten ah-bent/nukht* | Good evening/ <br> night. |
| **Bis bald/morgen.** <br> *biss balt/mor-gen* | See you soon/ <br> tomorrow. |
| **Auf Wiedersehen/ <br> Tschüss.** <br> *owf vee-der-zay- <br> en/tchews* | Goodbye. <br> (formal/ <br> informal) |

**Cultural tip** In addition to proper names, all nouns start with a capital letter in German - for example, **der Tag** (*the day*), as in **Guten Tag** (*good day*).

### 3  In conversation: formal (3 minutes)

**Guten Tag. Ich heiße Martina Li.**
*goo-ten tahk. ikh high-se mar-teen-a lee*

Hello. My name's Martina Li.

**Guten Tag. Michael Brand, freut mich.**
*goo-ten tahk. mikh-ah-ail brant, froyt mikh*

Hello. Michael Brand, pleased to meet you.

**Freut mich.**
*froyt mikh*

Pleased to meet you.

### 4 Put into practice (3 minutes)

Join in this conversation. Read the German beside the pictures on the left and then follow the instructions to make your reply. Then test yourself by concealing the answers with the cover flap.

**Guten Abend, Herr Gohl.**
*goo-ten ah-bent, hair goel*

Good evening, Mr Gohl.

**Guten Abend.**
*goo-ten ah-bent*

Say: Good evening.

**Ich heiße Ilse Gerlach.**
*ikh high-se ilze gair-lakh*

My name is Ilse Gerlach.

**Freut mich.**
*froyt mikh*

Say: Pleased to meet you.

### 5 Useful phrases (3 minutes)

Familiarize yourself with these words. Read them aloud several times and try to memorize them. Conceal the German with the cover flap and test yourself.

| | |
|---|---|
| What's your name? | **Wie heißen Sie?** *vee high-sen zee* |
| My name is Thomas. | **Ich heiße Thomas.** *ikh high-se toe-mass* |
| Pleased to meet you. | **Freut mich.** *froyt mikh* |
| Thank you. | **Danke.** *dun-ke* |

### 6 In conversation: informal (3 minutes)

**Also, bis morgen?**
*ull-zoe, biss mor-gen*

So, see you tomorrow?

**Ja, auf Wiedersehen.**
*yah, owf vee-der-zay-en*

Yes, goodbye.

**Tschüss. Bis bald.**
*tchews. biss balt*

Goodbye. See you soon.

# DIE VERWANDTEN
## Relatives

### 1 Warm up (1 minute)

Say "hello" and "goodbye" in German. (pp.8-9)

Now say "My name is...". (pp.8-9)

Say "Mr" and "Mrs". (pp.8-9)

In German things are masculine, feminine, or neuter, taking a different form of "the" according to gender: **der** (*masculine*), **die** (*feminine*), and **das** (*neuter*). There is no easy way of knowing the gender of a word; you will have to memorize them individually.

### 2 Match and repeat (5 minutes)

Look at the numbered family members in this scene and match them with the vocabulary list at the side. Read the German words aloud. Now, conceal the list with the cover flap and test yourself.

❶ **der Großvater**
*dair groes-fah-ter*

❷ **der Bruder**
*dair broo-der*

❸ **die Schwester**
*dee shvess-ter*

❹ **der Vater**
*dair fah-ter*

❺ **die Mutter**
*dee moot-ter*

❻ **die Großmutter**
*dee groes-moot-ter*

❼ **der Sohn**
*dair zoen*

❽ **die Tochter**
*dee tokh-ter*

❶ grandfather
brother ❷
❸ sister
❹ father
❺ mother

grandmother ❻   ❼ son   ❽ daughter

**Conversational tip** In German the word **ein** (*a/an*) changes according to the gender of the noun - for example, **Ich habe eine Schwester** (*I have a sister*), but **Ich habe einen Sohn** (*I have a son*).

### 3 Words to remember: relatives (4 minutes)

**der Ehemann**
*dair ay-amunn*
husband

**die Ehefrau**
*dee ay-afrow*
wife

Germans commonly refer to their spouses as **mein Mann** (*my man*) or **meine Frau** (*my woman*). This is not impolite, but a shortened version of **mein Ehemann** and **meine Ehefrau**.

| | |
|---|---|
| children | **dic Kinder** *dee kin-der* |
| brother-in-law/ sister-in-law | **der Schwager/die Schwägerin** *dair shvar-ger/ dee shvay-ge-rin* |
| half-brother/ half-sister | **der Halbbruder/ die Halbschwester** *dair hulp-broo-der/ dee hulp-shvess-ter* |
| stepson/stepdaughter | **der Stiefsohn/die Stieftochter** *dair shteef-zohn/ dee shteef-tokh-ter* |
| stepfather/stepmother | **der Stiefvater/die Stiefmutter** *dair shteef-fah-ter/ dee shteef-moot-ter* |
| I have two sons. | **Ich habe zwei Söhne.** *ikh hah-be tsvie zer-ne.* |

**Ich bin verheiratet.**
*ikh bin fer-hye-rah-tet*
I'm married.

### 4 Words to remember: numbers (3 minutes)

Memorize these words and then test yourself using the cover flap.

In German the plural is formed by adding an **en, e, er**, or **s** to the end of the word, as in **Frau/Frauen** (*woman/women*), **Tag/Tage** (*day/days*), **Mann/Männer** (*man/men*), **Auto/Autos** (*car/cars*). In many cases the main vowel changes to a vowel with an umlaut, as in **der Bruder/die Brüder** (*brother/brothers*). In others there is no change.

| | |
|---|---|
| one | **eins** *ients* |
| two | **zwei** *tsvie* |
| three | **drei** *drie* |
| four | **vier** *feer* |
| five | **fünf** *fewnf* |
| six | **sechs** *zeks* |
| seven | **sieben** *zee-ben* |
| eight | **acht** *akht* |
| nine | **neun** *noyn* |
| ten | **zehn** *tsayn* |

### 5 Say it (2 minutes)

One sister.

Three sons.

Two brothers.

# MEINE FAMILIE
## My family

**1** **Warm up** (1 minute)

Say the German for as many members of the family as you can. (pp.10-11)

Say "I have two sons". (pp.10-11)

There are two ways of saying *you* in German: **Sie** for people you have just met or don't know very well and **du** for family and friends. There are also different words for *your* (see below). It is best to use **Sie** when you first meet someone and wait until he or she invites you to use **du**.

**2** **Words to remember** (5 minutes)

The words for *my* and *your* change, depending on the gender and number of the word to which they relate.

| | |
|---|---|
| **mein** *mine* | my (with masculine or neuter) |
| **meine** *mye-ne* | my (with feminine) |
| **meine** *mye-ne* | my (with plural) |
| **dein** *dine* | your (informal, with masculine or neuter) |
| **deine** *dye-ne* | your (informal, with feminine) |
| **deine** *dye-ne* | your (informal, with plural) |
| **Ihr** *eer* | your (formal, with masculine or neuter) |
| **Ihre** *ee-re* | your (formal, with feminine or plural) |

**Das sind meine Eltern.**
*duss zint mye-ne ell-tern*
These are my parents.

**3** **In conversation** (4 minutes)

**Haben Sie Kinder?**
*hah-ben zee kin-der*

Do you have any children?

**Ja, ich habe zwei Töchter.**
*yah, ikh hah-be tsvie terkh-ter*

Yes, I have two daughters.

**Hier sind meine Töchter. Und Sie?**
*heer zint mye-ne terkh-ter. oont zee*

These are my daughters. And you?

**Conversational tip** The most common way to ask a question in German is to invert the verb and the subject: **Sie haben** (*you have*) becomes **Haben Sie...?** (*have you? or do you have?*). Similarly, **Sie möchten Kaffee** (*you want coffee*) becomes **Möchten Sie Kaffee?** (*Do you want coffee?*).

## 4 Useful phrases (3 minutes)

Read these phrases aloud several times and try to memorize them. Conceal the German with the cover flap and test yourself.

| | |
|---|---|
| Do you have any brothers? (formal) | **Haben Sie Brüder?** *hah-ben zee brew-der* |
| Do you have any brothers? (informal) | **Hast du Brüder?** *husst doo brew-der* |

| | |
|---|---|
| This is my husband. | **Hier ist mein Mann.** *heer isst mine munn* |
| That's my wife. | **Dort ist meine Frau.** *dort isst mye-ne frow* |

| | |
|---|---|
| Is that your sister? (formal) | **Ist das Ihre Schwester?** *isst duss ee-re shvess-ter* |
| Is that your sister? (informal) | **Ist das deine Schwester?** *isst duss dye-ne shvess-ter* |

## 5 Say it (2 minutes)

Do you have any brothers and sisters? (formal)

Do you have any children? (informal)

I don't have any sisters.

This is my wife.

**Nein, aber ich habe einen Stiefsohn.**
*nine, ah-ber ikh hah-be ie-nen shteef-zohn*

No, but I have a stepson.

## 1  Warm up (1 minute)

Say "See you soon".
(pp.8–9)

Say "I am married"
and "I have a wife".
(pp.10–11 and pp.12–13)

# SEIN UND HABEN
## To be and to have

German verbs have more forms than English ones, so learn them carefully. The verbs **sein** (to be) and **haben** (to have) are used in many expressions, often differently from English. For example, in English you say I'm hungry, but in German you say **Ich habe Hunger** (literally, I have hunger).

## 2  Sein: to be (5 minutes)

Familiarize yourself with the different forms of **sein** (to be). Use the cover flaps to test yourself and, when you are confident, practise the sample sentences below.

| | |
|---|---|
| **ich bin** *ikh bin* | I am |
| **du bist** *doo bisst* | you are (informal, singular) |
| **er/sie/es ist** *air/zee/ess isst* | he/she/it is |
| **wir sind** *veer zint* | we are |
| **ihr seid** *eer ziet* | you are (informal, plural) |
| **sie sind/Sie sind** *zee zint* | they are/you are (formal) |

**Ich bin Engländerin.**
*ikh bin ang-lan-darin*
I'm English.

| | |
|---|---|
| **Ich bin müde.** *ikh bin mew-de* | I'm tired. |
| **Du bist/Sie sind pünktlich.** *doo bisst/zee zint pewnkt-likh* | You're on time. |
| **Ist sie glücklich?** *isst zee glewk-likh* | Is she happy? |
| **Wir sind Deutsche.** *veer zind doitche* | We're German. |

## 3 Haben (5 minutes)

**Haben Sie Brokkoli?**
*hah-ben zee brokolee*
Do you have any broccoli?

Learn this verb and the sample sentences.
Use the flap to test yourself.

| | |
|---|---|
| I have | **ich habe** *ikh hah-be* |
| you have (informal, singular) | **du hast** *doo husst* |
| he/she/it has | **er/sie/es hat** *air/zee/ess hut* |
| we have | **wir haben** *veer hah-ben* |
| you have (informal, plural) | **ihr habt** *eer hahpt* |
| they have/you have (formal) | **sie haben/Sie haben** *zee hah-ben* |

| | |
|---|---|
| He has a meeting. | **Er hat eine Besprechung.** *air hut ie-ne be-shpre-khoong* |
| Do you have a mobile phone? | **Haben Sie ein Handy?** *hah-ben zee ine han-di* |
| They have a half-brother. | **Sie haben einen Halbbruder.** *zee hah-ben ie-nen hulp-broo-der* |

## 4 Negatives (4 minutes)

The most common way to make a sentence negative in German is to put **nicht** (*not*) in front of the word that is negated, much as in English: **Wir sind nicht verheiratet** (*We are not married*). Note the following special negative constructions: *not a/not any* becomes **kein/keine**, *not ever/never* becomes **nie**, and *not anywhere/nowhere* becomes **nirgendwo**.

**das Fahrrad**
*duss fahr-raht*
bicycle

**Ich habe kein Auto.**
*ikh hah-be kine ow-to*
I don't have a car.

| | |
|---|---|
| I'm not tired. | **Ich bin nicht müde.** *ikh bin nikht mew-de* |
| He's not married. | **Er ist nicht verheiratet.** *air isst nikht fer-hye-rah-tet* |
| We don't have any children. | **Wir haben keine Kinder.** *veer hah-ben kye-ne kin-der* |

# WIEDERHOLUNG
## Review and repeat

**Antworten**
*Answers* (Cover with flap)

### 1 How many?

**❶ drei**
*drie*

**❷ neun**
*noyn*

**❸ vier**
*feer*

**❹ zwei**
*tsvie*

**❺ acht**
*akht*

**❻ zehn**
*tsayn*

**❼ fünf**
*fewnf*

**❽ sieben**
*zee-ben*

**❾ sechs**
*zeks*

### 1 How many? (2 minutes)

Conceal the answers with the cover flap. Then say these numbers in German. Check you have remembered correctly.

3  ❷ 9  ❸ 4
❶
2 ❹  ❺ 8  10  ❻
5  7  6
❼  ❽  ❾

### 2 Hello

**❶ Guten Tag. Ich heiße...**
*goo-ten tahk. ikh high-se...*

**❷ Freut mich.**
*froyt mikh*

**❸ Ja, und ich habe zwei Söhne. Und Sie?**
*yah, oont ikh hah-be tsvie zer-ne. Oont zee?*

**❹ Auf Wiedersehen. Bis morgen.**
*owf vee-der-zay-en. biss mor-gen*

### 2 Hello (4 minutes)

You meet someone in a formal situation. Join in the conversation, replying in German according to the English prompts.

**Guten Tag. Ich heiße Claudia.**
❶ Answer the greeting and give your name.

**Das ist mein Mann, Norbert.**
❷ Say "Pleased to meet you".

**Sind Sie verheiratet?**
❸ Say "Yes, and I have two sons. And you?"

**Wir haben drei Töchter.**
❹ Say "Goodbye. See you tomorrow".

### To have or be (5 minutes)

Fill in the blanks with the correct form of **haben**
(*to have*) or **sein** (*to be*). Check you have
remembered the German correctly.

❶ Ich _____ verheiratet.

❷ Sie (*she*) _____ müde.

❸ Wir _____ Deutsche.

❹ _____ Sie eine Besprechung?

❺ Sie (*she*) _____ eine
Schwägerin.

❻ Ich _____ kein Handy.

❼ _____ du glücklich?

❽ Das _____ mein Mann.

### To have or be

❶ **bin**
*bin*

❷ **ist**
*isst*

❸ **sind**
*zint*

❹ **haben**
*hah-ben*

❺ **hat**
*hut*

❻ **habe**
*hah-be*

❼ **bist**
*bisst*

❽ **ist**
*isst*

### Family (4 minutes)

Say the German for each of the numbered family
members. Check you have remembered the
German correctly.

grandfather ❶
brother ❷
❸ sister
❹ father
❺ mother
grandmother ❻
❼ son
❽ daughter

### Family

❶ **der Großvater**
*dair groes-fah-ter*

❷ **der Bruder**
*dair broo-der*

❸ **die Schwester**
*dee shvess-ter*

❹ **der Vater**
*dair fah-ter*

❺ **die Mutter**
*dee moot-ter*

❻ **die Großmutter**
*dee groes-moot-ter*

❼ **der Sohn**
*dair zohn*

❽ **die Tochter**
*dee tokh-ter*

# IM CAFÉ
## In the café

**1 Warm up** (1 minute)

Count to ten.
(pp.10-11)

Say "hello" and
"goodbye". (pp.8-9)

Ask "Do you have a
brother?" (pp.12-13)

In a German **Café** the busiest time is the afternoon, when people stop for coffee and cake. Some savoury dishes are also usually available, but the emphasis is on pastries and gâteaux.

**der Zucker**
*dair tsook-ker*
sugar

**2 Match and repeat** (5 minutes)

Familiarize yourself with the words below. Then test yourself by hiding the German with the cover flap. Practise the words on the picture also.

| | |
|---|---|
| **der Kaffee ohne Milch** *dair kuf-fay oh-ne milkh* | black coffee |
| **der Tee mit Milch** *dair tay mit milkh* | tea with milk |
| **das Gebäck** *duss ge-beck* | pastry |
| **das Sandwich** *duss zent-vitch* | sandwich |

**der schwarze Tee**
*dair shvar-tse tay*
black tea

**Cultural tip** Coffee is always served with milk and sugar, but tea drinkers should specify if they want milk (**mit Milch**) or lemon (**mit Zitrone**).

**3 In conversation** (4 minutes)

**Ich hätte gern eine Tasse Tee mit Milch.**
*ikh het-te gairn ie-ne tuss-se tay mit milkh*

I would like a cup of tea with milk, please.

**Sonst noch etwas?**
*zonsst nokh et-vuss*

Anything else?

**Haben Sie Kuchen?**
*hah-ben zee koo-khen*

Do you have any cake?

## 4 Useful phrases (5 minutes)

Practise these phrases and then test yourself using the cover flap.

**ein Stück Kuchen**
*ine shtewck
koo-khen*
slice of cake

I'd like a cup of coffee, please.

**Ich hätte gern eine Tasse Kaffee, bitte.**
*ikh het-te gairn ie-ne tuss-se kuf-fay, bit-te*

Anything else?

**Sonst noch etwas?**
*zonsst nokh et-vuss*

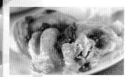

Yes, a Danish pastry, please.

**Ja, ein Teilchen, bitte.**
*yah, ine tile-khen, bit-te*

How much is that?

**Was macht das?**
*vuss mukht duss*

**der Kaffee**
*dair kuf-fay*
(white) coffee

---

**Ja, selbstverständlich.**
*yah, zelpst-fer-shtend-likh*

Yes, certainly.

**Danke. Was macht das?**
*dun-ke. vuss mukht duss*

Thank you. How much is that?

**Vier Euro, bitte.**
*feer oy-roe, bit-te*

Four euros, please.

## **1** Warm up (1 minute)

How do you say "I'd like"? (pp.18-19)

Say "I don't have a brother". (pp.14-15)

Is "der" masculine or feminine? When do you use "die"? (pp.10-11)

# IM RESTAURANT
## In the restaurant

There are many different eating places in Germany. A **Gaststätte** serves local or international dishes. In a **Gasthof** you'll get a more homely style of cooking. **Ratkeller**, in the basements of historic town halls, serve regional specialities. A **Weinstube** has local wine and snacks.

## **2** Words to remember (3 minutes)

Memorize these words. Conceal the German with the cover flap and then test yourself.

cup **7**

saucer **8**

**5** spoon

**6** knife

**4** fork

| | |
|---|---|
| **die Speisekarte** <br> *dee shpie-ze-kar-te* | menu |
| **die Weinkarte** <br> *dee vine-kar-te* | wine list |
| **die Vorspeisen** <br> *dee for-shpie-zen* | starters |
| **die Hauptgerichte** <br> *dee howpt-ge-rikh-te* | main courses |
| **der Nachtisch** <br> *dair nahkh-tish* | desserts |
| **das Mittagessen** <br> *duss mit-tahks-ess-sen* | lunch |
| **das Abendessen** <br> *duss ah-bent-ess-sen* | dinner |
| **das Frühstück** <br> *duss frew-shtewk* | breakfast |

## **3** In conversation (4 minutes)

**Einen Tisch für vier Personen.**
*ie-nen tish fewr feer pair-zoe-nen*

A table for four.

**Haben Sie reserviert?**
*hah-ben zee re-zair-veert*

Do you have a reservation?

**Ja, auf den Namen Schmidt.**
*yah, owf dayn nah-men shmitt*

Yes, in the name of Schmidt.

### 4 Match and repeat (5 minutes)

Look at the numbered items and match them with the German words at the side. Read the German words aloud. Now, conceal the German with the cover flap and test yourself.

**①** glass

**②** napkin

plate **③**

**①** das Glas
*duss glahss*

**②** die Serviette
*dee zair-vee-ett-te*

**③** der Teller
*dair tell-ler*

**④** die Gabel
*dee gah-bell*

**⑤** der Löffel
*dair lerff-fel*

**⑥** das Messer
*duss mess-ser*

**⑦** die Tasse
*dee tuss-se*

**⑧** die Untertasse
*dee unter-tuss-se*

### 5 Useful phrases (2 minutes)

Learn these phrases and then test yourself using the cover flap to conceal the German.

| | |
|---|---|
| What do you have for dessert? | **Was haben Sie zum Nachtisch?** *vuss hah-ben zee tsoom nahkh-tish* |
| May I have the bill, please. | **Könnte ich bitte die Rechnung haben.** *kern-te ikh bit-te dee rekh-noong hah-ben* |

**Welchen Tisch möchten Sie?**
*vel-khen tish merkh-ten zee*

Which table would you like?

**Am Fenster, bitte.**
*um fens-ter, bit-te*

Near the window, please.

**Selbstverständlich. Folgen Sie mir.**
*zelpst-fer-shtend-likh. fol-gen zee meer*

But of course. Follow me.

# MÖGEN
## To want

**1 Warm up** (1 minute)

What are "breakfast", "lunch", and "dinner" in German? (pp.20-1)

Say "I", "you" (informal, singular), "he", "she", "it", "we", "you" (formal), "they". (pp.14-15)

In this section, you will learn a verb, **mögen** (*to want*), which is essential to everyday conversation, as well as a useful polite expression, **ich hätte gern** (*I would like*). Remember to use this form when requesting something because **ich möchte** (*I want*) may sound too forceful.

**2 Mögen: to want** (6 minutes)

Say the different forms of **mögen** (*to want*) aloud and practise the sample sentences below. Use the cover flaps to test yourself.

| | |
|---|---|
| **ich möchte** <br> *ikh merkh-te* | I want |
| **du möchtest** <br> *doo merkh-test* | you want (informal, singular) |
| **er/sie/es möchte** <br> *air/zee/ess merkh-te* | he/she/it wants |
| **wir möchten** <br> *veer merkh-ten* | we want |
| **ihr möchtet** <br> *eer merkh-tet* | you want (informal, plural) |
| **sie möchten/Sie möchten** <br> *zee merkh-ten* | they want/you want (formal) |
| **Möchtest du Wein?** <br> *merkh-test doo vine* | Do you want some wine? |
| **Sie möchte ein neues Auto haben.** <br> *zee merkh-te ine noy-es ow-to hah-ben* | She wants a new car. |
| **Wir möchten in Urlaub fahren.** <br> *veer merkh-ten in oor-lowp fah-ren* | We want to go on holiday. |

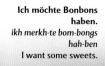

**Ich möchte Bonbons haben.**
*ikh merkh-te bom-bongs hah-ben*
I want some sweets.

**Conversational tip** In German you don't need to say *some* as in *We want some ice lollies* for **Wir möchten Eis am Stiel haben**. The phrase *some* is **ein paar**. It is generally used only when you want to imply some but not all, as in **Ich habe nur ein paar Bonbons gegessen**.

## ③ Polite requests (4 minutes)

It is polite to use the expression **ich hätte gern** (*I would like*) to explain what you would like.

| | |
|---|---|
| I'd like a beer. | **Ich hätte gern ein Bier.**<br>*ikh het-te gairn ine beer* |

| | |
|---|---|
| I'd like a table for tonight. | **Ich hätte gern einen Tisch für heute abend.**<br>*ikh het-te gairn ie-nen tish fewr hoy-te ah-bent* |

| | |
|---|---|
| I'd like the menu. | **Ich hätte gern die Speisekarte.**<br>*ikh het-te gairn dee shpie-ze-kar-te* |

## ④ Put into practice (4 minutes)

Join in this conversation. Read the German beside the pictures on the left and then follow the instructions to make your reply in German. Test yourself by concealing the answers with the cover flap.

**Guten Abend. Haben Sie reserviert?**
*goo-ten ah-bent. hah-ben zee re-zair-veert*

Good evening. Do you have a reservation?

Say: No, but I would like a table for three.

**Nein, aber ich hätte gern einen Tisch für drei Personen.**
*nine, ah-ber ikh het-te gairn ie-nen tish fewr drie per-zoe-nen*

**Sehr gut. Raucher oder Nichtraucher?**
*zair goot. row-kher oe-der nikht-row-kher*

Very good. Smoking or non-smoking?

Say: Non-smoking, please.

**Nichtraucher, bitte.**
*nikht-row-kher, bit-te*

## **DIE GERICHTE**
### Dishes

**Warm up** (1 minute)

Say "I am tired".
(pp.14-15)

Ask "Do you have
pastries?" (pp.18-19)

Say "I'd like a black
coffee". (pp.18-19)

Germany is famous for its sausages and meat dishes
as well as its sauerkraut and dumplings. Today's
restaurants, however, offer a wide selection of
international dishes. Although traditionally the
cuisine is meat-based, many restaurants now
offer vegetarian dishes.

**Cultural tip** In most restaurants at lunchtime you
will usually have the choice of eating a **Tagesgericht**
(*dish of the day*) or of choosing **à la carte** from the menu.

### **Match and repeat** (4 minutes)

Look at the numbered items and match them to the
German words in the panel on the left. Test yourself
using the cover flap.

❶ **das Gemüse**
*duss ge-mew-ze*

❷ **das Obst**
*duss opst*

❸ **der Käse**
*dair kay-ze*

❹ **die Nüsse**
*dee news-se*

❺ **die Suppe**
*dee zoop-pe*

❻ **das Geflügel**
*duss ge-flew-gel*

❼ **der Fisch**
*dair fish*

❽ **die Nudeln**
*dee noo-deln*

❾ **die Meeresfrüchte**
*dee mair-es-frewkh-te*

❿ **das Fleisch**
*duss fliesh*

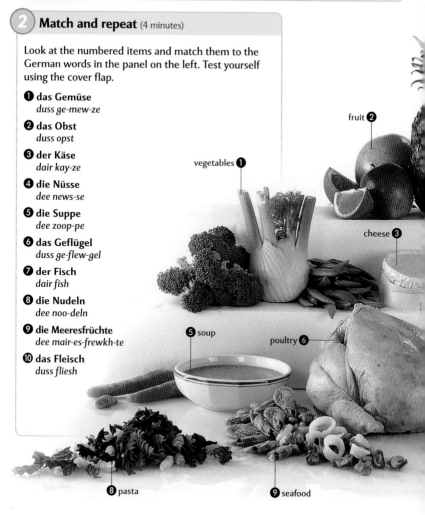

fruit ❷

vegetables ❶

cheese ❸

❺ soup

poultry ❻

❽ pasta

❾ seafood

## 3 Words to remember: cooking methods (3 minutes)

Familiarize yourself with these words and then test yourself.

| fried | **gebraten** |
| | *ge-brah-ten* |
| grilled | **gegrillt** |
| | *ge-grillt* |
| roasted | **geröstet** |
| | *ge-rerss-tet* |
| boiled | **gekocht** |
| | *ge-kokht* |
| steamed | **gedämpft** |
| | *ge-dempft* |
| rare | **blutig** |
| | *bloo-tikh* |

**Ich hätte mein Steak gern durchgebraten.**
*ikh het-te mine shtayk gairn doorkh-ge-brah-ten*
I'd like my steak well done.

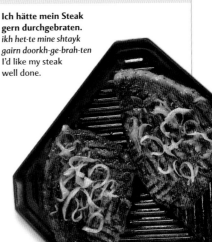

## 4 Say it (2 minutes)

What is **Sauerbraten**?

I'm allergic to seafood.

I'd like a fruit juice.

nuts

## 5 Words to remember: drinks (3 minutes)

Familiarize yourself with these words.

| water | **das Wasser** |
| | *duss vuss-ser* |
| fizzy water | **das Wasser mit Kohlensäure** |
| | *duss vuss-ser mit koe-len-zoy-re* |
| still water | **das Wasser ohne Kohlensäure** |
| | *duss vuss-ser oe-ne koe-len-zoy-re* |
| wine | **der Wein** |
| | *dair vine* |
| fruit juice | **der Fruchtsaft** |
| | *dair frookht-zufft* |

## 6 Useful phrases (2 minutes)

fish

Learn these phrases and then test yourself.

| I am a vegetarian. | **Ich bin Vegetarier/ Vegetarierin.** |
| | *ikh bin vay-ge-tah-ree-er/vay-ge-tah-ree-er-in* |
| I am allergic to nuts. | **Ich bin allergisch gegen Nüsse.** |
| | *ikh bin ull-lair-gish gay-gen news-se* |
| What is "Spätzle"? | **Was ist "Spätzle"?** |
| | *vuss isst shpets-le* |

❿ meat

# WIEDERHOLUNG
## Review and repeat

### 1 What food?

**1** die Nüsse
*dee news-se*

**2** die Meeresfrüchte
*dee mair-es-frewkh-te*

**3** das Fleisch
*duss fliesh*

**4** der Zucker
*dair tsook-ker*

**5** das Glas
*duss glahss*

### 1 What food? (4 minutes)

Name the numbered items.

**1** nuts

**2** seafood

**3** meat

**4** sugar

glass **5**

### 2 This is my...

**1** Das ist mein Ehemann.
*duss ist mine ay-emunn*

**2** Hier ist meine Tochter.
*heer ist mye-ne tokh-ter*

**3** Meine Kinder sind müde.
*mye-ne kin-der zint mew-de*

### 2 This is my... (4 minutes)

Say these phrases in German. Use **mein** or **meine**.

**1** This is my husband.

**2** Here is my daughter.

**3** My children are tired.

### 3 I'd like...

**1** Ich hätte gern Kuchen.
*ikh het-te gairn koo-khen*

**2** Ich hätte gern einen schwarzen Tee.
*ikh het-te gairn ie-nen shvar-tsen tay*

**3** Ich hätte gern einen Kaffee.
*ikh het-te gairn ie-nen kuf-fay*

### 3 I'd like... (3 minutes)

Say you'd like the following:

cake **1**

**2** black tea

coffee **3**

pasta **6**

knife **7**

**8** cheese

beer **10**

**9** napkin

**Antworten**
*Answers* (Cover with flap)

## What food?

**6** die Nudeln
*dee noo-deln*

**7** das Messer
*duss mess-ser*

**8** der Käse
*dair kay-ze*

**9** die Serviette
*dee zair-vee-ett-te*

**10** das Bier
*duss beer*

## 4  Restaurant (4 minutes)

You arrive at a restaurant. Join in the conversation, replying in German following the English prompts.

**Guten Tag.**
**1** Ask for a table for six.

**Raucher oder Nichtraucher?**
**2** Say: non-smoking.

**Folgen Sie mir, bitte.**
**3** Ask for the menu.

**Möchten Sie die Weinkarte?**
**4** Say: No. Fizzy water, please.

**Bitte schön.**
**5** Say: I don't have a glass.

## 4  Restaurant

**1** Guten Tag. Ich hätte
gern einen Tisch für
sechs Personen.
*goo-ten tahk. ikh het-
te gairn ie-nen tish
fewr zeks pair-zoe-nen*

**2** Nichtraucher.
*nikht-row-kher*

**3** Die Speisekarte,
bitte.
*dee shpie-ze-kar-te,
bit-te*

**4** Nein. Wasser mit
Kohlensäure, bitte.
*nine. vuss-ser mit koe-
len-zoy-re, bit-te*

**5** Ich habe kein Glas.
*ikh hah-be kine glahss*

# DIE TAGE UND DIE MONATE
## Days and months

Days of the week and months are all masculine. **Die Woche** (*week*) is feminine. You use **im** with months: **im April** (*in April*), and **am** with days: **am Montag** (*on Monday*). You also use **am** with **Wochenende** (*weekend*).

**2** **Words to remember: days of the week** (5 minutes)

Familiarize yourself with these words and test yourself using the flap.

| | |
|---|---|
| **Montag** *moen-tahk* | Monday |
| **Dienstag** *deens-tahk* | Tuesday |
| **Mittwoch** *mit-vokh* | Wednesday |
| **Donnerstag** *don-ners-tahk* | Thursday |
| **Freitag** *frie-tahk* | Friday |
| **Samstag** *zumss-tahk* | Saturday |
| **Sonntag** *zonn-tahk* | Sunday |
| **heute** *hoy-te* | today |
| **morgen** *mor-gen* | tomorrow |
| **gestern** *guess-tern* | yesterday |

**Morgen ist Montag.**
*mor-gen isst moen-tahk*
Tomorrow is Monday.

**3** **Useful phrases: days** (2 minutes)

Learn these phrases and then test yourself using the cover flap.

| | |
|---|---|
| **Die Besprechung ist am Dienstag.** *dee be-shpre-khoong isst am deens-tahk* | The meeting is on Tuesday. |
| **Ich arbeite sonntags.** *ikh ar-bie-te zonn-tahks* | I work on Sundays. |

## 4 Words to remember: months (5 minutes)

Familiarize yourself with these words and test yourself using the flap.

**Ostern ist im April.**
*oess-tairn isst im ah-prill*
Easter is in April.

**Weihnachten ist im Dezember.**
*vie-nahkh-ten isst im day-tsem-bair*
Christmas is in December.

| | | |
|---|---|---|
| January | **Januar** | *yunn-oo-ahr* |
| February | **Februar** | *fay-broo-ahr* |
| March | **März** | *mairts* |
| April | **April** | *ah-prill* |
| May | **Mai** | *mie* |
| June | **Juni** | *yoo-nee* |
| July | **Juli** | *yoo-lee* |
| August | **August** | *ow-goosst* |
| September | **September** | *zep-tem-bair* |
| October | **Oktober** | *ok-toe-bair* |
| November | **November** | *noe-vem-bair* |
| December | **Dezember** | *day-tsem-bair* |
| month | **der Monat** | *dair moenat* |
| day | **der Tag** | *dair tahk* |

## 5 Useful phrases: months (2 minutes)

Learn these phrases and then test yourself using the cover flap.

My children are on holiday in August.
**Meine Kinder haben im August Ferien.**
*mye-ne kin-der hah-ben im ow-goosst fay-ree-en*

My birthday is in June.
**Mein Geburtstag ist im Juni.**
*mine ge-boorts-tahk isst im yoo-nee*

# DIE ZEIT UND DIE ZAHLEN
## Time and numbers

## 1 Warm up (1 minute)

Count in German from 1 to 10. (pp.10–11)

Say "I have a reservation". (pp.20–1)

Say "The meeting is on Wednesday". (pp.28–9)

Germans use the 12-hour clock in everyday conversation and the 24-hour clock in official contexts such as timetables. Note that in German half past five is expressed as **halb sechs** (literally, *half six*).

## 2 Words to remember: time (4 minutes)

Familiarize yourself with these words.

| | |
|---|---|
| **ein Uhr** *ine oor* | one o'clock |
| **fünf nach eins** *fewnf nahkh ients* | five past one |
| **Viertel nach eins** *feer-tel nahkh ients* | quarter past one |
| **halbs zwei** *hulp tsvie* | half past one |
| **ein Uhr zwanzig** *ine oor tsvun-tsik* | twenty past one |
| **Viertel vor zwei** *feer-tel for tsvie* | quarter to two |
| **zehn Minuten vor zwei** *tsayn mee-noo-ten for tsvie* | ten to two |

## 3 Useful phrases (2 minutes)

Learn these phrases and then test yourself using the cover flap.

| | |
|---|---|
| **Wie spät ist es?** *vee shpayt isst es* | What time is it? |

| | |
|---|---|
| **Wann möchten Sie frühstücken?** *vunn merkh-ten zee frew-shtewk-ken* | What time do you want breakfast? |

| | |
|---|---|
| **Die Besprechung ist um 12 Uhr.** *dee be-shpre-khoong isst oom tsverlf oor* | The meeting is at midday. |

### 4 Words to remember: higher numbers (6 minutes)

In German, units are said before tens, so 32 is **zweiunddreißig** (literally, *two-plus-thirty*). Because of this, Germans often write numbers starting at the right and working towards the left.

**Ich habe viele Bücher.**
*ikh hah-be fee-le bew-kher*
I have many books.

**Das macht fünfundachtzig Euro.**
*duss makht fewnf-oont-akh-tsik oy-roe*
That's eighty-five euros.

| | | |
|---|---|---|
| eleven | **elf** | *elf* |
| twelve | **zwölf** | *tsverlf* |
| thirteen | **dreizehn** | *drie-tsayn* |
| fourteen | **vierzehn** | *feer-tsayn* |
| fifteen | **fünfzehn** | *fewnf-tsayn* |
| sixteen | **sechzehn** | *zekh-tsayn* |
| seventeen | **siebzehn** | *zeep-tsayn* |
| eighteen | **achtzehn** | *akh-tsayn* |
| nineteen | **neunzehn** | *noyn-tsayn* |
| twenty | **zwanzig** | *tsvun-tsik* |
| thirty | **dreißig** | *drie-ssik* |
| forty | **vierzig** | *feer-tsik* |
| fifty | **fünfzig** | *fewnf-tsik* |
| sixty | **sechzig** | *zekh-tsik* |
| seventy | **siebzig** | *zeep-tsik* |
| eighty | **achtzig** | *akh-tsik* |
| ninety | **neunzig** | *noyn-tsik* |
| hundred | **hundert** | *hoon-dairt* |
| three hundred | **dreihundert** | *drie-hoon-dairt* |
| thousand | **tausend** | *tow-zent* |
| ten thousand | **zehntausend** | *tsayn-tow-zent* |
| two hundred thousand | **zweihunderttausend** | *tsvie-hoon-dairt-tow-zent* |
| one million | **eine Million** | *ie-ne mill-ee-oen* |

### 5 Say it (2 minutes)

twenty-five

sixty-eight

eighty-four

ninety-one

It's five to ten.

It's half past eleven.

What time is lunch?

# DIE TERMINE
## Appointments

Say the days of the week. (pp.28-9)

Say "It's three o'clock". (pp.30-1)

What's the German for "today", "tomorrow", and "yesterday"? (pp.28-9)

Business in Germany is generally conducted more formally than in the UK or the US. Business associates generally call each other by their title and last name and use the formal form of *you*, **Sie**. Appointments are usually fixed using the 24-hour clock, **fünfzehn Uhr** (*3 pm*).

**Willkommen.**
*vil-komm-men*
Welcome.

**der Händedruck**
*dair hen-de-drook*
handshake

**2** **Useful phrases** (5 minutes)

Learn these phrases and then test yourself.

| | |
|---|---|
| **Können wir uns morgen treffen?** *kernen veer oons mor-gen treff-fen* | Can we meet tomorrow? |
| **Mit wem?** *mit vaym* | With whom? |
| **Wann sind Sie frei?** *vunn zint zee frie* | When are you free? |
| **Es tut mir Leid, ich bin beschäftigt.** *es toot meer liet, ikh bin be-sheff-tikht* | I'm sorry, I am busy. |
| **Wie wär's mit Donnerstag?** *vee vairs mit don-ners-tahk* | How about Thursday? |
| **Das passt mir gut.** *duss pusst meer goot* | That's good for me. |

**3** **In conversation** (4 minutes)

**Guten Tage. Ich habe einen Termin.**
*goo-ten tahk. ikh hah-be ie-nen terr-meen*

Hello. I have an appointment.

**Mit wem, bitte?**
*mit vaym, bit-te*

With whom, please?

**Mit Dieter Frenger.**
*mit dee-ter fren-ger*

With Dieter Frenger.

## 4 Put into practice (5 minutes)

Join in this conversation. Cover up the text on the right and say the answering part of the dialogue in German. Check your answers and repeat if necessary.

**Können wir uns am Donnertsag treffen?**
*kernen veer oons am don-ners-tahk treff-fen*
Shall we meet Thursday?

Say: Sorry, I'm busy.

**Es tut mir Leid, ich bin beschäftigt.**
*es toot meer liet, ikh bin be-sheff-tikht*

**Wann sind Sie frei?**
*vunn zint zee frie*
When are you free?

Say: Tuesday afternoon.

**Dienstag Nachmittag.**
*deens-tahk nahkh-mit-tahk*

**Das passt mir gut.**
*duss pusst meer goot*
That's good for me.

Ask: At what time?

**Um wieviel Uhr?**
*oom vee-feel oor*

**Um sechzehn Uhr, wenn es Ihnen passt.**
*oom zekh-tsayn oor, venn ess ee-nen pusst*
At 16.00 hours, if that's good for you.

Say: It's good for me.

**Das passt mir gut.**
*duss pusst meer goot*

---

**Sehr gut. Um wieviel Uhr?**
*zair goot. oom vee-feel oor*

Very good. What time?

**Um fünfzehn Uhr, aber ich bin etwas verspätet.**
*oom fewnf-tsayn oor, ah-ber ikh bin et-vuss fer-shpay-tet*

At 15.00 hours, but I'm a little late.

**Kein Problem. Setzen Sie sich, bitte.**
*kine pro-blaym. zet-sen zee zikh, bit-te*

Don't worry. Sit down, please.

# AM TELEFON
## On the telephone

## 1 Warm up (1 minute)

Say "I'm sorry". (pp.32-3)

What is the German for "I'd like an appointment"? (pp.32-3)

Ask "with whom?" in German. (pp.32-3)

Emergency phone numbers are: **Polizei** (*police*) 110; **Feuerwehr** (*fire service*) 112; and **Rettungsdienst** (*ambulance*) 192 22. Directory enquiries are 118 33 for inland numbers, 118 34 for abroad, and 118 37 for an English-speaking service.

## 2 Match and repeat (4 minutes)

Match the numbered items to the German.

❶ **das Ladegerät**
*duss lah-de-ge-rayt*

❷ **das Telefon**
*duss tay-lay-foen*

❸ **der Anrufbeantworter**
*dair un-roof-bay-unt-vor-ter*

❹ **die Kopfhörer**
*dee kopf-her-er*

❺ **das Handy**
*duss han-di*

❻ **die Telefonkarte**
*dee tay-lay-foen-kar-te*

❶ charger
❷ telephone
❺ mobile
❻ phonecard
❹ headphones

## 3 In conversation (4 minutes)

**Hallo. Elke Rubin am Apparat.**
*hul-lo. el-ke roo-been umm up-pa-raht*

Hello. Elke Rubin speaking.

**Guten Tag. Ich möchte bitte Peter Harnisch sprechen.**
*goo-ten tahk. ikh merkh-te bit-te peeter har-neesh shpre-khen*

Hello. I'd like to speak to Peter Harnisch.

**Mit wem spreche ich?**
*mit vaym shpre-khe ikh*

Who's speaking?

**Ich möchte ein R-Gespräch.**
*ikh merkh-te ine air-geshprekh*
I'd like to reverse the charges.

❸ answering machine

**5** **Say it** (2 minutes)

I'd like to speak to Mr Braun.

Hello, Gaby. Meyer speaking.

**4** **Useful phrases** (4 minutes)

Learn these phrases. Then test yourself using the cover flap.

**Ich möchte einen Amtsanschluss.**
*ikh merkh-te ie-nen umts-un-shlooss*

I'd like an outside line.

**Ich möchte mit Rita Wolbert sprechen.**
*ikh merkh-te mit ree-ta vol-bert shpre-khen*

I'd like to speak to Rita Wolbert.

**Kann ich eine Nachricht hinterlassen?**
*kunn ikh ie-ne nahkh-rikht hin-ter-luss-sen*

Can I leave a message?

**Es tut mir Leid, ich habe mich verwählt.**
*ess toot meer liet, ikh hah-be mikh fer-vaylt*

Sorry, I have the wrong number.

**Mit Norbert Lorenz von der Druckerei Knickmann.**
*mit nor-bert loe-rents fon dair drook-er-ie knick-munn*

Norbert Lorenz of Knickmann Printers.

**Es tut mir Leid. Es ist besetzt.**
*ess toot meer liet. ess isst be-zetst*

I'm sorry. The line is busy.

**Würden Sie ihn bitten, mich anzurufen?**
*vewr-den see een bit-ten, mikh un-tsoo-roo-fen*

Can he call me back, please?

# WIEDERHOLUNG
## Review and repeat

**Antworten**
*Answers* (Cover with flap)

### 1 Sums

❶ **sechzehn**
*zekh-tsayn*

❷ **neununddreißig**
*noyn-oont-drie-ssik*

❸ **dreiundfünfzig**
*drie-oont-fewnf-tsik*

❹ **vierundsiebzig**
*feer-oont-zeep-tsik*

❺ **neunundneunzig**
*noyn-oont-noyn-tsik*

❻ **einundvierzig**
*ine-oont-feer-tsik*

### 1 Sums (4 minutes)

Say the answers to these sums aloud in German. Then check if you have remembered correctly.

❶ 10 + 6 = ?

❷ 14 + 25 = ?

❸ 66 − 13 = ?

❹ 40 + 34 = ?

❺ 90 + 9 = ?

❻ 46 − 5 = ?

### 3 Telephones (3 minutes)

What are the numbered items in German?

mobile ❶

phonecard ❸

### 2 I want...

❶ **möchten**
*merkh-ten*

❷ **möchte**
*merkh-te*

❸ **möchten**
*merkh-ten*

❹ **möchtest**
*merkh-test*

❺ **möchte**
*merkh-te*

❻ **möchte**
*merkh-te*

### 2 I want... (3 minutes)

Fill the gaps with the correct form of **mögen** (*to want*).

❶ _____ Sie einen Kaffee?

❷ Sie (*singular*) _____ in Urlaub fahren.

❸ Wir _____ einen Tisch für drei Personen.

❹ Du _____ ein Bier.

❺ Ich _____ Bonbons.

❻ Er _____ Obst.

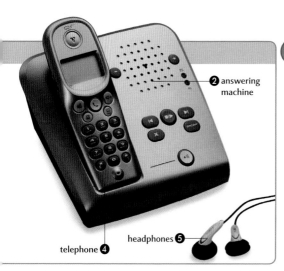

answering machine ②

telephone ④

headphones ⑤

### 3 Telephones

❶ **das Handy**
*duss han-di*

❷ **der Anrufbeantworter**
*dair un-roof-bay-unt-vor-ter*

❸ **die Telefonkarte**
*dee tay-lay-foen-kar-te*

❹ **das Telefon**
*duss tay-lay-foen*

❺ **die Kopfhörer**
*dee kopf-her-er*

### 4 When? (2 minutes)

What do these sentences mean?

❶ **Ich habe einen Termin am Montag, den zwanzigsten Mai.**

❷ **Mein Geburtstag ist im September.**

❸ **Ich arbeite freitags.**

❹ **Sie arbeiten nicht im August.**

### 4 When?

❶ I have an appointment on Monday 20th May.

❷ My birthday is in September.

❸ I work on Fridays.

❹ They don't work in August.

### 5 Time (3 minutes)

Say these times in German.

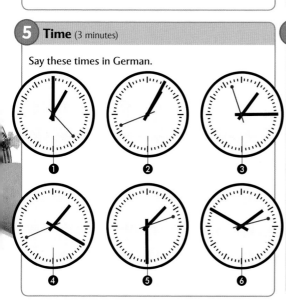

① ② ③
④ ⑤ ⑥

### 5 Time

❶ **ein Uhr**
*ine oor*

❷ **fünf nach eins**
*fewnf nahkh ients*

❸ **Viertel nach eins**
*feer-tel nahkh ients*

❹ **zwanzig Minuten nach eins**
*tsvun-tsik mee-noo-ten nahkh ients*

❺ **halb zwei**
*hulp tsvie*

❻ **zehn Minuten vor zwei (Uhr)**
*tsayn mee-noo-ten for tsvie (oor)*

## 1 Warm up (1 minute)

Count to 100 in tens.
(pp.10-11, pp.30-1)

Ask "At what time?"
(pp.32-3)

Say "Half-past one".
(pp.30-1)

# AM FAHRKARTENSCHALTER
## At the ticket office

On German trains, children under the age of four travel free, and children aged from 4 to 11 years pay half fare. There are also other concessions – for example, for senior citizens, groups, and weekend travel.

## 2 Words to remember (3 minutes)

Learn these words and then test yourself.

| | |
|---|---|
| **der Bahnhof** *dair bahn-hoef* | station |
| **der Zug** *dair tsook* | train |
| **der Fahrplan** *dair fahr-plahn* | timetable |
| **die Fahrkarte** *dee fahr-kar-te* | ticket |
| **eine einfache Fahrkarte** *ie-ne ine-fa-khe fahr-kar-te* | single ticket |
| **eine Rückfahrkarte** *ie-ne rewck-fahr-kar-te* | return ticket |
| **erster/zweiter Klasse** *airs-ter/tsvie-ter kluss-se* | first class/ second class |

der Bahnsteig
*dair bahn-shtiek*
platform

das Schild
*duss shilt*
sign

**Der Bahnhof ist überfüllt.**
*dair bahn-hoef isst ew-ber-fewllt*
The station is crowded.

## 3 In conversation (4 minutes)

**Zwei Fahrkarten nach Berlin, bitte.**
*tsvie fahr-kar-ten nahkh bair-leen, bit-te*

Two tickets for Berlin, please.

**Rückfahrkarten?**
*rewck-fahr-kar-ten*

Return?

**Ja. Muss ich die Sitze reservieren?**
*yah. mooss ikh dee zit-se re-zair-vee-ren*

Yes. Do I need to reserve seats?

## 4 Useful phrases (5 minutes)

**Der Zug hat zehn Minuten Verspätung.**
*dair tsook hut tsayn mee-noo-ten fer-shpay-toong*
The train is ten minutes late.

**der Fahrgast**
*dair fahr-gust*
passenger

Learn these phrases and then test yourself using the cover flap.

| | |
|---|---|
| How much is a ticket to Cologne? | **Was kostet eine Fahrkarte nach Köln?** *vuss kos-tet ie-ne fahr-kar-te nahkh kerln* |
| Can I pay by credit card? | **Kann ich mit Kreditkarte zahlen?** *kunn ikh mit kray-deet-kar-te tsah-len* |
| Do I have to change? | **Muss ich umsteigen?** *mooss ikh oomm-shtie-gen* |
| Which platform does the train leave from? | **Von welchem Bahnsteig fährt der Zug ab?** *fon vel-khem bahn-shtiek fairt dair tsook up* |
| Are there concessions? | **Gibt es Ermäßigungen?** *geept ess er-mays-si-goong-en* |
| What time does the train for Dresden leave? | **Wann fährt der Zug nach Dresden ab?** *vunn fairt dair tsook nahkh dres-den up* |

## 5 Say it (2 minutes)

Which platform does the train for Leipzig leave from?

Three return tickets to Hamburg, please.

**Cultural tip** Most stations have *automatic ticket machines* (**Fahrkartenautomaten**). If you are in a hurry, you can buy tickets on the train, but you won't be able to get any discounts.

**Nein. Vierzig Euro, bitte.**
*nine. feer-tsik oy-roe, bit-te*

No. Forty euros, please.

**Nehmen Sie Kreditkarten?**
*nay-men zee kray-deet-kar-ten*

Do you accept credit cards?

**Ja. Der Zug fährt auf Bahnsteig zehn ab.**
*yah. dair tsook fairt owf bahn-shtiek tsayn up*

Yes. The train leaves from platform ten.

# GEHEN UND NEHMEN
## To go and to take

**1** **Warm up** (1 minute)

Say "train" in German. (pp.38-9)

What does "von welchem Bahnsteig fährt der Zug ab?" mean? (pp.38-9)

Ask "When are you free?" (pp.32-3)

**Gehen** (to go) and **nehmen** (to take) are essential verbs in German, which form part of many useful expressions. Note that these verbs are not always used in the same way as in English and you need to learn phrases individually.

**2** **Gehen: to go** (6 minutes)

Say the different forms of **gehen** (to go) aloud. Use the cover flaps to test yourself and, when you are confident, practise the sample sentences below.

| | |
|---|---|
| **ich gehe** *ikh gay-e* | I go |
| **du gehst** *doo gayst* | you go (informal, singular) |
| **er/sie/es geht** *air/zee/ess gayt* | he/she/it goes |
| **wir gehen** *veer gay-en* | we go |
| **ihr geht** *eer gayt* | you go (informal, plural) |
| **sie gehen/Sie gehen** *zee gay-en* | they go/you go (formal) |
| **Wo gehen Sie hin?** *voe gay-en zee hin* | Where are you going? |
| **Ich gehe nach Bonn.** *ikh gay-e nahkh bonn* | I'm going to Bonn. |
| **Wie geht es Ihnen?** *vee gayt ess ee-nen* | How are you? |

**Ich gehe zum Brandenburger Tor.**
*ikh gay-e tsoom brun-den-boor-ger tor*
I'm going to the Brandenburg Gate.

**Conversational tip** German uses the same verb form for both *I go* and *I am going*. There is no equivalent of the English present continuous tense, which uses the *-ing* ending. For example, **Ich gehe nach Hamburg** means both *I am going to Hamburg* and *I go to Hamburg*. The same is true of other verbs: **Ich nehme den Zug** (*I am taking the train/I take the train*).

## 3 Nehmen: to take (6 minutes)

Say the different forms of **nehmen** (to take) aloud and then practise the sample sentences below. Use the cover flaps to test yourself.

**Ich nehme die Straßenbahn jeden Tag.**
*ikh nay-me dee shtrahs-sen-bahn yay-den tahk*
I take the tram every day.

| | |
|---|---|
| **ich nehme** <br> *ikh nay-me* | I take |
| **du nimmst** <br> *doo nimmst* | you take (informal, singular) |
| **er/sie/es nimmt** <br> *air/zee/ess nimmt* | he/she/it takes |
| **wir nehmen** <br> *veer nay-men* | we take |
| **ihr nehmt** <br> *eer naymt* | you take (informal, plural) |
| **sie nehmen/Sie nehmen** <br> *zee nay-men* | they take/you take (formal) |

| | |
|---|---|
| **Ich möchte kein Taxi nehmen.** <br> *ikh merkh-te kine tuck-see nay-men* | I don't want to take a taxi. |
| **Nehmen Sie die erste Straße links.** <br> *nay-men zee dee airs-te shtrahs-se links* | Take the first on the left. |
| **Er nimmt den Rehbraten.** <br> *air nimmt dayn ray-brah-ten* | He'll have the roast venison. |

## 4 Put into practice (2 minutes)

Cover the text on the right and complete the dialogue in German.

| | |
|---|---|
| **Wo gehen Sie hin?** <br> *voe gay-en zee hin* <br><br> Where are you going? <br><br> Say: I'm going to the station. | **Ich gehe zum Bahnhof.** <br> *ikh gay-e tsoom bahn-hoef* |
| **Möchten Sie die U-Bahn nehmen?** <br> *merkh-ten zee dee oo-bahn nay-men* <br><br> Do you want to take the metro? <br><br> Say: No, we want to go by bus. | **Nein, wir wollen den Bus nehmen.** <br> *nine. veer vol-len dayn booss nay-men* |

## Warm up (1 minute)

Ask "Where are you going?" (pp.40-1)

Say "I'm going to the station". (pp.40-1)

Say "fruit" and "cheese". (pp.24-5)

# TAXI, BUS, UND BAHN
## Public transport

The larger towns have *underground trains* (**U-Bahn**). Many also have *overground trams* (**Straßenbahn**) or *express trains* (**S-Bahn**). In most cases you need to buy and validate your ticket before you start the journey.

## 2 Words to remember (4 minutes)

Familiarize yourself with these words.

| | |
|---|---|
| **der Bus** *dair booss* | bus |
| **der Überlandbus** *dair ew-ber-lunt-boos* | coach |
| **der Busbahnhof** *dair booss-bahn-hoef* | bus station |
| **die Bushaltestelle** *dee booss-hal-te-shtel-le* | bus stop |
| **der Fahrpreis** *dair fahr-priess* | fare |
| **das Taxi** *duss tuck-see* | taxi |
| **der Taxistand** *dair tuck-see-shtunt* | taxi rank |
| **die U-Bahnstation** *dee oo-bahn-shta-tsee-oen* | underground station |

**Hält der Bus Nummer hundertzwanzig hier?**
*helt dair booss noom-mer hoon-dairt-tsvun-tsik heer*
Does the number 120 bus stop here?

## 3 In conversation: taxi (2 minutes)

**Zum Flughafen, bitte.**
*tsoom flook-hah-fen, bit-te*

The airport, please.

**Jawohl, kein Problem.**
*yah-voel. kine pro-blaym*

Yes, no problem.

**Können Sie mich bitte hier absetzen?**
*ker-nen zee mikh bit-te heer up-zet-sen*

Can you drop me here, please?

## 4 Useful phrases (4 minutes)

Practise these phrases and then test yourself using the cover flap.

| | |
|---|---|
| I would like a taxi to the cathedral. | **Ich hätte gern ein Taxi zum Dom.**<br>*ikh het-te gairn ine tuck-see tsoom doem* |
| When is the next bus? | **Wann fährt der nächste Bus?**<br>*vunn fairt dair nekh-ste booss* |
| How do you get to the museum? | **Wie komme ich zum Museum?**<br>*vee kom-me ikh tsoom moo-zay-oom* |
| How long is the journey? | **Wie lange dauert die Fahrt?**<br>*vee lan-ge dow-airt dee fahrt* |
| Please wait for me. | **Bitte warten Sie auf mich.**<br>*bit-te vahr-ten zee owf mikh* |

**Cultural tip** All taxis in Germany have meters. You can hail a taxi in the street when the lights are switched on, board one at a taxi rank, or phone for a taxi from your hotel or private address. Round up the fare to tip the driver.

## 5 Say it (2 minutes)

Do you go near the train station?

The bus station, please.

When's the next coach to Kiel?

## 6 In conversation: bus (2 minutes)

**Fahren Sie in der Nähe vom Museum entlang?**
*fah-ren zee in dair nay-e fom moo-zay-oom ent-lung*

Do you go near the museum?

**Ja. Das kostet achtzig Cent.**
*yah. duss kos-tet akh-tsik tsent*

Yes. That's 80 cents.

**Können Sie mir sagen, wann wir da sind?**
*ker-nen zee meer zah-gen, vunn veer dah zind*

Can you tell me when we arrive?

## 1 Warm up (1 minute)

How do you say "I have..."? (pp.14–15)

Say "my father", "my sister", and "my parents". (pp.10–11 and pp.12–13)

Say "I'm going to Berlin". (pp.40–1)

# AUF DER STRAßE
## On the road

German **Autobahnen** (*motorways*) are fast, but on many stretches there is now a speed limit of 130 km/h (80 mph). They are marked with the letter "A" on a blue sign, international expressways are "E" (**Europastraße**) on a green sign, and main roads "B" (**Bundesstraße**) on a white sign.

## 2 Match and repeat (4 minutes)

Match the numbered items to the list below and then test yourself.

**1** der Kofferraum
*dair kof-fer-rowm*

**2** die Windschutz-scheibe
*dee vint-shoots-shie-be*

**3** die Motorhaube
*dee mo-tor-how-be*

**4** der Reifen
*dair rie-fen*

**5** das Rad
*duss raht*

**6** die Tür
*dee tewr*

**7** die Stoßstange
*dee shtoess-shtange*

**8** die Scheinwerfer
*dee shien-vair-fer*

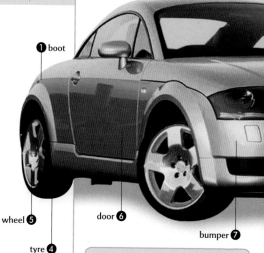

**1** boot

wheel **5**

door **6**

bumper **7**

tyre **4**

**Cultural tip** In Germany it is obligatory to carry with you in the car at all times your driving licence, car registration document, and a valid insurance certificate.

## 3 Road signs (2 minutes)

die Einbahnstraße
*dee ine-bahn-shtrah-se*

One way

der Kreisverkehr
*dair kries-fer-kair*

Roundabout

Vorfahrt achten
*for-fahrt akh-ten*

Give way

## 4 Useful phrases (4 minutes)

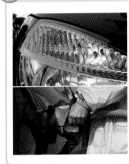

Learn these phrases and then test yourself using the cover flap.

| | |
|---|---|
| My indicator isn't working. | **Mein Blinker funktioniert nicht.** *mine blin-ker foonk-tsee-oe-neert nikht* |
| Fill it up, please. | **Volltanken, bitte.** *foll-tan-ken, bit-te* |

**2** windscreen

**3** bonnet

headlights **8**

## 5 Words to remember (3 minutes)

Familiarize yourself with these words and then test yourself using the flap.

| | |
|---|---|
| petrol | **das Benzin** *duss ben-tseen* |
| diesel | **der Diesel** *dair dee-zel* |
| oil | **das Öl** *duss erl* |
| engine | **der Motor** *dair moe-tor* |
| gearbox | **das Getriebe** *duss ge-tree-be* |
| indicator | **der Blinker** *dair blin-ker* |
| flat tyre | **ein Platten** *ine plutt-ten* |
| exhaust | **der Auspuff** *dair ows-pooff* |
| driving licence | **der Führerschein** *dair few-rer-shien* |

## 6 Say it (1 minute)

My gearbox isn't working.

I have a flat tyre.

**die Vorfahrtstraße**
*dee for-fahrt-shtrah-se*

Priority route

**Einfahrt verboten**
*ine-fahrt fer-boe-ten*

No entry

**Parken verboten**
*par-ken fer-boe-ten*

No parking

# WIEDERHOLUNG
## Review and repeat

**Antworten**
*Answers* (Cover with flap)

## 1 Transport

❶ der Bus
*dair booss*

❷ das Taxi
*duss tuk-see*

❸ das Auto
*duss ow-toe*

❹ das Fahrrad
*duss fahr-raht*

❺ der Zug
*dair tsook*

## 1 Transport (3 minutes)

Name these forms of transport in German.

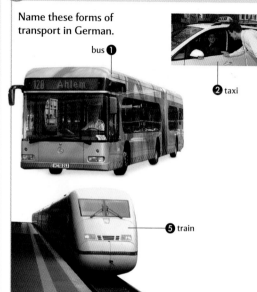

bus ❶

❷ taxi

❺ train

## 2 Go and take

❶ gehe
*gay-e*

❷ geht
*gayt*

❸ nehme
*nay-me*

❹ gehen
*gay-en*

❺ nehmen
*nay-men*

❻ gehen
*gay-en*

## 2 Go and take (4 minutes)

Use the correct form of the verb in brackets.

❶ Ich _____ zum Bahnhof. (gehen)

❷ Wie _____ es dir? (gehen)

❸ Ich _____ den Rehbraten. (nehmen)

❹ Wir _____ nach Berlin. (gehen)

❺ _____ Sie die erste Straße links. (nehmen)

❻ Wo _____ Sie hin? (gehen)

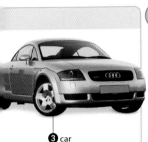

**3** car

**4** bicycle

## 3 Du or Sie?
(4 minutes)

Use the correct form of *you*.

**1** You are in a café. Ask "Do you have any cake?"

**2** You are with a friend. Ask "Do you want a beer?"

**3** A stranger approaches you at your company reception. Ask "Do you have an appointment?"

**4** You are on the bus. Ask "Do you go near the station?"

**5** Ask your mother where she's going.

## 3 Du or Sie?

**1** Haben Sie Kuchen?
*hah-ben zee koo-khen*

**2** Möchtest du ein Bier?
*merkh-test doo ine beer*

**3** Haben Sie einen Termin?
*hah-ben zee ie-nen terr-meen*

**4** Fahren Sie in der Nähe vom Bahnhof entlang?
*fah-ren zee in dair nay-e fom bahn-hoef ent-lung*

**5** Wo gehst du hin?
*voe gayst doo hin*

## 4 Tickets (4 minutes)

You're buying tickets at a train station. Follow the conversation, replying in German with the help of the numbered English prompts.

**Kann ich Ihnen helfen?**
**1** I'd like two tickets to Berlin.

**Rückfahrkarte oder einfach?**
**2** Return, please.

**Bitte schön. Fünfzig Euro, bitte.**
**3** What time does the train leave?

**Um dreizehn Uhr zehn.**
**4** What platform does the train leave from?

**Bahnsteig sieben.**
**5** Thank you very much. Goodbye.

## 4 Tickets

**1** Ich hätte gern zwei Fahrkarten nach Berlin.
*ikh het-te gairn tsvie fahr-kar-ten nahkh bair-leen*

**2** Rückfahrkarte, bitte.
*rewck-fahr-kar-te, bit-te*

**3** Wann fährt der Zug ab?
*vunn fairt dair tsook up*

**4** Von welchem Bahnsteig fährt der Zug ab?
*fon vel-khem bahn-shtiek fairt dair tsook up*

**5** Vielen Dank. Auf Wiedersehen.
*fee-len dunk. owf vee-der-zay-en*

# IN DER STADT
## About town

**Warm up** (1 minute)

Ask "How do you get to the museum?" (pp.42-3)

Say "I want to take the bus" and "I don't want to take a taxi". (pp.40-1)

Most German towns still have a market day and a thriving community of small shops. Even small villages tend to have a mayor and a town hall. Parking is usually regulated. Look out for blue parking zones, where you can park your car for a limited time without charge.

**2** **Match and repeat** (4 minutes)

Match the numbered locations to the words in the panel.

❶ **das Rathaus**
  *duss raht-hows*

❷ **die Brücke**
  *dee brew-ke*

❸ **die Kirche**
  *dee keer-khe*

❹ **der Parkplatz**
  *dair park-pluts*

❺ **das Stadtzentrum**
  *duss shtutt-tsen-troom*

❻ **der Platz**
  *dair pluts*

❼ **die Kunstgalerie**
  *dee koonst-gal-le-ree*

❽ **das Museum**
  *duss moo-zay-oom*

**3** **Words to remember** (4 minutes)

Familiarize yourself with these words.

| | |
|---|---|
| **die Tankstelle** <br> *dee tunk-shtel-le* | petrol station |
| **das Verkehrsbüro** <br> *duss fer-kairs-bew-roe* | tourist information |
| **die Werkstatt** <br> *dee vairk-shtutt* | car repairs |
| **das Schwimmbad** <br> *duss shvim-bad* | swimming pool |
| **die Bibliothek** <br> *dee beeb-lee-o-tayk* | library |

❶ town hall

church ❸

❷ bridge

square ❻

❼ art gallery

## 4 Useful phrases (4 minutes)

A useful expression for asking about public amenities is **es gibt** (*there is*). Notice that some words are often contracted in German – for example, **in dem** (*in the*) is contracted to **im**; **zu dem** (*to the*, masculine and neuter) becomes **zum**; and **zu der** (*to the*, feminine) contracts to **zur**.

Learn these phrases and then test yourself using the cover flap.

| | |
|---|---|
| Is there an art gallery in town? | **Gibt es eine Kunstgalerie in der Stadt?** *geept es ie-ne koonst-gal-le-ree in dair shtutt* |
| Is it far from here? | **Ist das weit von hier?** *isst duss viet fon heer* |
| There is a swimming pool near the bridge. | **Es gibt ein Schwimmbad bei der Brücke.** *es geept ien shvim-bad bie dair brew-ke* |
| There isn't a library. | **Es gibt keine Bibliothek.** *es geept kie-ne beeb-lee-o-tayk* |

## 5 Put into practice (2 minutes)

Join in this conversation. Conceal the text on the right with the cover flap and complete the dialogue in German. Check your answers and repeat if necessary.

car park ❹

❺ town centre

museum ❽

| | |
|---|---|
| **Kann ich Ihnen helfen?** *kunn ikh ee-nen hel-fen* Can I help you? | **Gibt es in der Stadt eine Bibliothek?** *geept es in dair shtutt ie-ne beeb-lee-o-tayk* |
| Ask: Is there a library in town? | |
| **Nein, aber es gibt ein Museum.** *nine, ah-ber es geept ine moo-zay-oom* No, but there's a museum. | **Wie komme ich zum Museum?** *vee kom-me ikh tsoom moo-zay-oom* |
| Ask: How do I get to the museum? | |
| **Es ist dort.** *es isst dort* It's over there. | **Vielen Dank.** *fee-len dunk* |
| Say: Thank you very much. | |

## DIE WEGBESCHREIBUNG
### Finding your way

### 1 Warm up (1 minute)

How do you say "near the station"? (pp.42-3)

Say "Take the first on the left". (pp.40-1)

Ask "Where are you going?" (pp.40-1)

In German you use **gehen** (*to go*) when talking about going somewhere on foot but **fahren** (*to drive*) when in a car. So *go left* is **Gehen Sie nach links** if you are on foot, but **Fahren Sie nach links** if you are travelling in a car.

### 2 Useful phrases (4 minutes)

Learn these phrases and then test yourself.

| | |
|---|---|
| **Gehen Sie nach links/rechts** *gay-en zee nahkh links/rekhts* | go left/right |
| **auf der linken Seite/ rechten Seite** *owf dair lin-ken zie-te/ rekh-ten zie-te* | on the left side/ right side |
| **geradeaus (weiter)** *ge-rah-de-ows (vieter)* | (continue) straight on |
| **Wie komme ich zum Schwimmbad?** *vee kom-me ikh tsoom shvim-bad* | How do I get to the swimming pool? |
| **die erste (Straße) links** *dee airs-te (shtrah-se) links* | first (street) on the left |

**die Bibliothek** *dee beeb-lee-o-tayk* library

**die Fußgängerzone** *dee foos-gen-ger-tsoe-ne* pedestrian zone

**Gehen Sie am Hauptplatz nach links.** *gay-en zee am howpt-pluts nahkh links* Turn left at the main square.

### 3 In conversation (4 minutes)

**Gibt es ein Restaurant in der Stadt?** *geept es ine res-to-rung in der shtutt*

Is there a restaurant in town?

**Ja, am Bahnhof.** *yah, um bahn-hoef*

Yes, near the station.

**Wie komme ich zum Bahnhof?** *vee kom-me ikh tsoom bahn-hoef*

How do I get to the station?

## 4 Words to remember (4 minutes)

**Ich habe mich verlaufen.**
*ikh hah-be mikh fer-low-fen*
I'm lost.

Familiarize yourself with these words and then test yourself using the flap.

| | |
|---|---|
| traffic lights | **die Ampel** *dee um-pel* |
| corner | **die Ecke** *dee ek-ke* |
| street/road | **die Straße** *dee shtrah-se* |
| main road | **die Hauptstraße** *dee howpt-shtrah-se* |
| at the end of the street | **am Ende der Straße** *um en-de dair shtrah-se* |
| (town) map | **der Stadtplan** *dair shtutt-plahn* |
| flyover | **die Überführung** *dee ew-ber-few-roong* |
| opposite | **gegenüber** *gay-gen-ew-ber* |

**Wir sind hier.**
*veer zint heer*
We are here.

**der Brunnen**
*dair broon-nen*
fountain

## 5 Say it (2 minutes)

Go right at the end of the street.

It's opposite the museum.

It's ten minutes by bus.

**Gehen Sie an der Ampel nach links.**
*gay-en zee un dair um-pel nahkh links*

Go left at the traffic lights.

**Ist es weit?**
*isst es viet*

Is it far?

**Nein, es ist fünf Minuten zu Fuß.**
*nine, es isst fewnf mee-noo-ten tsoo fooss*

No, it's five minutes on foot.

# DIE BESICHTIGUNG
## Sightseeing

Say the days of the week in German. (pp.28-9)

How do you say "at six o'clock"? (pp.30-1)

Ask "What time is it?" (pp.30-1)

Museums tend to stay open all day, but have more restricted opening hours in smaller villages where they are often closed on Sundays. Once a week, usually on Wednesdays or Thursdays, the larger museums will stay open till late, while many are closed on Mondays and on public holidays.

**2** **Words to remember** (4 minutes)

Familiarize yourself with these words and test yourself using the flap.

| | |
|---|---|
| **der Führer** *dair few-rer* | guidebook |
| **die Eintrittskarte** *dee ine-trits-kar-te* | entrance ticket |
| **die Öffnungszeiten** *dee erff-noongs-tsie-ten* | opening times |
| **der Feiertag** *dair fie-er-tahk* | public holiday |
| **die Ermäßigung** *dee er-mes-see-goong* | reduction/ discount |

**die Führung**
*dee few-roong*
guided tour

**Cultural tip** Germany observes a number of religious holidays in addition to Christmas and Easter - for example, Whit Monday and Ascension Day. The May bank holiday is always celebrated on 1st May, whatever day of the week it falls on. There are also additional regional holidays.

**3** **In conversation** (3 minutes)

**Sind Sie heute Nachmittag geöffnet?**
*zint zee hoy-te nahkh-mit-tahk ge-erff-net*

Do you open this afternoon?

**Ja, aber wir schließen um sechzehn Uhr.**
*yah, ah-ber veer shliee-sen oom zekh-tsayn oor*

Yes, but we close at 4 pm.

**Gibt es Zugang für Rollstuhlfahrer?**
*geept es tsoo-gung fewr roll-shtool-fah-rer*

Do you have wheelchair access?

## 4 Useful phrases (3 minutes)

**Öffnungszeiten:**
Di. - Fr.  11 - 18 Uhr
Sa. + So.  11 - 16 Uhr
(Montags geschlossen)

Learn these phrases and then test yourself using the cover flap.

| What time do you open/close? | **Wann öffnen/ schließen Sie?** *vunn erf-nen/shlee-sen zee* |
|---|---|
| Where are the toilets? | **Wo sind die Toiletten?** *voe zind dee twah-let-ten* |
| Is there wheelchair access? | **Gibt es Zugang für Rollstuhlfahrer?** *geept es tsoo-gung fewr roll-shtool-fah-rer* |

## 5 Put into practice (4 minutes)

Cover the text on the right and complete the dialogue in German.

**Das Museum ist geschlossen.**
*duss moo-zay-oom isst ge-shlos-sen*
The museum is closed.

Ask: Are you open on Mondays?

**Sind Sie am Montag geöffnet?**
*zint zee um moen-tahk ge-erff-net*

**Ja, aber wir schließen früh.**
*yah, ah-ber veer shlee-sen frew*

Yes, but we close early.

Ask: At what time?

**Um wieviel Uhr?**
*oom vee-feel oor*

**Ja, da drüben ist ein Fahrstuhl.**
*yah, dar drew-ben isst ine fahr-shtool*

Yes, there's a lift over there.

**Danke, ich hätte gern vier Eintrittskarten.**
*dun-ke, ikh het-te gairn feer ine-trits-kar-ten*

Thank you, I'd like four entrance tickets.

**Bitte sehr, und der Führer ist gratis.**
*bit-te zair, oont dair few-rer isst grah-tis*

Here you are, and the guidebook is free.

## 1 Warm up (1 minute)

Say "You're on time".
(pp.14–15)

What's the German for
"ticket"? (pp.38–9)

Say "I am going to New
York". (pp.40–1)

# IM FLUGHAFEN
## At the airport

Although the airport environment is largely signposted
in English, it will sometimes be useful to be able to ask
your way around the terminal in German. It's a good
idea to make sure you have a few one-euro coins when
you arrive at the airport; you may need to pay for a
baggage trolley.

## 2 Words to remember (4 minutes)

Familiarize yourself with these words and
test yourself using the flap.

| | |
|---|---|
| **die Gepäckausgabe** <br> *dee ge-peck-ows-gah-be* | baggage reclaim |
| **der Abflug** <br> *dair up-flook* | departures |
| **die Ankunft** <br> *dee un-koonft* | arrivals |
| **der Zoll** <br> *dair tsoll* | customs |
| **die Passkontrolle** <br> *dee puss-kon-trol-le* | passport control |
| **das Terminal** <br> *duss terr-mee-nahl* | terminal |
| **der Flugsteig** <br> *dair flook-shtiek* | gate |
| **die Flugnummer** <br> *dee flook-noom-mer* | flight number |

**Von welchem Flugsteig geht
der Flug 23?**
*fon vel-khem flook-shtiek gayt dair
flook drie-oont-tsvun-tsik*
What gate does flight 23 leave from?

## 3 Useful phrases (3 minutes)

Learn these phrases and then test yourself
using the cover flap.

| | |
|---|---|
| **Geht der Flug nach Hannover pünktlich ab?** <br> *gayt dair flook nahkh hun-no-fer pewnkt-likh up* | Will the flight for Hanover leave on time? |
| **Ich kann mein Gepäck nicht finden.** <br> *ikh kunn mine ge-peck nikht fin-den* | I can't find my baggage. |

## 4 Put into practice (3 minutes)

Join in this conversation. Read the German on the left and follow the instructions to make your reply. Then test yourself by concealing the answers with the cover flap.

**Guten Abend. Kann ich Ihnen helfen?**
*goo-ten ah-bent. kunn ikh ee-nen hel-fen*

Hello, can I help you?

**Geht der Flug nach Köln pünktlich ab?**
*gayt dair flook nahkh kerln pewnkt-likh up*

Ask: Is the flight to Cologne on time?

---

**Ja.**
*yah*

Yes.

**Von welchem Flugsteig geht er ab?**
*fon vel-khem flook-shtiek gayt air up*

Ask: What gate does it leave from?

## 5 Match and repeat (4 minutes)

Match the numbered items to the German words in the panel.

boarding ❶ pass

baggage ❷ check-in

ticket ❸

passport ❹

❺ suitcase    ❻ hand luggage    ❼ trolley

❶ **die Bordkarte**
*dee bort-kar-te*

❷ **der Abfertigungs-schalter**
*dair up-fer-ti-goongs-shull-ter*

❸ **das Flugticket**
*duss flook-tik-ket*

❹ **der Pass**
*dair puss*

❺ **der Koffer**
*dair kof-fer*

❻ **das Handgepäck**
*duss hunt-ge-peck*

❼ **der Kofferkuli**
*dair kof-fer-koo-li*

# WIEDERHOLUNG
## Review and repeat

**Antworten**
*Answers* (Cover with flap)

### 1 Places

❶ **das Museum**
*duss moo-zay-oom*

❷ **das Rathaus**
*duss raht-hows*

❸ **die Brücke**
*dee brew-ke*

❹ **die Kunstgalerie**
*dee koonst-gal-le-ree*

❺ **der Parkplatz**
*dair park-pluts*

❻ **der Dom**
*dair doem*

❼ **der Platz**
*dair pluts*

### 1 Places (4 minutes)

Name the numbered places in German.

❶ museum  ❷ town hall  ❸ bridge

❹ art gallery  ❺ car park

❻ cathedral

❼ square

### 2 Car parts

❶ **die Windschutz-scheibe**
*dee vint-shoots-shie-be*

❷ **der Blinker**
*dair blin-ker*

❸ **die Motorhaube**
*dee mo-tor-how-be*

❹ **der Reifen**
*dair rie-fen*

❺ **die Tür**
*dee tewr*

❻ **die Stoßstange**
*dee shtoess-shtange*

### 2 Car parts (3 minutes)

Name these car parts in German.

windscreen ❶

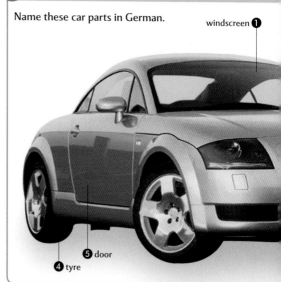

❺ door
❹ tyre

**Antworten**
*Answers* (Cover with flap)

## 3 Questions (4 minutes)

Ask the questions in German that match the
following answers:

❶ Der Bus fährt um acht Uhr ab.

❷ Kaffee, das macht zwei Euro fünfzig.

❸ Nein, ich möchte keinen Wein.

❹ Der Zug fährt von Bahnsteig fünf ab.

❺ Wir fahren nach Leipzig.

❻ Nein, es ist drei Minuten zu Fuß.

## 3 Questions

❶ **Wann fährt der Bus ab?**
*vunn fairt dair boos up*

❷ **Was kostet der Kaffee?**
*vuss kos-tet dair kuf-fay*

❸ **Möchten Sie Wein?**
*merkh-ten zee vine*

❹ **Von welchem Bahnsteig fährt der Zug ab?**
*fon vel-khem bahn-shtiek fairt dair tsook up*

❺ **Wo fahren Sie hin?**
*voe fah-ren zee hin*

❻ **Ist es weit?**
*isst es viet*

❷ indicator
❸ bonnet
bumper ❻

## 4 Verbs (4 minutes)

Choose the correct
words to fill the gaps.

❶ Ich _____ Deutsche(r).

❷ Wir _____ mit dem Bus.

❸ Sie *(she)* _____ nach Dresden.

❹ Er_____ drei Töchter.

❺ _____ du Tee?

❻ Wie viele Kinder _____ Sie?

❼ Wo _____ die Toiletten?

## 4 Verbs

❶ **bin**
*bin*

❷ **fahren**
*fah-ren*

❸ **geht**
*gayt*

❹ **hat**
*hut*

❺ **möchtest**
*merkh-test*

❻ **haben**
*hah-ben*

❼ **sind**
*zint*

**1** **Warm up** (1 minute)

How do you ask in German "Do you accept credit cards?" (pp.38–9)

Ask "How much is that?" (pp.18–19)

How do you ask "Do you have children?" (pp.12–13)

# DIE ZIMMER-RESERVIERUNG
## Booking a room

There are different types of accommodation: **das Hotel**, rated by one to five stars; **die Pension** or **der Gasthof**, which are traditional inns; and private accommodation where signs advertise **Zimmer frei** or **Fremdenzimmer**.

**2** **Useful phrases** (3 minutes)

Practise these phrases and then test yourself by concealing the German on the left with the cover flap.

**Ist das Frühstück inbegriffen?**
*isst duss frew-shtewk in-be-grif-fen*

Is breakfast included?

**Sind Tiere zugelassen?**
*zint tee-re tsoo-ge-luss-sen*

Are pets allowed?

**Haben Sie Zimmerservice?**
*hah-ben zee tsim-mer-sair-vis*

Do you have room service?

**Wann muss ich das Zimmer freimachen?**
*vunn mooss ikh duss tsim-mer frie-ma-khen*

When must I vacate the room?

**3** **In conversation** (5 minutes)

**Haben Sie noch Zimmer frei?**
*hah-ben zee nokh tsim-mer frie*

Do you have any vacancies?

**Ja, ein Doppelzimmer.**
*yah. ine dop-pel-tsim-mer*

Yes, a double room.

**Haben Sie ein Kinderbett?**
*hah-ben zee ine kin-der-bet*

Do you have a cot?

## 4 Words to remember (4 minutes)

Familiarize yourself with these words and test yourself by concealing the German on the right with the cover flap.

| | | |
|---|---|---|
| air-conditioning | **die Klimaanlage** | *dee klee-mah-un-lah-ge* |
| room | **das Zimmer** | *duss tsim-mer* |
| single room | **das Einzelzimmer** | *duss ine-tsel-tsim-mer* |
| double room | **das Doppelzimmer** | *duss dop-pel-tsim-mer* |
| twin beds | **die zwei Einzelbetten** | *dee tsvie ine-tsel-bet-ten* |
| bathroom | **das Badezimmer** | *duss bah-de-tsim-mer* |
| shower | **die Dusche** | *dee doo-she* |
| breakfast | **das Frühstück** | *duss frew-shtewk* |
| key | **der Schlüssel** | *dair shlews-sel* |
| balcony | **der Balkon** | *dair bull-kong* |

**Hat das Zimmer Blick auf den Park?**
*hut duss tsim-mer blick owf dayn park*
Does the room have a view over the park?

## 5 Say it (2 minutes)

Do you have a single room, please?

Does the room have a balcony?

**Cultural tip** Some, but not all, hotels and guest houses will include breakfast in the price of a room; in others you will be charged extra. Often breakfast is in the style of a **Frühstücksbüffet** (*breakfast buffet*) and includes cereals, a selection of breads, cooked meats, cheeses, jams, fruit juices, and a choice of coffee or tea.

**Wie lange möchten Sie bleiben?**
*vee lun-ge merkh-ten zee blie-ben*

How long will you be staying?

**Drei Nächte.**
*drie nekh-te*

For three nights.

**Sehr gut. Hier ist Ihr Schlüssel.**
*zair goot. heer isst eer shlews-sel*

Very good. Here's your key.

## 1 Warm up (1 minute)

How do you say "is there...?" and "there isn't..."? (pp.48-9)

What does "Haben Sie reserviert?" mean? (pp.20-1)

# IM HOTEL
## In the hotel

Although larger hotels almost always have bathrooms en suite, there are still some **Pensionen** and guest houses where you will have to share facilities with other guests. Prices are generally charged for the room, and not per person, so a family staying in one room can be a cheap option.

## 2 Match and repeat (6 minutes)

Match the numbered items in this hotel bedroom with the German text in the panel and then test yourself using the cover flap.

❶ **der Nachttisch**
*dair nukht-tish*

❷ **die Lampe**
*dee lum-pe*

❸ **die Musikanlage**
*dee moo-zik-an-lah-ge*

❹ **die Vorhänge**
*dee foer-hen-ge*

❺ **die Couch**
*dee kowtch*

❻ **das Kopfkissen**
*duss kopf-kis-sen*

❼ **das Kissen**
*duss kis-sen*

❽ **das Bett**
*duss bet*

❾ **die Tagesdecke**
*dee tah-ges-dek-ke*

❿ **die Decke**
*dee dek-ke*

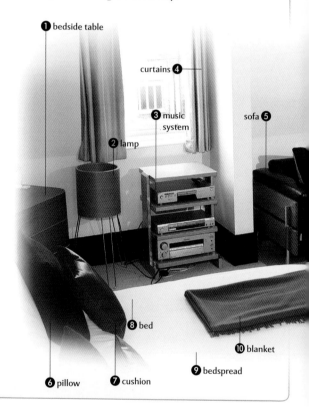

❶ bedside table

curtains ❹

❸ music system

sofa ❺

❷ lamp

❽ bed

❿ blanket

❾ bedspread

❻ pillow

❼ cushion

**Cultural tip** Hotel prices vary widely. They are higher during the season in summer or winter resorts. They are often much higher in cities during trade fairs and festivals, such as the Frankfurt Book Fair, the Berlinale Film Festival, the Cologne Carnival, the Hanover Computer Fair CEBIT, and the Munich Beer Festival in October.

## 3 Useful phrases (5 minutes)

Learn these phrases and then test yourself using the cover flap.

| | |
|---|---|
| The room is too warm/cold. | **Das Zimmer ist zu warm/kalt.** *duss tsim-mer isst tsoo varm/kullt* |
| There are no towels. | **Es gibt keine Handtücher.** *es geept kie-ne hunt-tew-kher* |
| I need some soap. | **Ich brauche Seife.** *ikh brow-khe zie-fe* |
| The shower doesn't work. | **Die Dusche funktioniert nicht.** *dee doo-she foonk-tsee-oe-neert nikht* |
| The lift is broken. | **Der Fahrstuhl ist kaputt.** *dair fahr-shtool isst ka-poott* |

## 4 Put into practice (3 minutes)

Cover the text on the right and complete the dialogue in German.

**Kann ich Ihnen helfen?**
*kunn ikh eenen hel-fen*

Can I help you?

Say: I need blankets.

**Ich brauche Decken.**
*ikh brow-khe dek-ken*

**Das Zimmermädchen wird sie bringen.**
*duss tsim-mer-met-khen virt zee brin-gen*

The maid will bring some.

Say: And the television is broken.

**Und der Fernseher ist kaputt.**
*oont dair fairn-zay-er isst ka-poott*

# BEIM CAMPING
## Camping

**1 Warm up** (1 minute)

Ask "Can I?" (pp.34–5)

What is English for "the shower"? (pp.60–1)

Say "I need some towels". (pp.60–1)

Camping has long been popular in Germany. There are numerous campsites all over the country, which tend to be of a high standard, usually equipped with washrooms, kitchens, shop, restaurant, and sometimes a swimming pool. Tourist offices have information about sites in their area.

**2 Useful phrases** (3 minutes)

Learn these phrases. Then test yourself by concealing the German with the cover flap.

**Kann ich ein Fahrrad ausleihen?**
*kunn ikh ine fahr-raht ows-lie-en*
Can I rent a bicycle?

**Ist das Wasser trinkbar?**
*isst duss vuss-ser trink-bahr*
Is this drinking water?

**Sind Lagerfeuer erlaubt?**
*zint lah-ger-foy-er er-lowpt*
Are campfires allowed?

**Radios sind verboten.**
*rah-dee-os zint fer-boe-ten*
Radios are forbidden.

**Der Campingplatz ist ruhig.**
*dair kam-ping-pluts isst roo-hik*
The campsite is quiet.

**das Campingplatz-büro**
*duss kamping-plutz-bew-roe*
campsite office

**das Überzelt**
*duss ew-ber-tselt*
fly sheet

**3 In conversation:** (5 minutes)

**Ich brauche einen Platz für zwei Tage.**
*ikh brow-khe ie-nen pluts fewr tsvie tah-ge*

I need a pitch for two days.

**Es gibt einen beim Schwimmbad.**
*es geept ie-nen bime shvim-bad*

There's one near the swimming pool.

**Wieviel kostet es für einen Wohnwagen?**
*vee-feel kos-tet es fewr ie-nen vohn-vah-gen*

How much is it for a caravan?

## 4 Say it (2 minutes)

I need a pitch for four days.

Can I rent a tent?

Where's the electrical hook-up?

**der Stromanschluss**
*dair shtrohm-un-shlooss*
electrical hook-up

**die Toiletten**
*dee twah-let-ten*
toilets

**die Zeltschnur**
*dee tselt-schnoor*
guy rope

**der Hering**
*dair hay-ring*
tent peg

## 5 Words to remember (4 minutes)

Familiarize yourself with these words and test yourself using the flap.

| | |
|---|---|
| tent | **das Zelt** <br> *duss tselt* |
| caravan | **der Wohnwagen** <br> *dair voen-vah-gen* |
| camper van | **das Wohnmobil** <br> *duss voen-moe-beel* |
| campsite | **der Campingplatz** <br> *dair kam-ping-pluts* |
| pitch | **der Platz** <br> *dair pluts* |
| campfire | **das Lagerfeuer** <br> *duss lah-ger-foy-er* |
| drinking water | **das Trinkwasser** <br> *duss trink-vuss-ser* |
| rubbish | **der Abfall** <br> *dair up-full* |
| showers | **die Duschen** <br> *dee doo-shen* |
| camping gas | **das Campinggas** <br> *duss kam-ping-gahs* |
| sleeping bag | **der Schlafsack** <br> *dair shlahf-zuck* |
| air mattress | **die Luftmatratze** <br> *dee looft-mah-trat-se* |
| ground sheet | **der Zeltboden** <br> *dair tselt-bo-den* |

**Fünfzig Euro, einen Tag im voraus.**
*fewnf-tsik oy-roe, ie-nen tahk im for-ows*

Fifty euros, one day in advance.

**Kann ich einen Grill mieten?**
*kunn ikh ie-nen grill mee-ten*

Can I rent a barbecue?

**Ja, aber sie müssen eine Kaution hinterlegen.**
*yah, ah-ber zee mews-sen ie-ne kow-tsee-oen hin-ter-lay-gen*

Yes, but you must pay a deposit.

# BESCHREIBUNGEN
## Descriptions

**1** **Warm up** (1 minute)

How do you say "hot" and "cold"? (pp.60-1)

What is the German for "room", "bed", and "pillow"? (pp.60-1)

Simple descriptive sentences are easily constructed in German: **Das Zimmer ist kalt** (*The room is cold*). Note that when adjectives are put first, they may have different endings, such as **-er**, **-e**, **-es**, or **-en** - for example, **ein kaltes Zimmer** (*a cold room*). Just learn these in context as you encounter them.

**2** **Words to remember** (7 minutes)

Learn these words and then test yourself.

| | |
|---|---|
| **hart**<br>*hart* | hard |
| **weich**<br>*viekh* | soft |
| **heiß**<br>*hiess* | hot |
| **kalt**<br>*kullt* | cold |
| **groß**<br>*groes* | big/tall |
| **klein**<br>*kline* | small/short |
| **schön**<br>*shern* | beautiful |
| **hässlich**<br>*hess-likh* | ugly |
| **laut**<br>*lowt* | noisy |
| **ruhig**<br>*roo-hig* | quiet |
| **gut**<br>*goot* | good |
| **schlecht**<br>*shlekht* | bad |
| **langsam**<br>*lung-zahm* | slow |
| **schnell**<br>*shnell* | fast |
| **dunkel**<br>*doon-kel* | dark |
| **hell**<br>*hell* | light |

**Die Berge sind hoch.**
*dee ber-ge zint hoekh*
The mountains are high.

**Der Hügel ist niedrig.**
*dair hew-gel isst nee-drikh*
The hill is low.

**Die Kirche ist alt.**
*dee kir-khe isst alt*
The church is old.

**Das Haus ist klein.**
*duss hows isst kline*
The house is small.

**Das Dorf ist sehr schön.**
*duss dorf isst zair shern*
The village is very beautiful.

## 3 Useful phrases (4 minutes)

To qualify a description add **sehr** (*very*) or **zu** (*too*) in front of the adjective, or surround it with **nicht... genug** (*not... enough*).

| | |
|---|---|
| This coffee is cold. | **Dieser Kaffee ist kalt.** <br> *dee-zer kuf-fay isst kullt* |
| My room is very noisy. | **Mein Zimmer ist sehr laut.** <br> *mine tsim-mer isst zair lowt* |
| My car is too small. | **Mein Auto ist zu klein.** <br> *mine ow-to isst tsoo kline* |
| The bed is not soft enough. | **Das Bett ist nicht weich genug.** <br> *das bet isst nikht viekh ge-nookh* |

## 4 Put into practice (3 minutes)

Join in this conversation. Cover the text on the right and complete the dialogue in German. Check and repeat if necessary.

| | |
|---|---|
| **Hier ist das Zimmer.** <br> *heer isst duss tsim-mer* <br> Here is the room. <br><br> Say: The view is very beautiful. | **Die Aussicht ist sehr schön.** <br> *dee ows-zikht isst zair shern* |
| **Dort ist das Badezimmer.** <br> *dort isst duss bah-de-tsim-mer* <br> There is the bathroom. <br><br> Say: It is too small. | **Es ist zu klein.** <br> *es isst tsoo kline* |
| **Wir haben sonst keins.** <br> *veer hah-ben zonst keins* <br> We haven't got another. <br><br> Say: Then we'll take the room. | **Dann nehmen wir das Zimmer.** <br> *dan nay-men veer duss tsim-mer* |

# WIEDERHOLUNG
## Review and repeat

### 1 Adjectives

❶ The room is too hot.

❷ My pillow is too small.

❸ The coffee is good.

❹ The bathroom is very cold.

❺ My car is not big enough.

### 1 Adjectives (3 minutes)

What do these sentences mean?

❶ Das Zimmer ist zu heiß.

❷ Mein Kopfkissen ist zu klein.

❸ Der Kaffee ist gut.

❹ Das Badezimmer ist sehr kalt.

❺ Mein Auto ist nicht groß genug.

### 2 Campsite

❶ der Stromanschluss
*dair shtrohm-un-shlooss*

❷ das Zelt
*duss tselt*

❸ die Zeltschnur
*dee tselt-shnoor*

❹ die Toiletten
*dee twah-let-ten*

❺ der Wohnwagen
*dair voen-vah-gen*

### 2 Campsite (3 minutes)

Name these items you might find in a campsite.

electrical ❶ hook-up

❷ tent

guy rope ❸

## 3 At the hotel (4 minutes)

You are booking a room in a hotel. Follow the conversation, replying in German following the English prompts.

**Kann ich Ihnen helfen?**
❶ Do you have any vacancies?

**Ja, ein Doppelzimmer.**
❷ Are pets allowed?

**Ja, wie lange möchten Sie bleiben?**
❸ Three nights.

**Das macht zweihundertfünfzig Euro.**
❹ Is breakfast included?

**Selbstverständlich, hier ist der Schlüssel.**
❺ Thank you very much.

## 3 At the hotel

❶ **Haben Sie noch Zimmer frei?**
*hah-ben zee nokh tsim-mer frie*

❷ **Sind Tiere zugelassen?**
*zint tee-re tsoo-ge-luss-sen*

❸ **Drei Nächte.**
*drie nekh-te*

❹ **Ist das Frühstück inbegriffen?**
*isst duss frew-shtewk in-be-grif-fen*

❺ **Vielen Dank.**
*fee-len dunk*

## 4 Negatives (5 minutes)

Make these sentences negative using the verb in brackets.

❶ Ich _____ Kinder. (haben)

❷ Sie _____ morgen nach Hamburg. (fahren)

❸ Er _____ Wein. (möchten)

❹ Ich _____ Zucker in meinem Kaffee. (nehmen)

❺ Die Aussicht _____ sehr schön. (sein)

## 4 Negatives

❶ **habe keine**
*hah-be kie-ne*

❷ **fährt nicht**
*fairt nikht*

❸ **möchte keinen**
*merkh-te kie-nen*

❹ **nehme keinen**
*nay-me kie-nen*

❺ **ist nicht**
*isst nikht*

❹ toilets

❺ caravan

## 1 Warm up (1 minute)

Ask "How do I get to the station?" (pp.50-1)

Say "Turn left at the traffic lights", "Go straight on", "The station is opposite the café". (pp.50-1)

# EINKAUFEN
## Shopping

Although shopping centres on the outskirts of the cities are increasingly important in Germany, there are still many smaller, traditional, specialized shops. Excellent local markets exist in large cities and small villages. Ask the **Verkehrsbüro** (*tourist office*) when the local market day is held.

## 2 Match and repeat (5 minutes)

Match the shops numbered 1-9 on the right to the German in the panel. Then test yourself using the cover flap.

❶ **die Bäckerei**
*dee bek-ke-rie*

❷ **die Konditorei**
*dee kon-dee-to-rie*

❸ **das Zeitungskiosk**
*duss tsie-toongs-kee-osk*

❹ **die Fleischerei**
*dee flie-she-rie*

❺ **das Feinkostgeschäft**
*duss fine-kost-ge-sheft*

❻ **die Buchhandlung**
*dee bookh-hund-loong*

❼ **das Fischgeschäft**
*duss fish-ge-sheft*

❽ **die Apotheke**
*dee a-po-tay-ke*

❾ **die Bank**
*dee bunk*

❶ baker

❷ cake shop

❹ butcher

❺ delicatessen

❼ fishmonger

❽ pharmacy

**Cultural tip** A German **Apotheke** (*pharmacy*) dispenses both prescription and over-the-counter medicines. It also sells a small range of upmarket health and beauty products. Everyday toiletries such as soap and shampoo are more usually obtained from the **Drogerie**, which is often a self-service supermarket. These shops do not, however, sell medicines of any kind.

## 3 Words to remember (4 minutes)

**Der Blumenladen**
*dair bloo-men-lah-den*
florist

Familiarize yourself with these words and test yourself using the flap.

| | |
|---|---|
| antique dealer | **der Antiquitätenladen** *dair an-ti-qvi-tay-ten-lah-den* |
| hairdresser | **der Friseur** *dair fri-zer* |
| jeweller | **der Juwelier** *dair yoo-ve-leer* |
| post office | **die Post** *dee posst* |
| shoe shop | **das Schuhgeschäft** *duss shoo-ge-sheft* |
| dry cleaner | **die Reinigung** *dee rie-nee-goong* |
| hardware shop | **der Eisenwarenhändler** *dair ie-zen-vah-ren-hend-ler* |

❸ newsagent

❻ bookshop

❾ bank

## 4 Useful phrases (3 minutes)

Familiarize yourself with these phrases.

| | |
|---|---|
| Where can I find the hairdresser? | **Wo ist der Friseur?** *voe isst dair fri-zer* |
| Where do I pay? | **Wo kann ich zahlen?** *voe kunn ikh tsah-len* |
| Thank you, I'm just looking. | **Danke, ich schaue mich nur um.** *dun-ke, ikh show-e mikh noor oomm* |
| Do you sell phonecards? | **Verkaufen Sie Telefonkarten?** *fer-kow-fen zee tay-lay-foen-kar-ten* |
| I'd like two of these. | **Ich hätte gern zwei von diesen.** *ikh het-te gairn tsvie fon dee-zen* |
| Is there a department store in town? | **Gibt es in der Stadt ein Kaufhaus?** *geept es in dair shtutt ine kowf-hows* |
| Can I place an order? | **Kann ich bitte bestellen?** *kunn ikh bit-te be-shtel-len* |

## 5 Say it (2 minutes)

Where can I find the bank?

Do you sell cheese?

I'd like three of these.

# AUF DEM MARKT
## At the market

### Warm up (1 minute)

What is German for 40, 56, 77, 82, and 94? (pp.30-1)

Say "I'd like a big room". (pp.64-5)

Ask "Do you have a small car?" (pp.64-5)

Germany uses the metric system of weights and measures. You need to ask for produce in kilogrammes or grammes. You may find that the older generation still use the term **ein Pfund** (*a pound*) meaning half a kilo. Larger items, such as melons, are sold **stückweise** or **am Stück** (*individually*).

### Match and repeat (4 minutes)

Match the numbered items in this scene with the text in the panel.

❶ **der Rhabarber**
*dair ra-bar-ber*

❷ **die Kartoffeln**
*dee kar-toff-eln*

❸ **die Radieschen**
*dee ra-dees-khen*

❹ **der Spinat**
*dair shpee-naht*

❺ **die Möhren**
*dee mer-ren*

❻ **der Kohl**
*dair koel*

❼ **der Lauch**
*dair lowk*

❽ **der Kohlrabi**
*dair koel-rah-bee*

radishes ❸
potatoes ❷
rhubarb ❶

cabbage ❻   ❽ kohlrabi

❼ leeks

### In conversation (3 minutes)

**Ich hätte gern Tomaten.**
*ikh het-te gairn to-mah-ten*

I'd like some tomatoes.

**Die großen oder die kleinen?**
*dee groe-sen oe-der dee klie-nen*

The large ones or the small ones?

**Zwei Kilo kleine, bitte.**
*tsvie kee-lo klie-ne, bit-te*

Two kilos of the small ones, please.

**Cultural tip** Germany uses the common European currency, the euro, divided into 100 cents. You will usually hear the price as **zehn Euro zwanzig** (€10.20). Often, the word **Euro** is also omitted: **zwei dreißig** (€2.30).

### 4 Say it (2 minutes)

Three kilos of potatoes, please.

The carrots are too expensive.

How much is the cabbage?

④ spinach

⑤ carrots

### 5 Useful phrases (5 minutes)

In German you don't need a word for *of* between the measurement unit (kilo) and the thing you are buying: **ein Kilo Kirschen** (*a kilo of cherries*).

These sausages are too expensive.

**Diese Würstchen sind zu teuer.**
*dee-ze vewrst-khen zint tsoo toy-er*

How much is a kilo of grapes?

**Was kostet ein Kilo Trauben?**
*vuss kos-tet ine kee-lo-trowben*

That's all.

**Das ist alles.**
*duss isst ull-les*

**Sonst noch etwas?**
*zonst nokh et-vuss*

Anything else?

**Das ist alles, danke. Was kostet das?**
*duss isst ull-les, dun-ke. vuss kos-tet duss*

That's all, thank you. How much?

**Drei Euro fünfzig.**
*drie oy-roe fewnf-tsik*

Three euros, fifty.

# IM SUPERMARKT
## At the supermarket

1

### Warm up (1 minute)

What are these items you could buy in a supermarket? (pp.24–5)

**das Fleisch**
**der Fisch**
**der Käse**
**der Fruchtsaft**
**der Wein**
**das Wasser**

Supermarkets in Germany range from the very well stocked at the expensive end of the market to much cheaper, budget chains. Some larger supermarkets, often in the basement of department stores, have small restaurants where you can sample the produce as you shop.

2

### Match and repeat (5 minutes)

Look at the numbered items and match them to the German words in the panel below. Then test yourself using the cover flap.

❶ **die Haushaltswaren**
*dee hows-hults-vah-ren*

❷ **das Obst**
*duss opst*

❸ **die Getränke**
*dee ge-tren-ke*

❹ **die Fertiggerichte**
*dee fair-tikh-ge-rikh-te*

❺ **die Kosmetika**
*dee kos-may-tee-ka*

❻ **die Milchprodukte**
*dee milkh-pro-dook-te*

❼ **das Gemüse**
*duss ge-mew-ze*

❽ **die Tiefkühlkost**
*dee teef-kewl-kost*

household products ❶

fruit ❷

drinks ❸

ready meals ❹

vegetables ❼

frozen foods ❽

**Cultural tip** In Germany it is unusual and frowned upon to ask for a plastic bag for your purchases, and you will have to pay for them. Instead, people use their own baskets or re-usable cotton bags that are sold at supermarkets.

## 3 Useful phrases (3 minutes)

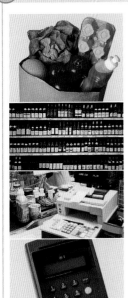

Learn these phrases and then test yourself using the cover flap.

| | |
|---|---|
| May I have a bag? | **Ich hätte gern eine Tragetasche.** *ikh het-te gairn ie-ne trah-ge-tush-e* |
| Where is the drinks aisle? | **Wo ist der Gang mit den Getränken?** *voe isst dair gung mit den ge-tren-ken* |
| Where is the check-out, please? | **Wo ist die Kasse, bitte?** *voe isst dee kuss-se, bit-te* |
| Please key in your PIN number. | **Bitte geben Sie Ihre Geheimzahl ein** *bit-te gay-ben zee ee-re ge-hime-tsahl ine* |

⑤ beauty products

⑥ dairy products

## 4 Words to remember (4 minutes)

Familiarize yourself with these words and then test yourself.

| | |
|---|---|
| bread | **das Brot** *duss broet* |
| milk | **die Milch** *dee milkh* |
| butter | **die Butter** *dee boott-ter* |
| ham | **der Schinken** *dair shin-ken* |
| salt | **das Salz** *duss zullts* |
| pepper | **der Pfeffer** *dair pfeff-fer* |
| washing powder | **das Waschpulver** *duss vush-pool-fer* |
| toilet paper | **das Toilettenpapier** *duss twah-let-ten-pa-peer* |
| washing-up liquid | **das Geschirrspülmittel** *duss ge-sheerr-shpewl-mit-tel* |

## 5 Say it (2 minutes)

Where's the dairy products aisle?

May I have some ham, please?

Where are the frozen foods?

# BEKLEIDUNG UND SCHUHE
## Clothes and shoes

**Warm up** (1 minute)

Say "I'd like…".
(pp.22-3)

Ask "Do you have…?"
(pp.12-13)

Say "38", "42", and
"46". (pp.30-1)

Say "big" and "small".
(pp.64-5)

When buying clothes, it is useful to know the colours. In German, colours can be adjectives or nouns; in the latter case they start with a capital: **Der Rock ist rot** (*The skirt is red*) but **Ich nehme diese in Rot** (*I'll take this in red*).

## 2 Match and repeat (4 minutes)

Match the numbered items of clothing to the German words in the panel below.

❶ **das Hemd**
*duss hemt*

❷ **die Krawatte**
*dee kra-vutt-te*

❸ **die Jacke**
*dee yuk-ke*

❹ **die Tasche**
*dee ta-she*

❺ **der Ärmel**
*dair airr-mel*

❻ **die Hose**
*dee hoe-ze*

❼ **der Rock**
*dair rok*

❽ **die Strumpfhose**
*dee shtroompf-hoe-ze*

❾ **die Schuhe**
*dee shoo-e*

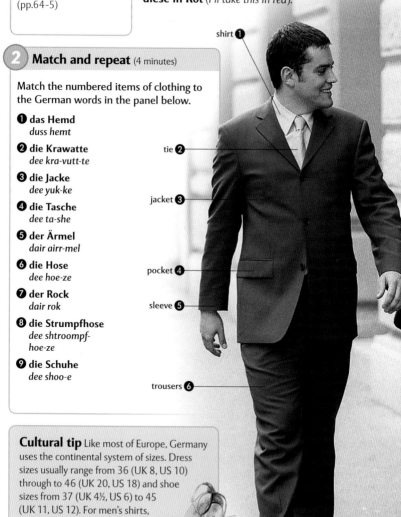

shirt ❶

tie ❷

jacket ❸

pocket ❹

sleeve ❺

trousers ❻

**Cultural tip** Like most of Europe, Germany uses the continental system of sizes. Dress sizes usually range from 36 (UK 8, US 10) through to 46 (UK 20, US 18) and shoe sizes from 37 (UK 4½, US 6) to 45 (UK 11, US 12). For men's shirts, a size 41 is a 16-inch collar, 43 is a 17-inch collar, and 45 is an 18-inch collar.

### 3 Useful phrases (3 minutes)

Learn these phrases and then test yourself using the cover flap.

| | |
|---|---|
| I'll take this in pink. | **Ich nehme das in Rosa.** *ikh nay-me duss in ro-sa* |
| Do you have this a size larger/smaller? | **Haben Sie das eine Nummer größer/kleiner?** *hah-ben zee duss ie-ne noom-mer grer-ser/klie-ner* |
| It's not what I'm looking for. | **Es ist nicht das, was ich suche.** *es isst nikht duss, vuss ikh zoo-khe* |

### 4 Words to remember (5 minutes)

Familiarize yourself with these words and test yourself using the cover flap.

| | |
|---|---|
| red | **rot** *roet* |
| white | **weiß** *vies* |
| blue | **blau** *blow* |
| yellow | **gelb** *gelp* |
| green | **grün** *grewn* |
| black | **schwarz** *shvarts* |

**7** skirt

**8** tights

**9** shoes

### 5 Say it (2 minutes)

Do you have this jacket in black?

Do you have this in a 38?

Do you have a size smaller?

# WIEDERHOLUNG
## Review and repeat

**Antworten**
*Answers* (Cover with flap)

### 1 Market

❶ **die Kartoffeln**
*dee kar-toff-eln*

❷ **die Radieschen**
*dee ra-dees-khen*

❸ **der Spinat**
*dair shpee-naht*

❹ **der Kohl**
*dair koel*

❺ **der Lauch**
*dair lowkh*

❻ **die Möhren**
*dee mer-ren*

### 1 Market (3 minutes)

Name the numbered items. Conceal the answers with the cover flap and then check if you have remembered the German correctly.

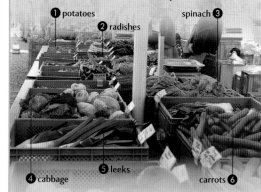

❶ potatoes
❷ radishes
spinach ❸
❹ cabbage
❺ leeks
carrots ❻

### 2 Description

❶ These shoes are too expensive.
❷ My room is very small.
❸ The bed is too hard.

### 2 Description (2 minutes)

What do these sentences mean?

❶ Diese Schuhe sind zu teuer.
❷ Mein Zimmer ist sehr klein.
❸ Das Bett ist zu hart.

### 3 Shops

❶ **die Bäckerei**
*dee bek-ke-rie*

❷ **die Bank**
*dee bunk*

❸ **die Buchhandlung**
*dee bookh-hund-loong*

❹ **das Fischgeschäft**
*duss fish-ge-sheft*

❺ **die Konditorei**
*dee kon-dee-to-rie*

❻ **die Fleischerei**
*dee flie-she-rie*

### 3 Shops (3 minutes)

Name the numbered shops in German. Then check your answers.

❶ baker
❷ bank
❸ bookshop

❹ fishmonger
❺ cake shop
❻ butcher

### 4 Supermarket (3 minutes)

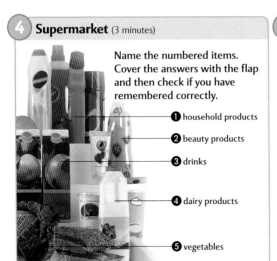

Name the numbered items. Cover the answers with the flap and then check if you have remembered correctly.

❶ household products

❷ beauty products

❸ drinks

❹ dairy products

❺ vegetables

### 4 Supermarket

❶ **die Haushalts-waren**
*dee hows-hults-vah-ren*

❷ **die Kosmetika**
*dee kos-may-tee-ka*

❸ **die Getränke**
*dee ge-tren-ke*

❹ **die Milchprodukte**
*dee milkh-pro-dook-te*

❺ **das Gemüse**
*duss ge-mew-ze*

### 5 Museum (4 minutes)

Follow this conversation, replying in German with the help of the numbered English prompts.

**Guten Tag. Kann ich Ihnen helfen?**
❶ I'd like five tickets.

**Das macht siebzig Euro.**
❷ That's very expensive!

**Wir geben keine Ermäßigung für Kinder.**
❸ How much is a guide?

**Fünfzehn Euro.**
❹ Five tickets and a guide, please.

**Fünfundachtzig Euro, bitte.**
❺ Here you are. Where are the toilets?

**Dort drüben.**
❻ Thank you very much.

### 5 Museum

❶ **Ich hätte gern fünf Eintrittskarten.**
*ikh het-te gairn fewnf ine-trits-kar-ten*

❷ **Das ist sehr teuer!**
*duss isst zair toy-er*

❸ **Was kostet der Führer?**
*vuss kos-tet dair few-rer*

❹ **Fünf Eintrittskarten und einen Führer, bitte.**
*fewnf ine-trits-kar-ten oont ie-nen few-rer, bit-te*

❺ **Bitte sehr. Wo sind die Toiletten?**
*bit-te zair. voe zint dee twah-let-ten*

❻ **Vielen Dank.**
*fee-len dunk*

## 1 Warm up (1 minute)

Ask "Which platform?"
(pp.38-9)

What is the German for
the following family
members: sister, brother,
mother, father, son, and
daughter? (pp.10-11)

# BERUFE
## Jobs

Most job titles are masculine. They can be turned
into the feminine equivalent by adding **-in**: for
example, **der Lehrer/die Lehrerin** (*male/female
teacher*). You don't need to use the indefinite
article *a* when you describe your job: **Ich bin
Buchhalter** (*I'm an accountant*).

## 2 Words to remember: jobs (7 minutes)

The feminine ending is shown in brackets. Some jobs
change the main vowel to an umlaut for the feminine
form: **Arzt/Ärztin** (*male/female doctor*).

| | |
|---|---|
| **Arzt/Ärztin**<br>*artst/airts-tin* | doctor |
| **Zahnarzt/Zahnärztin**<br>*tsahn-artst/*<br>*tsahn-airts-tin* | dentist |
| **Krankenpfleger/**<br>**Krankenschwester**<br>*krunk-en-pflay-ger/*<br>*krunk-en-shves-ter* | nurse |
| **Lehrer(in)**<br>*lay-rer(in)* | teacher |
| **Buchhalter(in)**<br>*bookh-hull-ter(in)* | accountant |
| **Rechtsanwalt/**<br>**Rechtsanwältin**<br>*rekhts-un-vullt/*<br>*rekhts-un-vel-tin* | lawyer |
| **Grafiker(in)**<br>*grah-fi-ker(in)* | designer |
| **Berater(in)**<br>*be-rah-ter(in)* | consultant |
| **Sekretär(in)**<br>*zek-re-tair(in)* | secretary |
| **Verkäufer(in)**<br>*fer-koy-fer(in)* | shop assistant |
| **Elektriker(in)**<br>*ay-lek-tree-ker(in)* | electrician |
| **Klempner(in)**<br>*klemp-ner(in)* | plumber |
| **selbstständig**<br>*zelpst-shten-dikh* | self-employed |

**Ich bin Klempner.**
*ikh bin klemp-ner*
I'm a plumber.

**Sie ist Lehrerin.**
*zee isst lay-re-rin*
She's a teacher.

## 3 Put into practice (4 minutes)

Practise these phrases. Then cover up the text on the right and complete the dialogue in German.

**Was machen Sie beruflich?**
*vuss ma-khen zee be-roof-likh*

What do you do?

Say: I am a consultant.

**Ich bin Berater.**
*ikh bin be-rah-ter*

**Bei welcher Firma arbeiten Sie?**
*bie vel-kher fir-ma ar-bie-ten zee*

What company do you work for?

Say: I'm self-employed.

**Ich bin selbstständig.**
*ikh bin zelpst-shten-dikh*

**Wie interessant!**
*vee in-tay-res-sunt*

How interesting!

Ask: And what do you do?

**Und was machen Sie beruflich?**
*oont vuss ma-khen zee be-roof-likh*

**Ich bin Zahnarzt.**
*ikh bin tsahn-artst*

I'm a dentist.

Say: My sister is a dentist too.

**Mein Schwester ist auch Zahnärztin.**
*mie-ne shves-ter isst owkh tsahn-airts-tin*

## 4 Words to remember: workplace (3 minutes)

Familiarize yourself with these words and test yourself.

| | |
|---|---|
| head office | **die Zentrale** *dee tsen-trah-le* |
| branch | **die Zweigstelle** *dee tsviek-shtel-le* |
| department | **die Abteilung** *dee up-tie-loong* |
| superior | **der/die Vorgesetzte** *dair/dee for-ge-zets-te* |
| trainee | **der Auszubildende** *dair ows-tsoo-bilden-de* |
| reception | **der Empfang** *dair emp-fung* |

**Die Zentrale ist in Bremen.**
*dee tsen-trah-le isst in bray-men*
Head office is in Bremen.

## 1 Warm up (1 minute)

Practise different ways of introducing yourself in different situations. Mention your name, your occupation, and any other information you'd like to give. (pp.8-9, pp.14-15, and pp.78-9)

# DAS BÜRO
## The office

In all countries, each company has its own special terms, but there are many items that are universal and the English word is often used. Note that the German keyboard has a different layout to the standard QWERTY convention, and that **das Handy** is a mobile phone.

## 2 Words to remember (5 minutes)

Familiarize yourself with these words. Read them aloud several times and try to memorize them. Conceal the German with the cover flap and test yourself.

| | |
|---|---|
| **der Monitor** <br> *dair mo-nee-tor* | monitor |
| **der Computer** <br> *dair kom-pyoo-ter* | computer |
| **die Maus** <br> *dee mows* | mouse |
| **die E-Mail** <br> *dee ee-mayle* | e-mail |
| **das Internet** <br> *duss in-ter-net* | internet |
| **das Passwort** <br> *duss puss-vort* | password |
| **die Voice-Mail** <br> *dee voyse-mayle* | voicemail |
| **das Fax** <br> *duss fux* | fax machine |
| **der Fotokopierer** <br> *dair fo-to-ko-pee-rer* | photocopier |
| **der Terminkalender** <br> *dair terr-meen-ka-len-der* | diary |
| **die Visitenkarte** <br> *dee vi-see-ten-kar-te* | business card |
| **die Besprechung** <br> *dee be-shpre-khoong* | meeting |
| **die Konferenz** <br> *dee kon-fay-rents* | conference |
| **die Tagesordnung** <br> *dee tah-ges-ort-noong* | agenda |

❶ lamp

keyboard ❺

screen ❹

❷ stapler

telephone ❸

pen ❿

⓬ drawer

⓫ notepad

### 3 Useful phrases (2 minutes)

Learn these phrases and then test yourself using the cover flap.

I need to photocopy something.
**Ich muss etwas fotokopieren.**
*ikh mooss et-vuss fo-to-ko-pee-ren*

I'd like to arrange an appointment.
**Ich möchte einen Termin ausmachen.**
*ikh merkh-te ie-nen tair-meen ows-ma-khen*

I want to send an e-mail.
**Ich möchte eine E-Mail schicken.**
*ikh merkh-te ie-ne ee-mayle shik-ken*

### 4 Say it (2 minutes)

I'd like to arrange a conference.

I need to send a fax.

Do you have a laptop?

### 5 Match and repeat (5 minutes)

Match the numbered items to the words in the panel and test yourself.

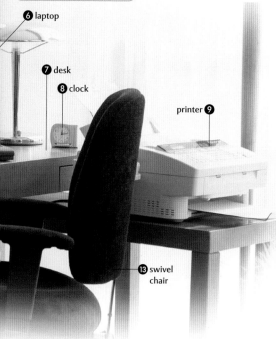

**6** laptop

**7** desk

**8** clock

printer **9**

**13** swivel chair

❶ **die Lampe**
*dee lum-pe*

❷ **das Heftgerät**
*duss heft-ge-rayt*

❸ **das Telefon**
*duss tay-lay-foen*

❹ **der Bildschirm**
*dair bilt-sheerm*

❺ **die Tastatur**
*dee tuss-tah-toor*

❻ **der Laptop**
*dair lap-top*

❼ **der Schreibtisch**
*dair shriep-tish*

❽ **die Uhr**
*dee oor*

❾ **der Drucker**
*dair drook-ker*

❿ **der Stift**
*dair shtift*

⓫ **der Notizblock**
*dair no-teets-blok*

⓬ **die Schublade**
*dee shoop-lah-de*

⓭ **der Drehstuhl**
*dair dray-shtool*

# DIE AKADEMISCHE WELT
## Academic world

### 1 Warm up (1 minute)

Say "How interesting!" (pp.78-9) and "library". (pp.48-9)

Ask "What do you do?" and answer "I'm an accountant". (pp.78-9)

At German universities, you have to collect credits, often over many years, before you can take the final exam. A first degree is either a **Staatsexamen** (*state exam*) or a **Magister** (*MA*), which can be followed by a **Doktorat** (*PhD*).

### 2 Useful phrases (3 minutes)

Learn these phrases and then test yourself using the cover flap.

| | |
|---|---|
| **Was ist Ihr Gebiet?** *vuss isst eer ge-beet* | What is your field? |
| **Ich betreibe Forschungen in Biochemie.** *ikh be-trie-be for-shoong-en in bee-oe-khay-mee* | I am doing research in biochemistry. |
| **Ich habe Jura studiert.** *ikh hah-be yoo-ra shtoo-deert* | I studied law. |
| **Ich halte einen Vortrag über moderne Architektur.** *ikh hul-te ie-nen vor-trahk ew-ber mo-dair-ne ar-khi-tek-toor* | I am giving a presentation on modern architecture. |

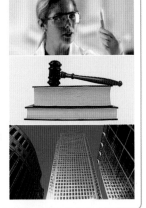

### 3 In conversation (5 minutes)

**Guten Tag, ich bin Professor Stein.**
*goo-ten tahk, ikh bin pro-fes-sor shtien*

Hello, I'm Professor Stein.

**An welcher Universität arbeiten Sie?**
*un vel-kher oo-nee-vair-zee-tayt ar-bie-ten zee*

What university do you work at?

**Ich bin Delegierte der Humboldt-Universität.**
*ikh bin day-lay-ge-ter dair hoomm-bolt-oo-nee-vair-zee-tayt*

I'm the delegate from Humboldt University.

### 4 Words to remember (4 minutes)

Familiarize yourself with these words and then test yourself.

**Wir haben einen Stand.**
*veer hah-ben ie-nen shtunt*
We have a stand.

| | |
|---|---|
| conference | **die Konferenz** *dee kon-fay-rents* |
| trade fair | **die Handelsmesse** *dee hun-dels-mes-se* |
| seminar | **das Seminar** *duss zay-mee-nahr* |
| lecture theatre | **der Vorlesungssaal** *dair for-lay-zoongs-zahl* |
| conference room | **das Konferenzzimmer** *duss kon-fay-rents-tsim-mer* |
| exhibition | **die Ausstellung** *dee ows-shtel-loong* |
| university lecturer | **der Dozent(in)** *dair do-tsent(in)* |
| professor | **der Professor(in)** *dair pro-fes-sor(in)* |
| medicine | **die Medizin** *dee may-dee-tseen* |
| science | **die Naturwissenschaften** *dee na-toor-vis-sen-shuff-ten* |
| humanities | **die Geisteswissen-schaften** *dee gies-tes-vis-sen-shuff-ten* |
| engineering | **die Technik** *dee tekh-nik* |

### 5 Say it (2 minutes)

I'm doing research in medicine.

I studied humanities.

She's the professor.

**Was ist Ihr Gebiet?**
*vuss isst eer ge-beet*

What's your field?

**Ich betreibe Forschungen in Technik.**
*ikh be-trie-be for-shoong-en in tekh-nik*

I'm doing research in engineering.

**Wie interessant!**
*vee in-tay-res-sunt*

How interesting!

## 1 Warm up (1 minute)

Ask "Can I...?" (pp.34–5)

Say "I want to send an e-mail". (pp.80–1)

Ask "Can you send a fax?" (pp.80–1)

# GESCHÄFTLICHES
## In business

You will receive a more friendly reception and make a good impression if you make the effort to begin a meeting with a short introduction in German, even if your vocabulary is limited. After that, all parties will probably be happy to continue the meeting in English.

## 2 Words to remember (6 minutes)

Familiarize yourself with these words and then test yourself by concealing the German with the cover flap.

| | |
|---|---|
| **der Zeitplan** *dair tsiet-plahn* | schedule |
| **die Lieferung** *dee lee-fe-roong* | delivery |
| **die Bezahlung** *dee be-tsah-loong* | payment |
| **das Budget** *duss bew-jay* | budget |
| **der Preis** *dair priez* | price |
| **die Akte** *dee ukk-te* | document |
| **die Rechnung** *dee rekh-noong* | invoice |
| **die Zahlen** *dee tsah-len* | figures |
| **der Kostenvoranschlag** *dair kos-ten-for-un-shlahk* | estimate |
| **der Gewinn** *dair ge-vinn* | profits |
| **der Absatz** *dair up-zuts* | sales |

**der Kunde**
*dair koonn-de*
client

**Cultural tip** Many German companies have **Gleitzeit** (*flexible working hours*). Generally, offices start at 9 am or before, break for lunch at 12 noon, and finish at about 5 pm or earlier. In larger firms and offices, lunch is often taken in a subsidized canteen together with colleagues.

## 3 Useful phrases (6 minutes)

Familiarize yourself with these phrases and then test yourself using the cover flap to conceal the German.

**Sollen wir den Vertrag unterzeichnen?**
*zol-len veer dayn fer-trahk oon-ter-tsiekh-nen*
Shall we sign the contract?

**die Managerin**
*dee man-a-je-rin*
executive

**der Vertrag**
*dair fer-trahk*
contract

**Bitte schicken Sie mir den Vertrag.**
*bit-te shik-ken zee meer dayn fer-trahk*

Please send me the contract.

**Haben wir uns auf einen Zeitplan geeinigt?**
*hah-ben veer oons owf ie-nen tsiet-plahn ge-ie-nikht*

Have we agreed a schedule?

**Wann können Sie liefern?**
*vunn kern-nen zee lee-fairn*

When can you deliver?

**Was ist das Budget?**
*vuss isst duss bew-jay*

What's the budget?

**der Bericht**
*dair be-rikht*
report

**Können Sie mir die Rechnung schicken?**
*kern-nen zee meer dee rekh-noong shik-ken*

Can you send me the invoice?

## 4 Say it (2 minutes)

Can you send me the estimate?

Have we agreed on a price?

What are the profits?

# WIEDERHOLUNG
## Review and repeat

### 1 At the office

❶ das Heftgerät
*duss heft-ge-rayt*

❷ die Lampe
*dee lum-pe*

❸ der Laptop
*dair lap-top*

❹ der Stift
*dair shtift*

❺ der Schreibtisch
*dair shriep-tish*

❻ der Notizblock
*dair no-teets-blok*

❼ die Uhr
*dee oor*

### 1 At the office (4 minutes)

Name these items.

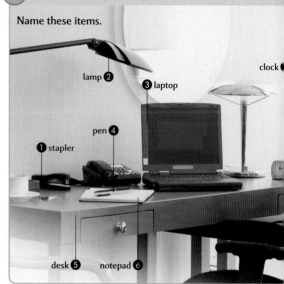

lamp ❷

❸ laptop

clock ❼

pen ❹

❶ stapler

desk ❺    notepad ❻

### 2 Jobs

❶ Arzt/Ärztin
*artst/airts-tin*

❷ Klempner(in)
*klemp-ner(in)*

❸ Verkäufer(in)
*fer-koy-fer(in)*

❹ Buchhalter(in)
*bookh-hull-ter(in)*

❺ Lehrer(in)
*lay-rer(in)*

❻ Rechtsanwalt/
Rechtsanwältin
*rekhts-un-vullt/*
*rekhts-un-vel-tin*

### 2 Jobs (3 minutes)

What are these jobs in German?

❶ doctor

❷ plumber

❸ shop assistant

❹ accountant

❺ teacher

❻ lawyer

## 3 Work (4 minutes)

Answer these questions following the numbered English prompts.

**Bei welcher Firma arbeiten Sie?**
❶ I work for myself.

**Von welcher Universität sind Sie?**
❷ I'm at the University of Köln.

**Was ist Ihr Gebiet?**
❸ I'm doing medical research.

**Haben wir uns auf einen Zeitplan geeinigt?**
❹ Yes, my secretary has the schedule.

## 3 Work

❶ **Ich bin selbstständig.**
*ikh bin zelpst-shten-dikh*

❷ **Ich bin von der Universität Köln.**
*ikh bin fon dair oo-nee-vair-zee-tayt kewln*

❸ **Ich betreibe Forschungen in der Medizin.**
*ikh be-trie-be for-shoong-en in dair may-dee-tseen*

❹ **Ja, meine Sekretärin hat den Zeitplan.**
*yah, mye-ne zek-re-tair-in hut dayn tsiet-plahn*

## 4 How much? (4 minutes)

Answer the question with the amount shown in brackets.

❶ **Was kostet der Kaffee?** (€2.50)

❷ **Was kostet das Zimmer?** (€47)

❸ **Was kostet das Kilo Tomaten?** (€3.25)

❹ **Was kostet der Parkplatz für drei Tage?** (€50)

## 4 How much?

❶ **Das macht zwei Euro fünfzig.**
*duss makht tsvie oy-roe fewnf-tsik*

❷ **Es kostet sieben-undvierzig Euro.**
*es kos-tet zee-ben-oont-feer-tsik oy-roe*

❸ **Das macht drei Euro fünfundzwanzig.**
*duss makht drie oy-roe fewnf-oont-tsvun-tsik*

❹ **Er kostet fünfzig Euro.**
*air kos-tet fewnf-tsik oy-roe*

# IN DER APOTHEKE
## At the chemist

## 1 Warm up (1 minute)

Say "I'm allergic to nuts".
(pp.24-5)

Say the verb **haben**
(to have) in all its forms
(**ich, du er/sie/es, wir,
ihr, sie/Sie**). (pp.14-15)

German *pharmacies* are indicated by a stylized red letter **A** for **Apotheke**. Pharmacists dispense a wide variety of medicines over the counter. They advise and can even give injections, if necessary. In larger towns, a rota ensures that there is always one pharmacy that is open.

## 2 Match and repeat (3 minutes)

Match the numbered items to the German words in the panel below and test yourself using the cover flap.

**1** der Verband
*dair fer-bunt*

**2** der Sirup
*dair zee-roop*

**3** die Tropfen
*dee trop-fen*

**4** das Pflaster
*duss pflus-ter*

**5** die Spritze
*dee shprit-se*

**6** die Salbe
*dee zull-be*

**7** das Zäpfchen
*duss tsepf-khen*

**8** die Tablette
*dee tub-let-te*

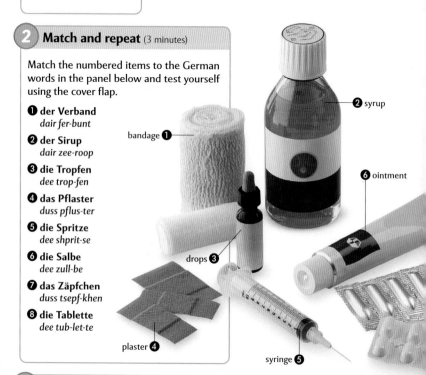

bandage **1**

**2** syrup

**6** ointment

drops **3**

plaster **4**

syringe **5**

## 3 In conversation (3 minutes)

**Guten Tag, Sie wünschen?**
*goo-ten tahk, zee vewn-shen*

Hello. What would you like?

**Ich habe Bauchschmerzen.**
*ikh hah-be bowkh-shmairt-sen*

I have a stomach ache.

**Haben Sie Durchfall?**
*hah-ben zee doorkh-full*

Do you have diarrhoea?

## 4 Words to remember (2 minutes)

In German you don't use the indefinite article *a* to describe a pain.

**Ich habe Kopfschmerzen.**
*ikh hah-be*
*kopf-shmairt-sen*
I have a headache.

| | |
|---|---|
| headache | **Kopfschmerzen** *kopf-shmairt-sen* |
| stomach ache | **Bauchschmerzen** *bowkh-shmairt-sen* |
| diarrhoea | **Durchfall** *doorkh-full* |
| cold (in the nose) | **der Schnupfen** *dair shnoop-fen* |
| cough | **der Husten** *dair hoos-ten* |
| sunburn | **der Sonnenbrand** *dair zon-nen-brunt* |
| toothache | **Zahnschmerzen** *tsahn-shmairt-sen* |

## 5 Say it (2 minutes)

I have a cold.

Do you have that as an ointment?

Do you have a cough?

**7** suppository

**8** tablet

## 6 Useful phrases (4 minutes)

Learn these phrases and then test yourself using the cover flap.

| | |
|---|---|
| I have sunburn. | **Ich haben einen Sonnenbrand.** *ikh hah-be ie-nen zon-nen-brunt* |
| Do you have that as a syrup? | **Haben Sie das auch als Sirup?** *hah-ben zee duss owkh ulls zee-roop* |
| I'm allergic to penicillin. | **Ich bin allergisch gegen Penizillin.** *ikh bin ull-lair-gish gay-gen pay-nee-tsee-leen* |

**Nein, aber ich habe auch Kopfschmerzen.**
*nine, ah-ber ikh hah-be owkh kopf-shmairt-sen*

No, but I also have a headache.

**Nehmen Sie dies.**
*nay-men zee dees*

Take this.

**Haben Sie das auch als Tabletten?**
*hah-ben zee duss owkh ulls tub-let-ten*

Do you have that as tablets?

# DER KÖRPER
## The body

**1** **Warm up** (1 minute)

Say " I have a toothache" and "I have sunburn". (pp.88-9)

Say the German for "red", "green", "black", and "yellow". (pp.74-5)

In German many expressions to do with health are reflexive, that is, the equivalent of *I am not feeling well* in German is **Ich fühle mich nicht wohl** (literally, *I am not feeling myself well*). As in English, the reflexive pronoun (*myself, yourself,* etc.) changes, depending on the context.

**2** **Match and repeat** (6 minutes)

Match the numbered parts of the body with the list below.

❶ **die Hand**
*dee hunt*

❷ **der Kopf**
*dair kopf*

❸ **die Schulter**
*dee shool-ter*

❹ **der Ellbogen**
*dair el-bo-gen*

❺ **das Haar, die Haare**
*duss hahr, dee hah-re*

❻ **der Arm**
*dair arm*

❼ **der Hals**
*dair hulls*

❽ **die Brust**
*dee broost*

❾ **der Bauch**
*dair bowkh*

❿ **das Bein**
*duss bine*

⓫ **das Knie**
*duss k-nee*

⓬ **der Fuß**
*dair fooss*

hand ❶    ❹ elbow
head ❷    ❺ hair
shoulder ❸    ❻ arm
   ❼ neck
   ❽ chest
   ❾ stomach
   ❿ leg
   ⓫ knee
   ⓬ foot

## 3 Match and repeat (3 minutes)

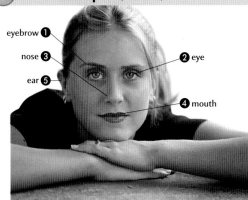

eyebrow **1**

nose **3**

ear **5**

**2** eye

**4** mouth

Match the numbered facial features with the list below.

**1** die Augenbraue
*dee ow-gen-brow-e*

**2** das Auge
*duss ow-ge*

**3** die Nase
*dee nah-ze*

**4** der Mund
*dair moont*

**5** das Ohr
*duss ohr*

## 4 Useful phrases (3 minutes)

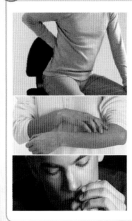

Learn these phrases and then test yourself using the cover flap.

| | |
|---|---|
| I have a pain in my back. | **Ich habe Schmerzen im Rücken.** *ikh hah-be shmairt-sen im rewk-ken* |
| I have a rash on my arm. | **Ich habe einen Ausschlag am Arm.** *ikh hah-be ie-nen ows-shluk um arm* |
| I don't feel well. | **Ich fühle mich nicht wohl.** *ikh few-le mikh nikht voel* |

## 5 Put into practice (2 minutes)

Join in this conversation and test yourself using the cover flap.

**Was ist denn los?**
*vuss isst denn loes*

What's the matter?

Say: I'm not feeling well.

**Ich fühle mich nicht wohl.**
*ikh few-le mikh nikht voel*

**Wo tut es denn weh?**
*voe toot es den vayh*

Where does it hurt?

Say: I have a pain in my shoulder.

**Ich haben Schmerzen in der Schulter.**
*ikh hah-be shmairt-sen in dair shool-ter*

## BEIM ARZT
### At the doctor

German doctors are titled according to their specialist qualifications, such as **Internist** (*internal medicine*) and **Kardiologe** (*heart specialist*). A *general practitioner* is known as **praktischer Arzt**. In most cases you'll need an appointment, or you can visit the hospital outpatients department.

### 1 Warm up (1 minute)

Say "I need some tablets" and "He needs some ointment". (pp.60-1 and pp.88-9)

What is the German for "I don't have a son"? (pp.10-15)

### 2 Useful phrases you may hear (3 minutes)

Learn these phrases and then test yourself using the cover flap to conceal the German.

| | |
|---|---|
| **Es ist nichts Ernsthaftes.** *es isst nikhts airnst-huff-tes* | It's not serious. |
| **Wir müssen ein paar Tests machen.** *veer mews-sen ine pahr tests ma-khen* | We need to do a few tests. |
| **Sie haben eine Niereninfektion.** *zee hah-ben ie-ne nee-ren-infek-tsee-oen* | You have an infection in your kidney. |
| **Sie müssen ins Krankenhaus gehen.** *zee mews-sen ins krunk-en-hows gay-en* | You need to go to hospital. |

**Nehmen Sie irgend-welche Medikamente?**
*nay-men zee ir-gent-vel-khe may-dee-ka-men-te*
Are you taking any medication?

### 3 In conversation (5 minutes)

**Was ist denn los?**
*vuss isst den loes*

What's the matter?

**Ich habe Schmerzen in der Brust.**
*ikh hah-be shmairt-sen in dair broost*

I have a pain in my chest.

**Ich werde Sie untersuchen.**
*ikh vair-de zee oon-ter-zoo-khen*

I'll examine you.

## 4 Useful phrases you may need to say (4 minutes)

**Ich bin schwanger.**
*ikh bin shvun-ger*
I am pregnant.

Learn these phrases and then test yourself using the cover flap.

| | |
|---|---|
| I am diabetic. | **Ich bin Diabetiker(in).** *ikh bin dee-ar-bay-ti-kair(in)* |
| I am epileptic. | **Ich bin Epileptiker(in).** *ikh bin ay-pee-lep-ti-kair(in)* |
| I have asthma. | **Ich habe Asthma.** *ikh hah-be ast-ma* |
| I have a heart condition. | **Ich bin herzkrank.** *ikh bin hairts-krunk* |
| I have a fever. | **Ich habe Fieber.** *ikh hah-be fee-ber* |
| It's urgent. | **Es ist dringend.** *es isst dring-ent* |
| I feel faint. | **Ich fühle mich schwach.** *ikh few-le mikh shvakh* |
| I feel sick. | **Mir ist schlecht.** *meer isst shlekht* |

### Cultural tip
If you are an EU national, you can obtain free emergency medical treatment in Germany on production of a valid European Health Insurance Card (EHIC).

## 5 Say it (2 minutes)

It is serious.

My son needs to go to hospital.

It's not urgent.

**Ist es etwas Ernsthaftes?**
*isst es et-vuss airnst-huff-tes*

Is it serious?

**Nein, nur Verdauungs-beschwerden.**
*nine, noor fer-dow-oongs-be-shvair-den*

No, only indigestion.

**Ein Glück!**
*ine glewkk*

What a relief!

## 1 Warm up (1 minute)

Say "how long" as in "how long is the journey?" (pp.42-3)

Ask "Do I need tests?" (pp.92-3)

Say "mouth" and "head". (pp.90-1)

# IM KRANKENHAUS
## At the hospital

It is useful to know a few basic phrases relating to hospitals for use in an emergency or in case you need to visit a friend or colleague in hospital. A *ward* in hospital is known as **die Station** and the equivalent of the *outpatient department* is known as **die Ambulanz**.

## 2 Useful phrases (5 minutes)

Familiarize yourself with these phrases. Conceal the German with the cover flap and test yourself.

| | |
|---|---|
| **Wann ist Besuchszeit?** *vunn isst be-zookhs-tsiet* | What are the visiting hours? |
| **Wie lange wird das dauern?** *vee lun-ge virt duss dow-ern* | How long will it take? |
| **Tut das weh?** *toot duss vayh* | Will it hurt? |
| **Bitte legen Sie sich hier hin.** *bit-te lay-gen zee zikh heer hin* | Please lie down here. |
| **Sie dürfen nichts essen.** *zee dewr-fen nikhts es-sen* | You must not eat. |
| **Bewegen Sie nicht den Kopf.** *be-vay-gen zee nikht dayn kopf* | Don't move your head. |
| **Bitte öffnen Sie Ihren Mund.** *bit-te erf-nen zee ee-ren moont* | Please open your mouth. |
| **Wir müssen eine Blutprobe machen.** *veer mews-sen ie-ne bloot-proe-be ma-khen* | We'll have to do a blood test. |

**Wo ist das Wartezimmer?**
*voe isst duss var-te-tsim-mer*
Where is the waiting room?

**die intravenöse Infusion**
*dee in-tra-vay-ner-ze in-foo-zee-oen*
intravenous drip

**Geht es Ihnen besser?**
*gayt es ee-nen bes-ser*
Are you feeling better?

### 3 Words to remember (4 minutes)

Memorize these words and test yourself using the cover flap.

| | |
|---|---|
| emergency department | **die Unfallstation**<br>*dee oon-full-shtah-tsee-oen* |
| x-ray department | **die Röntgenabteilung**<br>*dee rernt-gen-up-tie-loong* |
| children's ward | **die Kinderstation**<br>*dee kin-der-shtah-tsee-oen* |
| operating theatre | **der Operationssaal (der OP)**<br>*dair o-pay-rah-tsee-oens-zahl (dair oe-pay)* |
| corridor | **der Gang**<br>*dair gung* |
| stairs | **die Treppe**<br>*dee trep-pe* |

**Ihre Rötgenaufhahme ist normal.**
*ee-re rernt-gen-owf-nah-me isst nor-mal*
Your x-ray is normal.

### 4 Put into practice (3 minutes)

Join in this conversation. Read the German on the left and follow the instructions to make your reply. Then test yourself by concealing the answers with the cover flap.

**Sie haben eine Entzündung.**
*zee hah-ben ie-ne ent-tsewn-doong*

You have an infection.

Ask: Will you need to do tests?

**Müssen Sie Untersuchungen machen?**
*mews-sen zee oon-ter-zoo-khoong-en ma-khen*

**Zuerst machen wir eine Blutprobe.**
*tsoo-airst ma-khen veer ie-ne bloot-proe-be*

First we will do a blood test.

Ask: Will it hurt?

**Tut das weh?**
*toot duss vayh*

### 5 Say it (2 minutes)

Will you need to do a blood test?

Where is the children's ward?

**Nein, keine Angst.**
*nine, kie-ne unkst*

No. Don't worry.

Ask: How long will it take?

**Wie lange wird das dauern?**
*vee lun-ge virt duss dow-ern*

# WIEDERHOLUNG
## Review and repeat

### 1 The body

**1** der Kopf
*dair kopf*

**2** der Arm
*dair arm*

**3** die Brust
*dee broost*

**4** der Bauch
*dair bowkh*

**5** das Bein
*duss bine*

**6** das Knie
*duss k-nee*

**7** der Fuß
*dair fooss*

### 1 The body (4 minutes)

Name the numbered body parts in German.

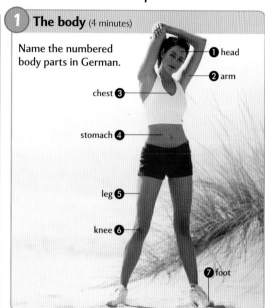

- **1** head
- **2** arm
- chest **3**
- stomach **4**
- leg **5**
- knee **6**
- **7** foot

### 2 On the phone

**1** Ich möchte bitte Venny Gerlach sprechen.
*ikh merkh-te bit-te ven-nee gair-lakh shpre-khen*

**2** Horst Richter von der Druckerei Gohl.
*horst rikh-ter fon dair drook-er-ie goel*

**3** Kann ich eine Nachricht hinterlassen?
*kunn ikh ie-ne nahkh-rikht hin-ter-luss-sen*

**4** Der Termin für Montag elf Uhr ist in Ordnung.
*dair terr-meen fewr mohn-tahk elf oor isst in ord-noong*

### 2 On the phone (4 minutes)

You are confirming an appointment with a business contact on the telephone. Join in the conversation, replying in German following the English prompts.

Hello, Firma Apex.
**1** I'd like to speak to Venny Gerlach.

Ja, mit wem spreche ich?
**2** Horst Richter of Gohl Printers.

Es tut mir Leid, da ist besetzt.
**3** Can I leave a message?

Aber selbstverständlich.
**4** The appointment on Monday at 11 am is fine.

### 3 Clothing (3 minutes)

Say the German words for the numbered items of clothing.

tie ❶
❷ jacket
❹ skirt
trousers ❸
❻ tights
shoes ❺

### 3 Clothing

❶ die Krawatte
*dee kra-vutt-te*

❷ die Jacke
*dee yuk-ke*

❸ die Hose
*dee hoe-ze*

❹ der Rock
*dair rok*

❺ die Schuhe
*dee shoo-e*

❻ die Strumpfhose
*dee shtroompf-hoe-ze*

### 4 At the doctor's (4 minutes)

Say these phrases in German.

❶ I don't feel well.
❷ Will you need to do tests?
❸ I have a heart condition.
❹ Do I need to go to hospital?
❺ I'm pregnant.

### 4 At the doctor's

❶ Ich fühle mich nicht wohl.
*ikh fewh-le mikh nikht voel*

❷ Müssen Sie Untersuchungen machen?
*mews-sen zee oon-ter-zoo-khoong-en ma-khen*

❸ Ich bin herzkrank.
*ikh bin hairts-krunk*

❹ Muss ich ins Krankenhaus gehen?
*mooss ikh ins krunk-en-hows gay-en*

❺ Ich bin schwanger.
*ikh bin shvun-ger*

# ZU HAUSE
## At home

Say the months of
the year in German.
(pp.28-9)

Ask "Is there...?"
(pp.48-9)

Most Germans live in *rented apartments*
(**die Wohnung**); only relatively few own their
*homes* (**das Eigenheim**). The size of a dwelling is
given in square metres and described in terms of the
number of rooms in addition to kitchen and bathroom:
**2 ZKB** means **2 Zimmer, Küche, Badezimmer**.

## 2 Match and repeat (5 minutes)

Match the numbered items to the list
below and test yourself using the flap.

**1** das Dach
*duss dukh*

**2** der Schornstein
*dair shorn-shtine*

**3** die Dachrinne
*dee dukh-rin-ne*

**4** der Blumenkasten
*dair bloo-men-kass-ten*

**5** die Mauer
*dee mow-er*

**6** das Fenster
*duss fens-ter*

**7** die Tür
*dee tewr*

**8** die Straße
*dee shtrah-se*

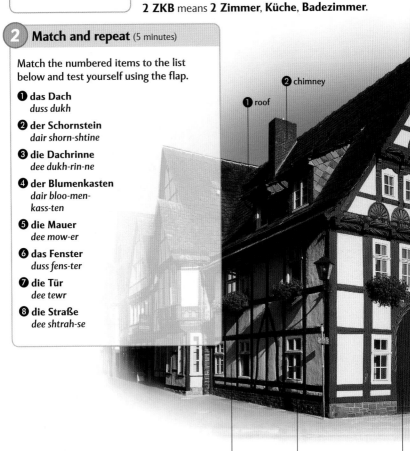

**2** chimney
**1** roof

wall **5**   window **6**   door **7**

**Conversational tip** In Germany, a detached house is
known as an **Einfamilienhaus** - literally a *one-family house*.
A semi-detached house is called a **Zweifamilienhaus**
(*two-family house*), while a terraced house is called a
**Reihenhaus** (*house in a row*). The *centre of town* is the
**Innenstadt**, and a *suburb* is a **Vorstadt** or **Vorort**.

## 3 Words to remember (4 minutes)

**Wie hoch ist die monatliche Miete?**
*vee hoekh isst dee mo-naht-li-khe mee-te*
What is the rent per month?

Familiarize yourself with these words and test yourself using the flap.

| | |
|---|---|
| room | **das Zimmer** *duss tsim-mer* |
| floor | **der Fußboden** *dair foos-bo-den* |
| ceiling | **die Decke** *dee dek-ke* |
| bedroom | **das Schlafzimmer** *duss shlahf-tsim-mer* |
| bathroom | **das Badezimmer** *duss bah-de-tsim-mer* |
| kitchen | **die Küche** *dee kew-khe* |
| dining room | **das Esszimmer** *duss ess-tsim-mer* |
| living room | **das Wohnzimmer** *duss vohn-tsim-mer* |
| cellar | **der Keller** *dair kel-ler* |
| attic | **der Dachboden** *dair dukh-boe-den* |

**3** gutter

**4** window box

**8** roadway

## 4 Useful phrases (3 minutes)

Learn these phrases and test yourself.

**Gibt es eine Garage?**
*geept es ie-ne ga-ra-je*

Is there a garage?

**Ab wann ist es frei?**
*up vunn isst es frie*

When is it available?

**Ist es möbliert?**
*isst es mer-bleert*

Is it furnished?

## 5 Say it (2 minutes)

Is there a dining room?

Is it large?

Is it available in July?

# IM HAUS
## In the house

### 1 Warm up (1 minute)

What is the German for "desk" (pp.80-1), "bed" (pp.60-1), and "window"? (pp.98-9)

How do you say "soft", "beautiful", and "big"? (pp.64-5)

If you're renting a flat or a house in Germany, the rent is often described as **kalt** (*cold*). This means that services such as electricity have to be paid for in addition to the basic rent. You will need to check this in advance. *Furnished apartments* in holiday resorts are known as **Ferienwohnung**.

### 2 Match and repeat (3 minutes)

Match the numbered items to the list in the panel below. Then test yourself by concealing the German with the cover flap.

❶ **die Arbeitsfläche**
*dee ar-biets-flay-khe*

❷ **das Spülbecken**
*duss shpewl-bek-ken*

❸ **die Mikrowelle**
*dee mee-kro-vel-le*

❹ **der Backhofen**
*dair bak-oe-fen*

❺ **der Herd**
*dair hairt*

❻ **der Kühlschrank**
*dair kewl-shrunk*

❼ **der Stuhl**
*dair shtool*

❽ **der Tisch**
*dair tish*

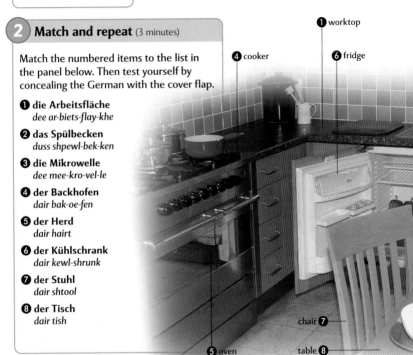

❶ worktop
❹ cooker
❻ fridge
chair ❼
❺ oven
table ❽

### 3 In conversation (3 minutes)

**Das ist der Herd.**
*duss isst dair hairt*

This is the cooker.

**Gibt es eine Geschirrspül-maschine?**
*geept es ie-ne ge-sheerr-spewl-mah-shee-ne*

Is there a dishwasher?

**Ja, und der Gefrierschrank ist groß.**
*yah, oont dair ge-freer-shrunk isst groes*

Yes, and the freezer is big.

## 4 Words to remember (2 minutes)

Familiarize yourself with these words and test yourself using the flap.

**Die Couch ist neu.**
*dee kowtch isst noy*
The sofa is new.

microwave ❸

sink ❷

| | |
|---|---|
| wardrobe | **der Schrank** *dair shrunk* |
| armchair | **der Sessel** *dair zes-sel* |
| carpet | **der Teppich** *dair tep-pikh* |
| bathtub | **die Badewanne** *dee bah-de-vunn-ne* |
| toilet | **die Toilette (das WC)** *dee twah-let-te (duss vay-tsay)* |
| wash basin | **das Waschbecken** *duss vush-bek-ken* |
| curtains | **die Gardine** *dee gar-dee-ne* |

## 5 Useful phrases (4 minutes)

Learn these phrases and then test yourself.

| | |
|---|---|
| The cooker doesn't work. | **Der Herd funktioniert nicht.** *dair hairt foonk-tsee-oe-neert nikht* |
| I don't like the curtains. | **Die Gardinen gefallen mir nicht.** *dee gar-dee-nen ge-fall-en meer nikht* |
| Is electricity included? | **Ist der Strom inbegriffen?** *isst dair shtroem in-be-grif-fen* |

## 6 Say it (2 minutes)

Is there a microwave?

I like the carpet.

The bathroom is beautiful!

**Ist das Spülbecken neu?**
*isst duss spewl-bek-ken noy*

Is the sink new?

**Und hier ist die Waschmaschine.**
*oont heer isst dee vush-mah-shee-ne*

And here's the washing machine.

**Die Kacheln sind schön!**
*dee ka-kheln zint shern*

The tiles are beautiful!

# DER GARTEN
## The garden

### 1 Warm up (1 minute)

Say "I need" and "you need". (pp.92–3)

What is the German for "day" and "month"? (pp.28–9)

Ask "Is there a garage?" (pp.98–9)

Many Germans who live in apartments rent allotment gardens. But rather than just growing fruits and vegetables there, they often turn these into attractive leisure gardens with extensive flowerbeds and ponds as well as terraces, decks, and barbecues for casual entertaining.

### 2 Words to remember (3 minutes)

Familiarize yourself with these words and test yourself using the flap.

| | |
|---|---|
| **der Rasenmäher** *dair rah-zen-may-er* | lawnmower |
| **die Gabel** *dee gah-bel* | fork |
| **der Spaten** *dair shpah-ten* | spade |
| **der Rechen** *dair re-khen* | rake |
| **das Gartencenter** *duss gar-ten-tsen-ter* | garden centre |

terrace ❶

❷ tree

plants ❻

❽ weeds

path ❾   ❸ soil

## 3 Useful phrases (4 minutes)

Learn these phrases and then test yourself using the cover flap.

| | |
|---|---|
| The gardener comes once a week. | **Der Gärtner kommt einmal in der Woche.** *dair gairt-ner komt ine-mahl in dair vo-khe* |
| Can you please mow the lawn? | **Können Sie bitte den Rasen mähen?** *kern-nen zee bit-te dayn rah-zen may-en* |
| Is the garden private? | **Ist der Garten privat?** *isst dair gar-ten pree-vaht* |
| The garden needs watering. | **Der Garten muss gegossen werden.** *dair gar-ten mooss ge-gos-sen vair-den* |

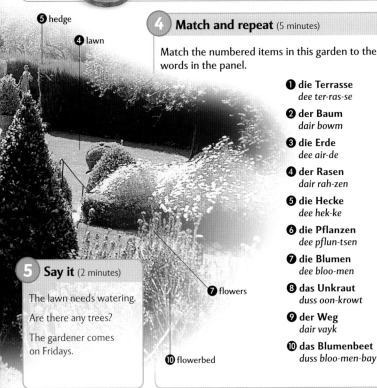

❺ hedge

❹ lawn

## 4 Match and repeat (5 minutes)

Match the numbered items in this garden to the words in the panel.

❶ **die Terrasse** *dee ter-ras-se*

❷ **der Baum** *dair bowm*

❸ **die Erde** *dee air-de*

❹ **der Rasen** *dair rah-zen*

❺ **die Hecke** *dee hek-ke*

❻ **die Pflanzen** *dee pflun-tsen*

❼ **die Blumen** *dee bloo-men*

❽ **das Unkraut** *duss oon-krowt*

❾ **der Weg** *dair vayk*

❿ **das Blumenbeet** *duss bloo-men-bayt*

❼ flowers

❿ flowerbed

## 5 Say it (2 minutes)

The lawn needs watering.

Are there any trees?

The gardener comes on Fridays.

# DIE HAUSTIERE
## Pets

**1 Warm up** (1 minute)

Say "My name's John".
(pp.8–9)

How do you say "Don't
worry"? (pp.94–5)

What's "your" in
German? (pp.12–13)

Pet passports are now available to enable
holiday-makers and commuters to take their
pets with them to Germany and avoid quarantine
on return to the United Kingdom. Consult your
vet for details of how to obtain the necessary
vaccinations and paperwork.

## 2 Match and repeat (3 minutes)

Match the numbered animals to the
German words below. Test yourself
using the cover flap.

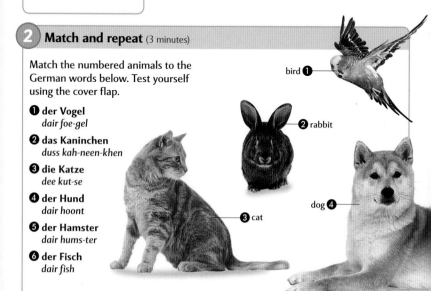

bird **1**

**2** rabbit

dog **4**

**3** cat

**1** der Vogel
*dair foe-gel*

**2** das Kaninchen
*duss kah-neen-khen*

**3** die Katze
*dee kut-se*

**4** der Hund
*dair hoont*

**5** der Hamster
*dair hums-ter*

**6** der Fisch
*dair fish*

## 3 Useful phrases (4 minutes)

Familiarize yourself with these phrases and
then test yourself using the cover flap.

| | |
|---|---|
| **Ist dieser Hund gutartig?** *isst dee-zer hoont goot-ar-tikh* | Is this dog friendly? |
| **Kann ich meinen Hund mitbringen?** *kunn ikh mie-nen hoont mit-bring-en* | Can I bring my dog? |
| **Ich habe Angst vor Katzen.** *ikh hah-be unkst foer kut-tsen* | I'm frightened of cats. |
| **Mein Hund beißt nicht.** *mine hoont biesst nikht* | My dog doesn't bite. |

**Diese Katze hat Flöhe.**
*dee-ze kut-se hut fler-we*
This cat has fleas.

**Cultural tip** Many dogs in Germany are working dogs and you may encounter them tethered or roaming free. Approach rural houses with particular care. Look out for warning notices such as **Warnung vor dem Hunde** (*Beware of the dog*).

---

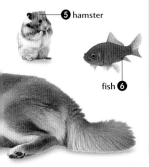

**Meinem Hund geht es nicht gut.**
*mie-nem hoont gayt es nikht goot*
My dog is not well.

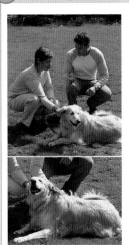

**5** hamster

fish **6**

### 4 Words to remember (4 minutes)

Familiarize yourself with these words and test yourself using the flap.

| | |
|---|---|
| basket | **der Korb** <br> *dair korp* |
| cage | **der Käfig** <br> *dair kay-fik* |
| bowl | **die Schüssel** <br> *dee shews-sel* |
| collar | **das Halsband** <br> *duss hulls-bunt* |
| lead | **die Leine** <br> *dee lie-ne* |
| vet | **der Tierarzt** <br> *dair teer-artst* |
| vaccination | **die Impfung** <br> *dee imp-foong* |
| pet passport | **der Tierpass** <br> *dair teer-puss* |
| fleas | **die Flöhe** <br> *die fler-we* |

### 5 Put into practice (3 minutes)

Join in this conversation. Read the German on the left and follow the instructions to make your reply. Then test yourself by concealing the answers with the cover flap.

**Ist das Ihr Hund?**
*isst duss eer hoont*

Is this your dog?

Say: Yes, he's called Hasso.

**Ja, er heißt Hasso.**
*yah, er hiesst hus-so*

---

**Ich habe Angst vor Hunden.**
*ikh hah-be unkst foer hoon-den*

I'm frightened of dogs.

Say: Don't worry, he's well behaved.

**Keine Angst, er ist gutartig.**
*kie-ne unkst, er isst goot-ar-tikh*

# WIEDERHOLUNG
## Review and repeat

**Antworten**
*Answers* (Cover with flap)

### 1 Colours

❶ **schwarz**
*shvarts*

❷ **weiß**
*vies*

❸ **rot**
*roet*

❹ **grün**
*grewn*

❺ **gelb**
*gelp*

### 1 Colours (4 minutes)

Complete the sentences with the German word for the colour in brackets.

❶ Haben Sie diese Jacke in _____ . (*black*)

❷ Ich nehme den Rock in _____ . (*white*)

❸ Haben Sie die Hose in _____ ? (*red*)

❹ Nein, aber ich habe eine in _____ . (*green*)

❺ Ich möchte diese Schuhe in _____ . (*yellow*)

### 2 Kitchen

❶ **der Herd**
*dair hairt*

❷ **der Kühlschrank**
*dair kewl-shrunk*

❸ **das Spülbecken**
*duss spewl-bek-ken*

❹ **die Mikrowelle**
*dee mee-kro-vel-le*

❺ **der Backofen**
*dair bak-oe-fen*

❻ **der Stuhl**
*dair shtool*

❼ **der Tisch**
*dair tish*

### 2 Kitchen (4 minutes)

Say the German words for the numbered items.

cooker ❶

fridge ❷

chair ❻

❺ oven

table ❼

### 3 House (4 minutes)

You are being shown around a house in Germany. Join in the conversation, replying in German following the numbered English prompts.

**Hier ist das Wohnzimmer.**
**1** What a lovely sofa.

**Ja, und da ist auch eine große Küche.**
**2** How many rooms?

**Es gibt drei Zimmer.**
**3** Do you have a garage?

**Nein, aber da ist ein großer Garten.**
**4** When is the house available?

**Ab Juli.**
**5** What is the rent per month?

### 3 House

**1** Was für eine schöne Couch!
*vuss fewr ie-ne shern-ne kowtch*

**2** Wie viele Zimmer gibt es?
*vee fee-le tsim-mer geept es*

**3** Haben Sie eine Garage?
*hah-ben zee ie-ne ga-ra-je*

**4** Ab wann ist das Haus frei?
*up vunn isst duss hows frie*

**5** Wie hoch ist die monatliche Miete?
*vee hoekh isst dee mo-naht-li-khe mee-te*

### 4 At home (3 minutes)

microwave **4**

**3** sink

Say the German for the following items:

**1** washing machine
**2** sofa
**3** attic
**4** dining room
**5** tree
**6** garden

### 4 At home

**1** die Waschmaschine
*dee vush-mah-shee-ne*

**2** die Couch
*dee kowtch*

**3** der Dachboden
*dair dukh-boe-den*

**4** das Esszimmer
*duss es-tsim-mer*

**5** der Baum
*dair bowm*

**6** der Garten
*dair gar-ten*

# BANK UND POST
## Bank and post office

### 1 Warm up (1 minute)

Ask "Where can I find the bank?" (pp.68-9)

What's the German for "passport"? (pp.54-5)

Ask "What time?" (pp.30-1)

German post offices have machines that print stamps on demand, weigh parcels automatically, and explain their services in several languages. Most banks have cash machines (ATMs) with multiple language options. However, banks also offer a cashier service, if you need help.

### 2 Words to remember: post (3 minutes)

| | |
|---|---|
| **der Umschlag** *dair oom-shlahk* | envelope |
| **die Postkarte** *dee posst-kar-te* | postcard |
| **das Paket** *duss pa-kayt* | parcel |
| **per Luftpost** *pair looft-posst* | by air mail |
| **per Einschreiben** *pair ine-shrie-ben* | by registered post |
| **der Briefkasten** *dair breef-kuss-ten* | post box |
| **die Postleitzahl** *dee posst-lite-tsahl* | postcode |
| **der Briefträger** *dair breef-tray-ger* | postman |

Familiarize yourself with these words and test yourself using the cover flap to conceal the German on the left.

**die Briefmarken**
*dee breef-mar-ken*
stamps

**Wie hoch ist das Porto nach England?**
*vee hoekh isst duss por-toe nahkh eng-lant*
What is the postage for England?

### 3 In conversation (3 minutes)

**Ich möchte Geld abheben.**
*ikh merkh-te gelt up-hay-ben*

I'd like to withdraw some money.

**Können Sie sich ausweisen?**
*kern-nen zee zikh ows-vie-zen*

Do you have any ID?

**Ja, ich habe meinen Pass dabei.**
*Yah, ikh hah-be mye-nen puss da-bie*

Yes, I have my passport with me.

**Wie kann ich zahlen?**
*vee kunn ikh tsah-len*
How can I pay?

### 4 Words to remember: bank (2 minutes)

Familiarize yourself with these words and test yourself using the cover flap.

| | |
|---|---|
| PIN | **die Geheimnummer** *dee ge-hime-noom-mer* |
| bank | **die Bank** *dee bunk* |
| cashier | **der Kassierer(in)** *dair kuss-see-rer(in)* |
| ATM | **der Geldautomat** *dair gelt-ow-to-maht* |
| notes | **die Banknoten** *dee bunk-noe-ten* |
| coin | **die Münze** *dee mewn-tse* |
| credit card | **die Kreditkarte** *dee kray-deet-kar-te* |

### 5 Useful phrases (4 minutes)

Learn these phrases and then test yourself using the cover flap.

| | |
|---|---|
| I'd like to change some money. | **Ich möchte Geld wechseln.** *ikh merkh-te gelt vek-zeln* |
| What is the exchange rate? | **Wie ist der Wechselkurs?** *vee isst dair vek-zel-koors* |
| I'd like to withdraw some money. | **Ich möchte Geld abheben.** *ikh merkh-te gelt up-hay-ben* |

### 6 Say it (2 minutes)

I'd like a stamp.

Where can I find a post box?

I have ID.

**Bitte geben Sie Ihre Geheimzahl ein**
*bit-te gay-ben zee ee-re ge-hime-tsahl ine*

Please key in your PIN.

**Muss ich auch unterschreiben?**
*mooss ikh owkh oon-ter-shrie-ben*

Do I need to sign as well?

**Nein, das ist nicht nötig.**
*nine, duss isst nikht ner-tikh*

No, that's not necessary.

# DIENSTLEISTUNGEN
## Services

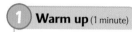

### 1 Warm up (1 minute)

What is the German for "doesn't work"? (pp.60-1)

What's the German for "today" and "tomorrow"? (pp.28-9)

You can combine the German words on these pages with the vocabulary you learned in week 10 to help you explain basic problems and cope with arranging most repairs. When organizing building work or a repair, it's a good idea to agree the price and method of payment in advance.

### 2 Words to remember (4 minutes)

Familiarize yourself with these words and test yourself using the flap.

| | |
|---|---|
| **Klempner(in)** *klemp-ner(in)* | plumber |
| **Elektriker(in)** *ay-lek-tree-ker(in)* | electrician |
| **Mechaniker(in)** *me-khah-nee-ker(in)* | mechanic |
| **Bauarbeiter(in)** *bow-ar-bie-ter(in)* | builder |
| **die Putzfrau** *dee poots-frow* | cleaning lady |
| **Maler(in)** *mah-ler(in)* | painter/decorator |
| **Schreiner(in)** *shrie-ner(in)* | carpenter |
| **die Telefonnummer** *dee tay-lay-foen-noom-mer* | telephone number |

**der Radschüssel**
*dair raht-shlews-sel*
wheel brace

**Ich brauche keinen Mechaniker.**
*ikh brow-khe kie-nen me-khah-nee-ker*
I don't need a mechanic.

### 3 In conversation (3 minutes)

**Die Waschmachine funktioniert nicht.**
*dee vush-mah-shee-ne foonk-tsee-oen-eert nikht*

The washing machine is not working.

**Ja, die Pumpe ist kaputt.**
*yah, dee poom-pe isst ka-poott*

Yes, the pipe is broken.

**Können Sie die reparieren?**
*kern-nen zee dee re-pah-ree-ren*

Can you repair it?

## 4 Useful phrases (3 minutes)

Learn these phrases and then test yourself using the cover flap.

| | |
|---|---|
| Can you clean the bathroom? | **Können Sie das Badezimmer putzen?**<br>*kern-nen zee duss bah-de-tsim-mer poot-tsen* |
| Can you repair the boiler? | **Können Sie den Boiler reparieren?**<br>*kern-nen zee dayn boi-ler re-pah-ree-ren* |
| Do you know a good electrician? | **Kennen Sie einen guten Elektriker?**<br>*ken-nen zee ie-nen goo-ten ay-lek-tree-ker* |

**Wo kann ich das reparieren lassen?**
*voe kunn ikh duss re-pah-ree-ren luss-sen*
Where can I get this repaired?

## 5 Put into practice (4 minutes)

Learn these phrases. Cover up the text on the right and complete the dialogue in German. Check your answers and repeat if necessary.

| | |
|---|---|
| **Ihr Tor ist kaputt.**<br>*eer tohr isst ka-poott*<br>Your gate is broken.<br><br>Ask: Do you know a good carpenter? | **Kennen Sie einen guten Schreiner?**<br>*ken-nen zee ie-nen goo-ten shrie-ner* |
| **Ja, es gibt einen im Ort.**<br>*yah, es geept ie-nen im ort*<br>Yes, there is one in the village.<br><br>Ask: Do you have the telephone number? | **Haben Sie die Telefonnummer?**<br>*hah-ben zee dee tay-lay-foen-noom-mer* |

**Nein, Sie brauchen eine neue.**
*nine, zee brow-khen ie-ne noy-e*

No, you'll need a new one.

**Können Sie das heute machen?**
*kern-nen zee duss hoy-te ma-khen*

Can you do it today?

**Nein, ich komme morgen wieder.**
*nine, ikh kom-me mor-gen vee-der*

No. I'll come back tomorrow.

## 1 Warm up (1 minute)

Say the days of the week in German. (pp.28-9)

How do you say "builder"? (pp.110-11)

Say "It's 9.30", "10.45", and "12.00". (pp.10-11, pp.30-1)

# KOMMEN
## To come

The verb **kommen** (*to come*) is another important verb. Apart from its literal meaning, it can mean *happen* as in *how come?* It can be combined with adverbs such as **her** (*here*) or **herein** (*in*). It also occurs in many expressions, such as **das kommt davon, dass...** (*That's because...*).

## 2 Kommen: to come (6 minutes)

Say the different forms of **kommen** (*to come*) aloud. Use the cover flap to test yourself and, when you are confident, practise the sample sentences below.

| | |
|---|---|
| **ich komme**<br>*ikh kom-me* | I come |
| **du kommst**<br>*doo komst* | you come (informal) |
| **er/sie/es kommt**<br>*air/zee/es komt* | he/she/it comes |
| **wir kommen**<br>*veer kom-men* | we come |
| **ihr kommt**<br>*eer komt* | you come (informal, plural) |
| **sie/Sie kommen**<br>*zee kom-men* | they come/you come (plural or formal) |
| **Ich komme aus London.**<br>*ikh kom-me ows london* | I come from London. |
| **Wir kommen jeden Dienstag.**<br>*veer kom-men yay-den deens-tahk* | We come every Tuesday. |
| **Sie kommen mit dem Zug.**<br>*zee kom-men mit daym tsook* | They come by train. |

**Er kommt aus China.**
*air komt ows khee-nah*
He comes from China.

**Conversational tip Kommen** is used in many (usually friendly) commands such as **komm her** (*come here*) or **kommen Sie herein** (*come in*). It also often appears together with another verb, when in English we might link the two verbs with *and*, as in: **komm setz dich** (*come and sit down*), **kommt essen** (*come and eat*).

## 3 Useful phrases (4 minutes)

Learn these phrases and then test yourself using the cover flap.

| | |
|---|---|
| When can I come? | **Wann kann ich kommen?** *vunn kunn ikh kom-men* |
| Where does she come from? | **Woher kommt sie?** *vo-hair komt zee* |
| The cleaner comes every Monday. | **Die Putzfrau kommt jeden Montag.** *dee poots-frow komt yay-den moen-tahk* |
| Come with me. (informal/formal) | **Komm mit/ Kommen Sie mit.** *kom mit/ kom-men zee mit* |

**Bitte setzen Sie sich.**
*bit-te zet-sen zee zikh*
Come and sit down.

## 4 Put into practice (4 minutes)

Join in this conversation. Read the German on the left and follow the instructions to make your reply. Then test yourself by concealing the answers with the cover flap.

**Guten Tag, Friseursalon Hannelore.**
*goo-ten tahk, fri-zer-zah-long hun-ne-loe-re*

Hello, this is Hannelore's hair salon.

Say: I'd like an appointment.

**Ich hätte gern einen Termin.**
*ikh het-te gairn ie-nen terr-meen*

**Wann möchten Sie kommen?**
*vunn merkh-ten zee kom-men*

When would you like to come?

Say: Can I come today?

**Kann ich heute kommen?**
*kunn ikh hoy-te kom-men*

**Natürlich. Um wieviel Uhr?**
*na-tewr-likh. oomm vee-feel oor*

Yes, of course. What time?

Say: At 10.30.

**Um halb elf.**
*oomm hulp elf*

# POLIZEI UND VERBRECHEN
## Police and crime

### 1 Warm up (1 minute)

What's the German for "big/tall" and "small/short"? (pp.64-5)

Say "The room is big" and "The bed is small". (pp.64-5)

*German traffic police (***Verkehrspolizei***) carry out checks and impose fines for violations of the traffic regulations. If you are the victim of a crime or are in a traffic accident in Germany, report it to the nearest police station.*

### 2 Words to remember: crime (4 minutes)

Familiarize yourself with these words.

**Ich brauche einen Rechtsanwalt.**
*ikh brow-khe ie-nen rekhts-un-vullt*
I need a lawyer.

| | |
|---|---|
| **der Diebstahl** *dair deep-shtahl* | robbery |
| **der Polizeibericht** *dair po-lee-tsie-be-rikht* | police report |
| **der Dieb** *dair deep* | thief |
| **die Polizei** *dee po-lee-tsie* | police |
| **die Aussage** *dee ows-zah-ge* | statement |
| **Rechtsanwalt/-wältin** *rekhts-un-vullt/-vael-tin* | lawyer |
| **Zeuge/Zeugin** *tsoy-ge/tsoy-gin* | witness |

### 3 Useful phrases (3 minutes)

Memorize these phrases and then test yourself.

| | |
|---|---|
| **Ich bin bestohlen worden.** *ikh bin be-shtoe-len vor-den* | I've been robbed. |
| **Was ist gestohlen worden?** *vuss isst ge-shtoe-len vor-den* | What was stolen? |
| **Haben Sie den Täter gesehen?** *hah-ben zee den tay-ter ge-zay-en* | Did you see who did it? |
| **Wann ist es passiert?** *vunn isst es puss-seert* | When did it happen? |

**die Wertsachen**
*dee vairt-zakh-en*
valuables

### 4 Words to remember: appearance (5 minutes)

Learn these words for describing people.

**Er hat eine Glatze und einen Bart.**
*air hut ie-ne glut-se oont ie-nen bart*
He is bald and has a beard.

**Er hat kurze, schwarze Haare.**
*air hut koor-tse, shvar-tse hah-re*
He has short, black hair.

| | | |
|---|---|---|
| man | **der Mann** | *dair munn* |
| woman | **die Frau** | *dee frow* |
| tall | **groß** | *groes* |
| short | **klein** | *kline* |
| young | **jung** | *yoong* |
| old | **alt** | *ullt* |
| fat | **dick** | *dick* |
| thin | **dünn** | *dewnn* |
| long/short hair | **lange/kurze Haare** | *lun-ge/koor-tse hah-re* |
| glasses | **die Brille** | *dee bril-le* |
| beard | **der Bart** | *dair bart* |

**Cultural tip** If you have a car accident or serious breakdown on a motorway, use one of the special telephones that you can find at regular intervals. Elsewhere, phone 112, which is free from all telephones in Germany. The operator will inform the appropriate service (police, fire service, or ambulance) immediately.

### 5 Put into practice (2 minutes)

Practise these phrases. Then cover up the text on the right and follow the instructions to make your reply in German.

**Wie sah er aus?** **Klein und dick.**
*vee zah air ows* *kline oont dick*

What did he look like?

Say: Short and fat.

---

**Und die Haare?** **Lang, mit Bart.**
*oont dee hah-re* *lung, mit bart*

And the hair?

Say: Long, with a beard.

# WIEDERHOLUNG
## Review and repeat

**Antworten**
*Answers* (Cover with flap)

### 1 To come

❶ **komme**
*kom-me*

❷ **kommt**
*komt*

❸ **kommen**
*kom-men*

❹ **kommt**
*komt*

❺ **kommen**
*kom-men*

### 1 To come (3 minutes)

Put the correct form of **kommen** (*to come*) into the gaps.

❶ Ich _____ um vier Uhr.

❷ Der Gärtner _____ einmal in der Woche.

❸ Wir _____ Dienstag zum Essen.

❹ _____ ihr mit?

❺ Meine Eltern _____ mit dem Zug.

### 2 Bank and post

❶ **die Banknoten**
*dee bunk-noe-ten*

❷ **das Paket**
*duss pa-kayt*

❸ **die Postkarte**
*dee posst-kar-te*

❹ **die Briefmarken**
*dee breef-mar-ken*

### 2 Bank and post (4 minutes)

Name the numbered items in German.

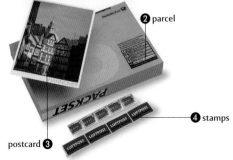

❶ notes

❷ parcel

❹ stamps

postcard ❸

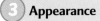

### 3 Appearance (4 minutes)

What do these descriptions mean?

1. Der Mann ist groß und dünn.
2. Sie hat kurze Haare und eine Brille.
3. Ich bin klein und habe lange Haare.
4. Sie ist alt und dick.
5. Er hat blaue Augen und einen Bart.

### 3 Appearance

1. The man is tall and thin.
2. She has short hair and glasses.
3. I'm short and I have long hair.
4. She is old and fat.
5. He has blue eyes and a beard.

### 4 The pharmacy (4 minutes)

You are asking a pharmacist for advice. Join in the conversation, replying in German where you see the numbered English prompts.

**Guten Tag, kann ich Ihnen helfen?**
1. I have a cough.

**Und haben Sie auch Schnupfen?**
2. No, but I have a headache.

**Nehmen Sie diese Tabletten.**
3. Do you have that as a syrup?

**Selbstverständlich. Bitte sehr.**
4. Thank you. How much is that?

**Sechs Euro.**
5. Here you are. Goodbye.

### 4 The pharmacy

1. Ich habe Husten.
   *ikh hah-be hoos-ten*

2. Nein, aber ich habe Kopfschmerzen.
   *nine, ah-ber ikh hah-be kopf-shmairt-sen*

3. Haben Sie das auch als Sirup?
   *hah-ben zee duss owkh ulls zee-roop*

4. Danke. Was macht das?
   *dun-ke. vuss mukht duss*

5. Bitte sehr. Auf Wiedersehen.
   *bit-te zair. owf vee-der-zay-en*

# DIE FREIZEIT
## Leisure time

What is the German for "museum" and "art gallery"? (pp.48-9)

Say "I don't like the curtains". (pp.100-1)

Ask "Do you want...?" informally. (pp.22-3)

In Germany the arts, from opera and classic drama to performance art and cabaret, and from great composers to folk and avant-garde music, are keenly followed and receive public support. **Lust haben** is a useful expression, meaning to *like the idea of doing something*.

**2 Words to remember** (4 minutes)

Familiarize yourself with these words.

| | |
|---|---|
| **das Theater** *duss tay-ah-ter* | theatre |
| **das Kino** *duss kee-no* | cinema |
| **das Ballett** *duss bull-let* | ballet |
| **die Musik** *dee moo-zeek* | music |
| **die Kunst** *dee koonst* | art |
| **der Sport** *dair shport* | sport |
| **die Besichtigungen** *dee be-zikh-tee-goong-en* | sightseeing |
| **die Computerspiele** *dee com-pyoo-ter-shpee-le* | computer games |

**Ich liebe Opern.**
*ikh lee-be oh-pairn*
I love opera.

**das Publikum**
*duss poo-blee-koomm*
audience

**3 In conversation** (4 minutes)

**Hast du Lust, heute Tennis zu spielen?**
*husst doo loost, hoy-te ten-nis tsoo shpee-len*

Do you want to play tennis today?

**Nein, ich mag keinen Sport.**
*nine, ikh mahk kie-nen shport*

No, I don't like sport.

**Wofür interessierst du dich denn?**
*voe-fewr in-ter-es-seerst doo dikh den*

So what are you interested in?

**Ich hasse Gitarrenmusik.**
*ikh hus-se gee-tar-ren-moo-zeek*
I hate guitar music.

**der Rang**
*dair rung*
circle

**das Parkett**
*duss par-ket*
stalls

### 4 Useful phrases (4 minutes)

Learn these phrases and then test yourself using the cover flap.

| | |
|---|---|
| I like the theatre. | **Ich liebe das Theater.** *ikh lee-be duss tay-ah-ter* |
| I prefer the cinema. | **Ich ziehe das Kino vor.** *ikh tsee-e duss kee-no for* |
| I'm interested in art. | **Ich interessiere mich für die Kunst.** *ikh in-ter-es-see-re mikh fewr dee koonst* |
| What are your (formal/informal) interests? | **Wofür interessierst du dich/interessieren Sie sich?** *vo-fewr in-ter-es-seerst doo dikh/in-ter-es-see-ren zee zikh* |
| That bores me. | **Das finde ich langweilig.** *duss fin-de ikh lung-vie-likh* |

### 5 Say it (2 minutes)

I'm interested in music.

I prefer sport.

I don't like computer games.

**Ich mache lieber Besichtigungen.**
*ikh ma-khe lee-ber be-zikh-tee-goong-en*

I prefer sightseeing.

**Das interessiert mich nicht.**
*duss in-ter-es-seert mikh nikht*

That doesn't interest me.

**Kein Problem. Ich gehe allein.**
*kine pro-blaym. ikh gay-he ull-line*

No problem. I'll go on my own.

## 1 Warm up (1 minute)

Ask "Do you (informal) want to play tennis?" (pp.118-19)

Say "I like the cinema", "I prefer sightseeing", and "That doesn't interest me". (pp.118-19)

# SPORT UND HOBBYS
## Sport and hobbies

Germany is a nation of sports enthusiasts. Many people cycle, jog, swim, or work out at the gym, and many follow sport as spectators. Football is very popular, but so are boxing, ice hockey, tennis, and skiing. The verb **spielen** (to play) is mainly used for ball games.

## 2 Words to remember: sports (5 minutes)

Familiarize yourself with these words and test yourself using the flap.

| | |
|---|---|
| **der Fußball** *dair foos-bull* | football |
| **das Boxen** *duss box-en* | boxing |
| **das Tennis** *duss ten-nis* | tennis |
| **das Schwimmen** *duss shvim-men* | swimming |
| **das Segeln** *duss zay-geln* | sailing |
| **das Angeln** *duss ung-eln* | fishing |
| **das Radfahren** *duss raht-fah-ren* | cycling |
| **das Wandern** *duss vunn-dairn* | hiking |

**der Bunker**
*dair boon-ker*
bunker

**der Golfspieler**
*dair golf-shpee-ler*
golfer

**Ich spiele jeden Tag Golf.**
*ikh shpee-le yay-den tahk golf*
I play golf every day.

## 3 Useful phrases (2 minutes)

Familiarize yourself with these phrases.

| | |
|---|---|
| **Ich spiele Fußball.** *ikh shpee-le foos-bull* | I play football. |
| **Wir spielen gern Tennis.** *veer shpee-len gairn ten-nis.* | We like playing tennis. |
| **Sie malt.** *zee mahlt.* | She paints. |

## 4 Words to remember: hobbies (4 minutes)

**Ich begesitere mich für das Fotografieren.**
*ikh be-gesi-tair mikh fewr foe-to-grah-fee-ayren*
I'm keen on photography.

die Flagge
*dee flug-ge*
flag

der Golfplatz
*dair golf-pluts*
golf course

Learn these words and phrases, and then test yourself using the cover flap.

| | |
|---|---|
| do-it-yourself | **das Basteln** *duss bass-teln* |
| pottery | **die Töpferei** *dee ter-pfe-rie* |
| flower arranging | **das Blumenstecken** *duss bloo-men-shtek-en* |
| gardening | **die Gartenarbeit** *dee gar-ten-ar-biet* |
| singing | **das Singen** *duss zing-en* |
| Can I join a club? | **Kann ich einem Klub beitreten?** *kunn ikh ien-em kloop bie-tray-ten* |
| Do I have to be a member? | **Muss man Mitglied sein?** *moos munn mit-gleet zine* |
| Can I hire the equipment? | **Kann ich die Ausrüstung mieten?** *kumm ikh dee ows-rews-toong mee-ten* |

## 5 Put into practice (3 minutes)

Join in this conversation. Conceal the text on the right and complete the dialogue in German using the cover flap. Check your answers.

**Was machst du gern?**
*vuss mukhst doo gairn*

What do you like doing?

Say: I like playing tennis.

**Ich spiele gern Tennis.**
*ikh shpee-le gairn ten-nis*

**Spielst du auch Golf?**
*speelst doo owkh golf*

Do you also play golf?

Say: No, I play football.

**Nein, ich spiele Fußball.**
*nine, ikh shpee-le foos-bull*

**Spielst du oft?**
*speelst doo oft*

Do you play often?

Say: Yes, I play every week.

**Ja, ich spiele jede Woche.**
*yah, ikh shpee-le yay-de vokh-e*

# BESUCHEN
## Socializing

Say "my husband" and "my wife". (pp.10-11)

How do you say "lunch" and "dinner" in German? (pp.20-1)

Say "Sorry, I'm busy". (pp.32-3)

In Germany, much socializing takes place outside the home. People meet up to go to a play, a film, or a sports event together, or they go out for a meal or a drink. Friends and family also invite each other for meals, especially for special occasions such as birthdays.

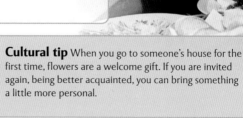

**der Gast**
*dair gust*
guest

**2　Useful phrases** (3 minutes)

Learn these phrases and then test yourself.

| | |
|---|---|
| **Ich möchte Sie zum Abendessen einladen.** *ikh merkh-te zee tsoom ah-bent-ess-sen ine-lah-den* | I'd like to invite you for dinner. |
| **Sind Sie nächsten Mittwoch frei?** *zint zee nayks-ten mit-vokh frie* | Are you free next Wednesday? |
| **Vielleicht ein andermal.** *feel-liekht ine un-der-mahl* | Perhaps another time. |

**Cultural tip** When you go to someone's house for the first time, flowers are a welcome gift. If you are invited again, being better acquainted, you can bring something a little more personal.

**3　In conversation** (3 minutes)

**Möchten Sie zum Mittagessen kommen?**
*merkh-ten zee tsoom mit-tahk-ess-sen kom-men*

Would you like to come to lunch?

**Mit Vergnügen. Wann?**
*mit fer-g-new-gen. vunn*

I'd be delighted. When?

**Wie wär's mit Donnerstag?**
*vee vairs mit don-ners-tahk*

What about Thursday?

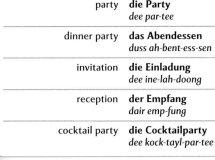

**die Gastgeberin**
*dee gust-gay-be-rin*
hostess

### 4 Words to remember (3 minutes)

Familiarize yourself with these words and test yourself using the flap.

| | |
|---|---|
| party | **die Party** *dee par-tee* |
| dinner party | **das Abendessen** *duss ah-bent-ess-sen* |
| invitation | **die Einladung** *dee ine-lah-doong* |
| reception | **der Empfang** *dair emp-fung* |
| cocktail party | **die Cocktailparty** *dee kock-tayl-par-tee* |

### 5 Put into practice (5 minutes)

Join in this conversation.

**Können Sie heute Abend zu einem Empfang kommen?**
*ker-nen zee hoy-te ah-bent tsoo ie-nem emp-fung kom-men*

Can you come to a reception tonight?

Say: Yes, I'd love to.

**Ja, gerne.**
*yah, gair-ne*

**Es fängt um zwanzig Uhr an.**
*es fengt oom tsvun-tsik oor un*

It starts at eight o'clock.

Ask: What should I wear?

**Was trägt man?**
*vuss traygt munn*

**Danke für die Einladung.**
*dun-ke fewr dee ine-lah-doonk.*
Thank you for inviting us.

**Das passt mir gut.**
*duss pusst meer goot*

That's good for me.

**Bringen Sie Ihren Mann mit.**
*brin-gen zee ee-ren munn mit*

Bring your husband.

**Danke. Um wieviel Uhr?**
*dun-ke. oom vee-feel oor*

Thank you. At what time?

**Antworten**
*Answers* (Cover with flap)

# WIEDERHOLUNG
## Review and repeat

### 1 Animals

❶ **der Fisch**
*dair fish*

❷ **der Vogel**
*dair foh-gel*

❸ **der Hamster**
*dair hums-ter*

❹ **die Katze**
*dee kut-se*

❺ **das Kaninchen**
*duss kah-neen-khen*

❻ **der Hund**
*dair hoont*

### 1 Animals (3 minutes)

Name the animals.

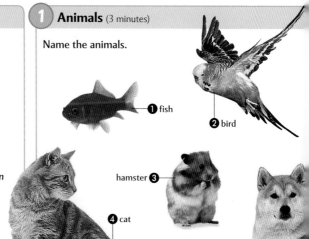

❶ fish
❷ bird
hamster ❸
❹ cat

### 2 I like...

❶ **Ich spiele gern Fußball.**
*ikh shpee-le gairn foos-bull*

❷ **Ich spiele nicht gern Golf.**
*ikh shpee-le nikht gairn golf*

❸ **Ich male gern.**
*ikh mah-le gairn*

❹ **Blumenstecken mache ich nicht gern.**
*bloo-men-shtek-ken makh-e ikh nikht gairn*

### 2 I like... (4 minutes)

Say the following in German.

❶ I like playing football.
❷ I don't like playing golf.
❸ I like to paint.
❹ I don't like flower arranging.

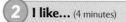

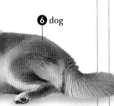

**5** rabbit

**6** dog

### **3** Leisure (4 minutes)

What is the German for these sports and leisure activities?

**1** sailing
**2** art
**3** sightseeing
**4** cinema
**5** hiking
**6** swimming

### **3** Leisure

**1** das Segeln
*duss zay-geln*

**2** die Kunst
*dee koonst*

**3** die Besichtigungen
*dee be-zikh-tee-goong-en*

**4** das Kino
*duss kee-no*

**5** das Wandern
*duss vunn-dairn*

**6** das Schwimmen
*duss shvim-men*

### **4** An invitation (4 minutes)

You are invited for dinner. Join in the conversation, replying in German following the English prompts.

**Möchten Sie am Freitag zum Essen kommen?**
**1** I'm sorry, I'm busy.

**Wie wär's mit Samstag?**
**2** I'd be delighted.

**Bringen Sie Ihre Kinder mit.**
**3** Thank you. At what time?

**Um halb eins.**
**4** That's good for me.

### **4** An invitation

**1** Es tut mir Leid, ich habe schon etwas vor.
*es toot meer liet, ikh hah-be shoen et-vuss for*

**2** Mit Vergnügen.
*mit fer-g-new-gen*

**3** Danke. Um wieviel Uhr?
*dun-ke. oom vee-feel oor*

**4** Ja, das passt mir.
*yah, duss pusst meer*

# Reinforce and progress

Regular practice is the key to maintaining and advancing your language skills. In this section you will find a variety of suggestions for reinforcing and extending your knowledge of German. Many involve returning to exercises in the book and using the dictionaries to extend their scope. Go back through the lessons in a different order, mix and match activities to make up your own 15-minute daily programme, or focus on topics that are of particular relevance to your current needs.

**1 Warm up** (1 minute)

Say "I'm sorry". (pp.32-3)

What is the German for "I'd like an appointment"? (pp.32-3)

Ask "with whom?" in German. (pp.32-3)

**Keep warmed up**
Re-visit the Warm Up boxes to remind yourself of key words and phrases. Make sure you work your way through all of them on a regular basis.

**2 I'd like...** (3 minutes)

Say you'd like the following:

cake ❶

❷ black tea

coffee ❸

**Review and repeat again**
Work through a Review and Repeat lesson as a way of reinforcing words and phrases presented in the course. Return to the main lesson for any topic on which you are no longer confident.

**Carry on conversing**
Re-read the In Conversation panels. Say both parts of the conversation, paying attention to the pronunciation. Where possible, try incorporating new words from the dictionary.

**3 In conversation: taxi** (2 minutes)

**Zum Flughafen, bitte.**
*tsoom flook-hah-fen, bit-te*

The airport, please.

**Jawohl, kein Problem.**
*yah-voel, kine pro-blaym*

Yes, no problem.

**Können Sie mich bitte hier absetzen?**
*ker-nen zee mikh bit-te heer up-zet-sen*

Can you drop me here, please?

**4 Useful phrases** (3 minutes)

**Öffnungszeiten:**
Di. - Fr. 11-18 Uhr
Sa.+So. 11-16 Uhr
(Montags geschlossen)

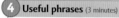

**Toilette**

Learn these phrases and then test yourself using the cover flap.

| What time do you open/close? | **Wann öffnen/ schließen Sie?** *vunn erf-nen/shlee-sen zee* |
|---|---|
| Where are the toilets? | **Wo sind die Toiletten?** *voe zind dee twah-let-ten* |
| Is there wheelchair access? | **Gibt es Zugang für Rollstuhlfahrer?** *geept es tsoo-gung fewr roll-shtool-fah-rer* |

**Practise phrases**
Return to the Useful Phrases and Put into Practice exercises. Test yourself using the cover flap. When you are confident, devise your own versions of the phrases, using new words from the dictionary.

**Match, repeat, and extend**
Remind yourself of words related to specific topics by returning to the Match and Repeat and Words to Remember exercises. Test yourself using the cover flap. Discover new words in that area by referring to the dictionary and menu guide.

**5 Match and repeat** (4 minutes)

Match the numbered items in this scene with the text in the panel.

**1 der Rhabarber**
*dair ra-bar-ber*

**2 die Kartoffeln**
*dee kar-toff-eln*

**3 die Radieschen**
*dee ra-dees-khen*

**4 der Spinat**
*dair shpee-naht*

**5 die Möhren**
*dee mer-ren*

**6 der Kohl**
*dair koel*

**7 der Lauch**
*dair lowk*

**8 der Kohlrabi**
*dair koel-rah-bee*

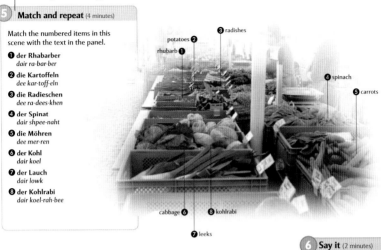

radishes **3**
potatoes **2**
rhubarb **1**
spinach **4**
carrots **5**
cabbage **6**   **8** kohlrabi
**7** leeks

**Say it again**
The Say it exercises are a useful instant reminder for each lesson. Practise these, using your own vocabulary variations from the dictionary or elsewhere in the lesson.

**6 Say it** (2 minutes)

The lawn needs watering.

Are there any trees?

The gardener comes on Fridays.

---

## Using other resources

In addition to working with this book, try the following language extension ideas:

**Visit a German-speaking country** and try out your new skills with native speakers. Find out if there is a German community near you. There may be shops, cafés, restaurants, and clubs. Try to visit some of these and use your German to order food and drink and strike up conversations. Most native speakers will be happy to speak German to you.

**Join a language class or club.** There are usually evening and day classes available at a variety of different levels. Or you could start a club yourself if you have friends who are also interested in keeping up their German.

**Look at German magazines** and newspapers. The pictures will help you to understand the text. Advertisements are also a useful way of expanding your vocabulary.

**Use the Internet,** where you can find all kinds of websites for learning languages, some of which offer free online help and activities. You can also find German websites for anything from renting a house to shampooing your pet. You can even access German radio and TV stations online. Start by going to a German search engine, such as *excite.de*, and keying a subject that interests you, or set yourself a challenge, for example, finding a two-bedroom apartment for rent in Hamburg.

# MENU GUIDE

This guide lists the most common terms you may encounter on German menus or when shopping for food. If you can't find an exact phrase, try looking up its component parts.

## A

**Aal** *eel*
**am Spieß** *on the spit*
**Ananas** *pineapple*
**Äpfel** *apple*
**Apfel im Schlafrock** *baked apple in puff pastry*
**Apfelsaft** *apple juice*
**Apfelsinen** *oranges*
**Apfelstrudel** *apple strudel*
**Apfeltasche** *apple turnover*
**Apfelwein** *cider*
**Aprikosen** *apricots*
**Arme Ritter** *bread soaked in milk and egg, then fried*
**Artischocken** *artichokes*
**Auberginen** *aubergines*
**Auflauf** *baked pudding or omelette*
**Aufschnitt** *cold meats*
**Austern** *oysters*

## B

**Backobst** *dried fruit*
**Backpflaume** *prune*
**Baiser** *meringue*
**Balkansalat** *cabbage and pepper salad*
**Bananen** *bananas*
**Bandnudeln** *ribbon noodles*
**Basilikum** *basil*
**Bauernauflauf** *bacon and potato omelette*
**Bauernfrühstück** *fried potato, bacon, and egg*
**Bauernomelett** *bacon and potato omelette*
**Bechamelkartoffeln** *potatoes in creamy sauce*
**Bedienung** *service*
**Beilagen** *side dishes*
**Berliner** *jam doughnut*
**Bier** *beer*
**Birnen** *pears*
**Biskuit** *sponge cake*
**Bismarckhering** *filleted pickled herring*
**Blätterteig** *puff pastry*
**blau** *cooked in vinegar; virtually raw (steak)*

**Blumenkohl** *cauliflower*
**blutig** *rare*
**Blutwurst** *black pudding*
**Bockwurst** *large frankfurter*
**Bohnen** *beans*
**Bouillon** *clear soup*
**Braten** *roast meat*
**Brathering** *pickled and fried herring, served cold*
**Bratkartoffeln** *fried potatoes*
**Bratwurst** *grilled pork sausage*
**Brot** *bread*
**Brötchen** *roll*
**Brühwurst** *large frankfurter*
**Brust** *breast*
**Bückling** *smoked red herring*
**Buletten** *burgers; rissoles*
**Bunte Platte** *mixed platter*
**Burgundersoße** *Burgundy wine sauce*
**Buttercremetorte** *cream cake*
**Buttermilch** *buttermilk*

## C, D

**Champignons** *mushrooms*
**Cordon bleu** *veal cordon bleu*
**Currywurst mit Pommes frites** *curried pork sausage with chips*
**Dampfnudeln** *sweet yeast dumpling*
**Deutsches Beefsteak** *minced meat or patty*
**Dicke Bohnen** *broad beans*
**Dillsoße** *dill sauce*
**durchgebraten** *well-done*
**durchwachsen** *with fat*
**durchwachsener Speck** *streaky bacon*

## E

**Eier** *eggs*
**Eierauflauf** *omelette*
**Eierkuchen** *pancake*
**Eierpfannkuchen** *egg pancake*
**Eierspeise** *egg dish*
**eingelegt** *pickled*
**Eintopf** *stew*
**Eintopfgericht** *stew*
**Eis** *ice*

**Eisbecher** *sundae*
**Eisbein** *knuckles of pork*
**Eisschokolade** *iced chocolate*
**Eissplittertorte** *ice chip cake*
**Endiviensalat** *endive salad*
**englisch** *rare*
**Entenbraten** *roast duck*
**entgrätet** *bones (fish)*
**Erbsen** *peas*
**Erdbeertorte** *strawberry cake*
**Essig** *vinegar*

## F

**Falscher Hase** *meat loaf*
**Fasan** *pheasant*
**Fenchel** *fennel*
**Fett** *fat*
**Filet** *fillet (steak)*
**Fisch** *fish*
**Fischfrikadellen** *fishcakes*
**Fischstäbchen** *fish fingers*
**Flädlesuppe** *consommé with pancake strips*
**flambiert** *flambéed*
**Fleischbrühe** *bouillon*
**Fleischkäse** *meat loaf*
**Fleischklößchen** *meatball(s)*
**Fleischpastete** *meat vol-au-vent*
**Fleischsalat** *diced meat salad with mayonnaise*
**Fleischwurst** *pork sausage*
**Fond** *meat juices*
**Forelle** *trout*
**Forelle Müllerin (Art)** *breaded trout with butter and lemon*
**Frikadelle** *rissole*
**Frikassee** *fricassee*
**fritiert** *(deep-) fried*
**Froschschenkel** *frog's legs*
**Fruchtsaft** *fruit juice*
**Frühlingsrolle** *spring roll*

## G

**Gans** *goose*
**Gänseleberpastete** *goose-liver pâté*
**garniert** *garnished*
**Gebäck** *pastries, cakes*
**gebacken** *baked*
**gebraten** *roast*

**gedünstet** steamed
**Geflügel** poultry
**Geflügelleberragout** chicken liver ragoût
**gefüllt** stuffed
**gefüllte Kalbsbrust** veal roll
**gekocht** boiled
**Gelee** jelly
**gemischter Salat** mixed salad
**Gemüse** vegetable(s)
**Gemüseplatte** assorted vegetables
**gepökelt** salted, pickled
**geräuchert** smoked
**Gericht** dish
**geschmort** braised, stewed
**Geschnetzeltes** strips of fried meat in cream sauce
**gespickt** larded
**Getränke** beverages
**Gewürze** spices
**Gewürzgurken** gherkins
**Goldbarsch** type of perch
**Götterspeise** jelly
**gratiniert** au gratin
**Grieß** semolina
**Grießklößchen** semolina dumplings
**grüne Bohnen** French beans
**grüne Nudeln** green pasta
**grüner Aal** fresh eel
**Grünkohl** (curly) kale
**Gulasch** goulash
**Gulaschsuppe** goulash soup
**Gurkensalat** cucumber salad

## H

**Hackfleisch** mince
**Hähnchen** chicken
**Hähnchenkeule** chicken leg
**Haifischflossensuppe** shark-fin soup
**Hammelbraten** roast mutton
**Hammelfleisch** mutton
**Hammelkeule** leg of mutton
**Hammelrücken** saddle of mutton
**Hartkäse** hard cheese
**Haschee** hash
**Hasenkeule** haunch of hare
**Hasenpfeffer** hare casserole
**Hauptspeisen** main courses
**Hecht** pike
**Heidelbeeren** bilberries, blueberries
**Heilbutt** halibut
**Heringsstipp** herring salad
**Heringstopf** pickled herrings in sauce
**Herz** heart
**Herzragout** heart ragoût
**Himbeeren** raspberries

**Himmel und Erde** potato and apple purée with black pudding or liver sausage
**Hirn** brains
**Hirschbraten** roast venison
**Honig** honey
**Honigmelone** honeydew melon
**Hoppelpoppel** bacon and potato omelette
**Hüfte** haunch
**Huhn** chicken
**Hühnerbrühe** chicken broth
**Hühnerfrikassee** chicken fricassee
**Hülsenfrüchte** peas and beans, pulses
**Hummer** lobster

## J, K

**Jägerschnitzel** cutlet with mushrooms
**Kabeljau** cod
**Kaffee** coffee
**Kaiserschmarren** sugared pancake with raisins
**Kakao** cocoa
**Kalbfleisch** veal
**Kalbsbries** sweetbread
**Kalbsfrikassee** veal fricassee
**Kalbshaxe** leg of veal
**Kalbsnierenbraten** roast veal with kidney
**Kalbsschnitzel** veal cutlet
**kalte Platte** cold platter
**kaltes Büfett** cold buffet
**Kaltschale** cold, sweet fruit soup
**Kaninchen** rabbit
**Kapern** capers
**Karamelpudding** caramel blancmange
**Karotten** carrots
**Karpfen** carp
**Kartoffelbrei** mashed potato
**Kartoffeln** potatoes
**Kartoffelpuffer** potato fritters
**Kartoffelpüree** mashed potato
**Käse** cheese
**Käsegebäck** cheese savouries
**Käsekuchen** cheesecake
**Käseplatte** selection of cheeses
**Käse-Sahne-Torte** cream cheesecake
**Käsespätzle** home-made noodles with cheese
**Kasseler Rippenspeer** smoked pork loin
**Kasserolle** casserole
**Kassler** smoked pork loin
**Kastanien** chestnuts
**Katenrauchwurst** smoked sausage
**Keule** leg, haunch
**Kieler Sprotten** smoked sprats

**Kirschen** cherries
**klare Brühe** consommé
**Klöße** dumplings
**Knäckebrot** crispbread
**Knacker** spicy fried sausage
**Knackwurst** spicy fried sausage
**Knoblauch** garlic
**Knochen** bone
**Knochenschinken** ham on the bone
**Knödel** dumplings
**Kognak** brandy
**Kohl** cabbage
**Kohlrouladen** stuffed cabbage leaves
**Kohl und Pinkel** cabbage, potatoes, sausage, and smoked meat
**Kompott** stewed fruit
**Konfitüre** jam
**Königinpastete** chicken vol-au-vent
**Königsberger Klopse** meatballs in caper sauce
**Königskuchen** type of fruit cake
**Kopfsalat** lettuce
**Kotelett** chop
**Krabben** shrimps; prawns
**Krabbencocktail** prawn cocktail
**Kraftbrühe** beef consommé
**Kräuter** herbs
**Krautsalat** coleslaw
**Krautwickel** stuffed cabbage leaves
**Krebs** crayfish
**Kresse** cress
**Kroketten** croquettes
**Kruste** crust
**Kuchen** cake
**Kürbis** pumpkin

## L

**Labskaus** meat, fish, and potato stew
**Lachs** salmon
**Lachsersatz** sliced, salted pollack (fish)
**Lachsforelle** sea trout
**Lachsschinken** smoked rolled fillet of ham
**Lamm** lamb
**Lammrücken** saddle of lamb
**Langusten** crayfish
**Lauch** leek
**Leber** liver
**Leberkäse** baked pork and beef loaf
**Leberpastete** liver pâté
**Leberwurst** liver pâté
**Lebkuchen** gingerbread
**Leipziger Allerlei** mixed vegetables
**Linsen** lentils

## M

mager *lean*
Majoran *marjoram*
Makrele *mackerel*
Makronen *macaroons*
Mandeln *almonds*
mariniert *marinaded, pickled*
Markklößchen
    *marrow dumplings*
Marmelade *jam*
Maronen *sweet chestnuts*
Matjes(hering) *young herring*
Medaillons *small fillets*
Meeresfische *seafish*
Meeresfrüchte *seafood*
Meerrettich *horseradish*
Miesmuscheln *mussels*
Milch *milk*
Milchmixgetränk *milk shake*
Milchreis *rice pudding*
Mineralwasser *(sparkling)*
    *mineral water*
Mohnkuchen *poppyseed cake*
Möhren *carrots*
Mohrrüben *carrots*
Most *fruit wine*
Mus *purée*
Muscheln *mussels*
Muskat(nuss) *nutmeg*
MWSt (Mehrwertsteuer) *VAT*

## N, O

nach Art des Hauses
    *of the house*
nach Hausfrauenart
    *home-made*
Nachspeisen *desserts*
Nachtisch *dessert*
Napfkuchen *ring-shaped*
    *poundcake*
natürlich *natural*
Nieren *kidneys*
Nudeln *pasta, noodles*
Nüsse *nuts*
Obstsalat *fruit salad*
Ochsenschwanzsuppe
    *oxtail soup*
Öl *oil*
Oliven *olives*
Orangen *oranges*
Orangensaft *orange juice*

## P

Palatschinken *stuffed pancakes*
paniert *with breadcrumbs*
Paprika *peppers*
Paprikaschoten *peppers*
Paradiesäpfel *tomatoes*
Pastete *vol-au-vent*
Pellkartoffeln *potatoes boiled*
    *in their jackets*

Petersilie *parsley*
Pfannkuchen *pancake(s)*
Pfeffer *pepper*
Pfifferlinge *chanterelles*
Pfirsiche *peaches*
Pflaumen *plums*
Pflaumenkuchen *plum tart*
Pflaumenmus *plum jam*
Pichelsteiner Topf *vegetable*
    *stew with beef*
pikant *spicy*
Pilze *mushrooms*
Platte *selection*
pochiert *poached*
Pökelfleisch *salt meat*
Pommes frites
    *French fried potatoes*
Porree *leek*
Potthast *braised beef*
    *with sauce*
Poularde *young chicken*
Preiselbeeren *cranberries*
Presskopf *brawn*
Pumpernickel *black rye bread*
Püree *mashed potato*
püriert *puréed*
Putenschenkel *turkey leg*
Puter *turkey*

## Q, R

Quark *curd cheese*
Radieschen *radishes*
Rahm *(sour) cream*
Räucheraal *smoked eel*
Räucherhering *kipper,*
    *smoked herring*
Räucherlachs *smoked salmon*
Räucherspeck *smoked bacon*
Rauchfleisch *smoked meat*
Rehbraten *roast venison*
Rehgulasch *venison goulash*
Rehkeule *haunch of venison*
Rehrücken *saddle of venison*
Reibekuchen *potato waffles*
Reis *rice*
Reisbrei *creamed rice*
Reisrand *with rice*
Remoulade *mayonnaise*
    *flavoured with herbs, mustard,*
    *and capers*
Renke *whitefish*
Rettich *radish*
Rhabarber *rhubarb*
Rheinischer Sauerbraten
    *roast pickled beef*
Rinderbraten *pot roast*
Rinderfilet *fillet steak*
Rinderrouladen *beef olives*
Rinderzunge *ox tongue*
Rindfleisch *beef*
Rippchen *spareribs*
Risi-Pisi *rice and peas*
roh *raw*

Rohkostplatte *selection*
    *of salads*
Rollmops *rolled-up pickled*
    *herring, rollmops*
rosa *rare to medium*
Rosenkohl *Brussels sprouts*
Rosinen *raisins*
Rostbraten *roast*
Rostbratwurst
    *barbecued sausage*
Rösti *fried potatoes*
    *and onions*
Röstkartoffeln *fried potatoes*
Rotbarsch *type of perch*
Rote Bete *beetroot*
rote Grütze *red fruit jelly*
Rotkohl *red cabbage*
Rotkraut *red cabbage*
Rotwein *red wine*
Rühreier *scrambled eggs*
Russische Eier
    *egg mayonnaise*

## S

Sahne *cream*
Salate *salads*
Salatplatte *selection of salads*
Salatsoße *salad dressing*
Salz *salt*
Salzburger Nockerln
    *sweet soufflés*
Salzheringe *salted herrings*
Salzkartoffeln *boiled potatoes*
Salzkruste *salty crusted skin*
Sandkuchen *type of*
    *Madeira cake*
sauer *sour*
Sauerbraten *roast pickled beef*
Sauerkraut *pickled white*
    *cabbage*
Sauerrahm *sour cream*
Schaschlik *(shish-)kebab*
Schattenmorellen
    *morello cherries*
Schellfisch *haddock*
Schildkrötensuppe *real*
    *turtle soup*
Schillerlocken *smoked*
    *haddock rolls*
Schinken *ham*
Schinkenröllchen *rolled ham*
Schlachtplatte *selection of*
    *fresh sausages*
Schlagsahne *whipped cream*
Schlei *tench*
Schmorbraten *pot roast*
Schnecken *snails*
Schnittlauch *chives*
Schnitzel *breaded escalope*
Schokolade *chocolate*
Scholle *plaice*
Schulterstück *slice of shoulder*
Schwarzbrot *brown rye bread*

**Schwarzwälder Kirschtorte**
  *Black Forest cherry gâteau*
**Schwarzwurzeln** *salsify*
**Schwein** *pork*
**Schweinebauch** *belly of pork*
**Schweinefleisch** *pork*
**Schweineripp** *cured pork chop*
**Schweinerollbraten** *rolled roast of pork*
**Schweineschmorbraten**
  *roast pork*
**Schweineschnitzel** *breaded pork cutlet*
**Schweinshaxe** *knuckle of pork*
**Seelachs** *pollack (fish)*
**Seezunge** *sole*
**Sekt** *sparkling wine*
**Sellerie** *celeriac*
**Semmel** *bread roll*
**Senf** *mustard*
**Senfsahnesoße** *mustard and cream sauce*
**Senfsoße** *mustard sauce*
**Serbisches Reisfleisch**
  *diced pork, onions, tomatoes, and rice*
**Soleier** *pickled eggs*
**Soße** *sauce, gravy*
**Soufflé** *soufflé*
**Spanferkel** *suckling pig*
**Spargel** *asparagus*
**Spätzle** *home-made noodles*
**Speck** *fatty bacon*
**Speisekarte** *menu*
**Spezialität des Hauses**
  *house speciality*
**Spiegeleier** *fried eggs*
**Spießbraten** *joint roasted on a spit*
**Spinat** *spinach*
**Spitzkohl** *white cabbage*
**Sprotten** *sprats*
**Sprudel(wasser)** *mineral water*
**Stachelbeeren** *gooseberries*
**Stangen(weiß)brot**
  *French bread*
**Steinbutt** *turbot*
**Steinpilze** *cep mushrooms*
**Stollen** *Christmas fruit loaf*
**Strammer Max** *ham and fried egg on bread*
**Streuselkuchen** *cake with crumble topping*
**Sülze** *brawn*
**Suppen** *soups*
**Suppengrün** *mixed herbs and vegetables (used in soup)*
**süß** *sweet*
**süß-sauer** *sweet-and-sour*
**Süßspeisen** *sweet dishes*
**Süßwasserfische**
  *freshwater fish*
**Szegediner Gulasch** *goulash with pickled cabbage*

# T

**Tafelwasser (still)**
  *mineral water*
**Tafelwein** *table wine*
**Tagesgericht** *dish of the day*
**Tageskarte** *menu of the day*
**Tagessuppe** *soup of the day*
**Tatar** *steak tartare*
**Taube** *pigeon*
**Tee** *tea*
**Teigmantel** *pastry case*
**Thunfisch** *tuna*
**Tintenfisch** *squid*
**Tomaten** *tomatoes*
**Törtchen** *tart(s)*
**Torte** *gâteau*
**Truthahn** *turkey*

# U, V

**überbacken** *au gratin*
**Ungarischer Gulasch**
  *Hungarian goulash*
**ungebraten** *not fried*
**Vanille** *vanilla*
**Vanillesoße** *vanilla sauce*
**verlorene Eier** *poached eggs*
**Vollkornbrot** *dark whole grain bread*
**vom Grill** *grilled*
**vom Kalb** *veal*
**vom Rind** *beef*
**vom Rost** *grilled*
**vom Schwein** *pork*
**Vorspeisen** *hors d'oeuvres, starters*

# W

**Waffeln** *waffles*
**Waldorfsalat** *salad with celery, apples, and walnuts*
**Wasser** *water*
**Wassermelone** *watermelon*
**Weichkäse** *soft cheese*
**Weinbergschnecken** *snails*
**Weinbrand** *brandy*
**Weincreme** *pudding with wine*
**Weinschaumcreme** *creamed pudding with wine*
**Weinsoße** *wine sauce*
**Weintrauben** *grapes*
**Weißbier** *wheat beer*
**Weißbrot** *white bread*
**Weißkohl** *white cabbage*
**Weißkraut** *white cabbage*
**Weißwein** *white wine*
**Weißwurst** *veal sausage*
**Weizenbier** *fizzy, light-coloured beer made with wheat*
**Wiener Schnitzel** *veal in breadcrumbs*
**Wild** *game*

**Wildschweinkeule** *haunch of wild boar*
**Wildschweinsteak**
  *wild boar steak*
**Windbeutel** *cream puff*
**Wirsing** *savoy cabbage*
**Wurst** *sausage*
**Würstchen** *frankfurter(s)*
**Wurstplatte** *selection of sausages*
**Wurstsalat** *sausage salad*
**Wurstsülze** *sausage brawn*
**würzig** *spicy*

# Z

**Zander** *pike-perch, zander*
**Zigeunerschnitzel** *veal with peppers and relishes*
**Zitrone** *lemon*
**Zitronencreme** *lemon cream*
**Zucchini** *courgettes*
**Zucker** *sugar*
**Zuckererbsen** *mangetout*
**Zunge** *tongue*
**Zungenragout** *tongue ragoût*
**Zutaten** *ingredients*
**Zwiebeln** *onions*
**Zwiebelringe** *onion rings*
**Zwiebelsuppe** *onion soup*
**Zwiebeltorte** *onion tart*
**Zwischengerichte** *entrées*

# DICTIONARY
## English to German

In German, the gender of a noun is indicated by the word for *the*: **der** for a masculine noun, **die** for feminine, and **das** for neuter. **Die** is also used with plural nouns, and the abbreviations *m pl*, *f pl*, and *nt pl* are used to indicate their gender here. The feminine form of most occupations and personal attributes is made by adding **-in** to the masculine form: *accountant* **Buchhalter(in)**, for example. Exceptions to this rule are listed separately. Where necessary, adjectives are denoted by the abbreviation *adj*.

### A

*about:* about 16 **etwa 16**
*accelerator* **das Gaspedal**
*accident* **der Unfall**
*accommodation* **die Unterkunft**
*accountant* **der/die Buchhalter(in)**
*ache* **der Schmerz**
*adaptor* **der Adapter**
*address* **die Adresse**
*admission charge* **der Eintrittspreis**
*after* **nach**
*aftershave* **das Rasierwasser**
*again* **nochmal**
*against* **gegen**
*agenda* **die Tagesordnung**
*agent* **der Vertreter**
*air* **die Luft**
*air conditioning* **die Klimaanlage**
*aircraft* **das Flugzeug**
*airline* **die Fluglinie**
*airmail* **die Luftpost**
*air mattress* **die Luftmatratze**
*airport* **der Flughafen**
*airport bus* **der Flughafenbus**
*aisle* **der Gang**
*alarm clock* **der Wecker**
*alcohol* **der Alkohol**
*all* **alle(s)**; all the streets **alle Straßen**; that's all **das ist alles**
*allergic* **allergisch**
*almost* **fast**
*alone* **allein**
*already* **schon**
*always* **immer**
*am:* I am **ich bin**
*ambulance* **der Krankenwagen**
*America* **Amerika**
*American* **der/die Amerikaner(in)**; (adj) **amerikanisch**
*and* **und**
*ankle* **der Knöchel**

*another* (different) **ein anderer**; (one more) **noch ein**; another time **ein andermal**; another room **ein anderes Zimmer**; another coffee, please **noch einen Kaffee, bitte**
*answering machine* **der Anrufbeanworter**
*antique shop* **das Antiquitätengeschäft**
*antiseptic* **das Antiseptikum**
*apartment* **die Wohnung**
*aperitif* **der Aperitif**
*appetite* **der Appetit**
*apple* **der Apfel**
*application form* **das Antragsformular**
*appointment* **der Termin**
*apricot* **die Aprikose**
*are:* you are (singular informal) **du bist**; (singular formal; plural formal) **sie sind**; (plural informal) **ihr seit**; we are **wir sind**; they are **sie sind**
*arm* **der Arm**
*armchair* **der Sessel**
*arrivals* **die Ankunft**
*art* **die Kunst**
*art gallery* **die Kunstgalerie**
*artist* **der/die Künstler(in)**
*as:* as soon as possible **so bald wie möglich**
*ashtray* **der Aschenbecher**
*asthma* **das Asthma**
*at:* at the post office **auf der Post**; at the station **am Bahnhof**; at night **in der Nacht**; at 3 o'clock **um 3 Uhr**
*ATM* **der Geldautomat**
*attic* **der Dachboden**
*attractive* **attraktiv**
*August* **August**
*aunt* **die Tante**
*Australia* **Australien**

*Australian* **der/die Australier(in)**; (adj) **australisch**
*Austria* **Österreich**
*Austrian* **der/die Österreicher(in)**; (adj) **österreichisch**
*automatic* **automatisch**
*away:* is it far away? **ist es weit von hier?**; go away! **gehen sie weg!**
*awful* **furchtbar**

### B

*baby* **das Baby**
*back* (not front) **die Rückseite**; (part of body) **der Rücken**
*bacon* **der Speck**; bacon and eggs **Eier mit Speck**
*bad* **schlecht**
*bag* **die Tasche**
*baggage* **das Gepäck**; baggage claim **die Gepäckausgabe**
*bait* **der Köder**
*bake* **backen**
*baker* **der Bäcker**
*bakery* **die Bäckerei**
*balcony* **der Balkon**
*ball* **der Ball**
*ballet* **das Ballett**
*Baltic* **die Ostsee**
*banana* **die Banane**
*band* (musicians) **die Band**
*bandage* **der Verband**
*bank* **die Bank**
*banknote* **der (Geld)schein**
*bar* (drinks) **die Bar**
*barbecue* **der Grill**
*barber's* **der Herrenfriseur**
*bargain* **das Sonderangebot**
*basement* **das Untergeschoss**
*basin* (sink) **das Becken**
*basket* **der Korb**
*bath* **das Bad**; (tub) **die Badewanne**; to have a bath **ein Bad nehmen**

bathroom **das Badezimmer**
bathtub **die Badewanne**
battery **die Batterie**
Bavaria **Bayern**
beach **der Strand**
beans **die Bohnen**
beard **der Bart**
beautiful **schön**
because **weil**
bed **das Bett**; bed linen
  **die Bettwäsche**
bedroom **das Schlafzimmer**
bedside table **der Nachttisch**
bedspread **die Tagesdecke**
beef **das Rindfleisch**
beer **das Bier**
before... **vor...**
beginner **der Anfänger**
behind... **hinter...**
beige **beige**
Belgian **der/die Belgier(in)**;
  (adj) **belgisch**
Belgium **Belgien**
bell (church) **die Glocke**;
  (door) **die Klingel**
below... **unter...**
belt **der Gürtel**
beside **neben**
best **bester**
better **besser**
between... **zwischen...**
bicycle **das Fahrrad**
big **groß**
bikini **der Bikini**
bill **die Rechnung**
bin liner **der Müllsack**
biochemistry **die Biochemie**
bird **der Vogel**
birthday **der Geburtstag**;
  happy birthday! **Herzlichen**
  **Glückwunsch!**
birthday card **die**
  **Geburtstagskarte**
birthday present **das**
  **Geburtstagsgeschenk**
biscuit **das Keks**
bite (by dog) **der Biss**;
  (by insect) **der Stich**;
  (verb: by dog) **beißen**;
  (by insect) **stechen**
bitter **bitter**
black **schwarz**
blackberry **die Brombeere**
blackcurrant **die schwarze**
  **Johannisbeere**
Black Forest **der Schwarzwald**
blanket **die Decke**
bleach **das Bleichmittel**;
  (verb: hair) **bleichen**
blind (unsighted) **blind**
blinds **die Jalousie**

blister **die Blase**
blond (adj) **blond**
blood **das Blut**; blood test
  **die Blutprobe**
blouse **die Bluse**
blue **blau**
boarding pass **die Bordkarte**
boat **das Schiff**;
  (small) **das Boot**
body **der Körper**;
  (corpse) **die Leiche**
boil (verb) **kochen**
boiled **gekocht**
boiler **der Boiler**
bolt (on door) **der Riegel**;
  (verb) **verriegeln**
bone **der Knochen**
bonnet (car) **die Motorhaube**
book **das Buch**; (verb) **buchen**
bookshop **die Buchhandlung**
boot (car) **der Kofferraum**;
  (footwear) **der Stiefel**
border **die Grenze**
boring **langweilig**
born: I was born in...
  **ich bin in... geboren**
both **beide**; both of us
  **wir beide**; both... and...
  **sowohl... als auch...**
bottle **die Flasche**
bottle opener **der**
  **Flaschenöffner**
bottom **der Boden**;
  (sea) **der Grund**
bowl **die Schüssel**
box **die Schachtel**
boxing **das Boxen**
box office **die Kasse**
boy **der Junge**
boyfriend **der Freund**
bra **der Büstenhalter**
bracelet **das Armband**
braces **die Hosenträger** (nt pl)
brake **die Bremse**;
  (verb) **bremsen**
branch **die Zweigstelle**
brandy **der Weinbrand**
bread **das Brot**
breakdown (car) **die Panne**
breakfast **das Frühstück**
breathe **atmen**
bridge **die Brücke**; (game)
  **das Bridge**
briefcase **die Aktentasche**
Britain **Großbritannien**
British **britisch**
brochure **die Broschüre**
broken (arm, etc.) **gebrochen**;
  (vase, etc.) **zerbrochen**;
  (machine, etc.) **kaputt**;
  broken leg **der Beinbruch**

brooch **die Brosche**
brother **der Bruder**
brother-in-law **der Schwager**
brown **braun**
bruise **der blaue Fleck**
brush **die Bürste**; (paint)
  **der Pinsel**; (verb: hair)
  **bürsten**; (floor) **kehren**
Brussels **Brüssel**
bucket **der Eimer**
budget **das Budget**
builder **der/die Bauarbeiter(in)**
building **das Gebäude**
bumper **die Stoßstange**
burglar **der Einbrecher**
burn **die Verbrennung**;
  (verb) **brennen**
bus **der Bus**; bus station
  **der Busbahnhof**
business **das Geschäft**;
  it's none of your business
  **das geht Sie nichts an**
business card **die Visitenkarte**
busy (occupied) **beschäftigt**;
  (bar, etc.) **voll**
but **aber**
butcher's **die Metzgerei**
butter **die Butter**
button **der Knopf**
buy **kaufen**
by: by the window **am Fenster**;
  by Friday **bis Freitag**

## C
cabbage **der Kohl**
cable car **die Drahtseilbahn**
café **das Café**
cage **der Käfig**
cake **der Kuchen**
cake shop **die Konditorei**
calculator **der Rechner**
call: what's it called?
  **wie heißt das?**
camera **die Kamera**
camper van **das Wohnmobil**
campfire **das Lagerfeuer**
camping gas **das Campinggas**
campsite **der Campingplatz**;
  campsite office **die**
  **Campingplatzverwaltung**
camshaft **die Nockenwelle**
can (vessel) **die Dose**;
  (verb: to be able) can I
  have...? **kann ich...haben?**;
  can you...? **können Sie...?**
Canada **Kanada**
Canadian **der/die Kanadier(in)**;
  (adj) **kanadisch**
canal **der Kanal**
candle **die Kerze**

canoe das Kanu

cap (bottle) der Verschluss; (hat) die Mütze

car das Auto

caravan der Wohnwagen

carburettor der Vergaser

card die Karte

careful sorgfältig; be careful! passen Sie auf!

caretaker der/die Hausmeister(in)

car park der Parkplatz

carpenter der/die Schreiner(in)

carpet der Teppich

car repairs die Werkstatt

carriage (train) der Wagen

carrot die Möhre, die Karotte

car seat (for baby) der Kindersitz

case (suitcase) der Koffer

cash das Bargeld; (verb) einlösen; to pay cash bar bezahlen

cashier der/die Kassierer(in)

cash machine der Geldautomat

cassette die Kassette; cassette player der Kassettenrecorder

castle das Schloss, die Burg

cat die Katze

cathedral der Dom

cauliflower der Blumenkohl

cave die Höhle

ceiling die Decke

cellar der Keller

cemetery der Friedhof

central heating die Zentralheizung

centre (middle) die Mitte

certificate die Bescheinigung

chair der Stuhl

change (money) das Kleingeld; (verb: money) wechseln; (clothes) sich umziehen

Channel der Kanal; Channel Tunnel der Kanaltunnel

charger das Ladegerät

cheap billig

check in (desk) der Abfertigungsschalter, die Abfertigung; (verb) einchecken

checkout die Kasse

cheers! prost!

cheese der Käse

chemist's (shop) die Apotheke

cheque der Scheck; cheque card die Scheckkarte; chequebook das Scheckheft

cherry die Kirsche

chess Schach

chest (part of body) die Brust; (furniture) die Truhe

chest of drawers die Kommode

chewing gum der Kaugummi

chicken das Huhn; (cooked) das Hähnchen

child das Kind

children die Kinder (nt pl)

children's ward die Kinderstation

chimney der Schornstein

china das Porzellan

chips die Fritten, die Pommes (m pl)

chocolate die Schokolade; box of chocolates die Schachtel Pralinen

chop (food) das Kotelett; (verb: to cut) kleinschneiden

Christmas Weihnachten

church die Kirche

cigar die Zigarre; (thin) das Zigarillo

cigarette die Zigarette

cinema das Kino

circle der Rang

city die (Groß)stadt; city centre das Stadtzentrum

class die Klasse

classical music die klassische Musik

clean (adj) sauber

cleaner die Putzfrau

clear klar

clever klug

client der Kunde

clock die Uhr

close (near) nah; (stuffy) stickig; (verb) schließen

closed geschlossen

clothes die Kleider (nt pl)

club der Klub

clubs (cards) Kreuz

clutch die Kupplung

coach der Überlandbus, der Reisebus; (train) der Wagen; coach station der Busbahnhof

coat der Mantel

coat hanger der (Kleider)bügel

coffee der Kaffee; black coffee der Kaffee ohne Milch

coin die Münze

cold (illness) die Erkältung; (adj) kalt; I have a cold ich bin erkältet; I am cold mir ist kalt

collar das Halsband, der Kragen

collection (stamps, etc.) die Sammlung; (postal) die Leerung

Cologne Köln

colour die Farbe;

colour film der Farbfilm

comb der Kamm

come kommen; I come from... ich komme aus...; come here! kommen Sie her! come back zurückkommen

compact disc die Compact-Disc, die CD

compartment das Abteil

complicated kompliziert

computer der Computer; computer games die Computerspiele (nt pl)

concert das Konzert

conditioner (hair) die Haarspülung

condom das Kondom

conductor (bus) der Schaffner; (orchestra) der Dirigent

conference die Konferenz; conference room das Konferenzzimmer

congratulations! herzlichen Glückwunsch!

consulate das Konsulat

consultant der/die Berater(in)

contact lenses die Kontaktlinsen

contraceptive das Verhütungsmittel

contract der Vertrag

cook der Koch; (verb) kochen

cooker der Herd

cool kühl

cork der Korken

corkscrew der Korkenzieher

corner die Ecke

corridor der Korridor

cosmetics die Kosmetika

cost (verb) kosten; what does it cost? was kostet das?

cot das Kinderbett

cotton (fabric) die Baumwolle

cotton wool die Watte

cough der Husten; (verb) husten

country das Land

cousin (male) der Vetter; (female) die Kusine

crab die Krabbe

cramp der Krampf

crayfish der Krebs

cream (for cake, etc.) die Sahne; (lotion) die Creme

credit card die Kreditkarte

crisps die Chips

crowded überfüllt

cruise die Kreuzfahrt

crutches die Krücken (f pl)

cry (weep) weinen; (shout) rufen

cucumber die Gurke

*cufflinks* die Manschettenknöpfe (m pl)
*cup* die Tasse
*cupboard* der Schrank
*curls* die Locken (f pl)
*curry* das Curry
*curtain* der Vorhang
*cushion* das Kissen
*Customs* der Zoll
*cut* der Schnitt; (verb) schneiden
*cycling* das Radfahren

# D

*dad* der Papa
*dairy products* die Molkereiprodukte (nt pl)
*damp* feucht
*dance* der Tanz; (verb) tanzen
*Dane* (man) der Däne; (woman) die Dänin
*dangerous* gefährlich
*Danish* dänisch
*Danish pastry* das Teilchen
*Danube* die Donau
*dark* dunkel
*daughter* die Tochter
*day* der Tag
*dead* tot
*deaf* taub
*dear* (person) lieb; (expensive) teuer
*December* Dezember
*deck chair* der Liegestuhl
*decorator* der/die Maler(in)
*deep* tief
*delayed* verspätet
*delegate* der/die Delegierte(r)
*deliberately* absichtlich
*delicatessen* das Feinkostgeschäft
*delivery* die Lieferung
*Denmark* Dänemark
*dentist* der Zahnarzt
*dentures* die Prothese, das Gebiss
*deny* bestreiten
*deodorant* das Deodorant
*department* die Abteilung
*department store* das Kaufhaus
*departure* die Abfahrt
*departure lounge* die Abflughalle
*departures* der Abflug
*deposit* die Kaution
*designer* der/die Grafiker(in)
*desserts* der Nachtisch
*develop* (film) entwickeln
*diabetic* der/die Diabetiker(in)
*diamond* (gem) der Diamant
*diamonds* (cards) Karo

*diarrhoea* der Durchfall
*diary* das Tagebuch
*dictionary* das Wörterbuch
*die* sterben
*diesel* der Diesel
*different* verschieden; *that's different!* das ist etwas anderes!; *I'd like a different kind* ich möchte gern eine andere Sorte
*difficult* schwierig
*dining room* der Speiseraum
*dinner* das Abendessen
*directory* (telephone) das Telefonbuch
*dirty* schmutzig
*disabled* behindert
*discounts* die Ermäßigungen
*dishwasher* die Geschirrspülmaschine
*disposable nappies* die Einwegwindeln
*dive* der Sprung; (verb) tauchen
*diving board* das Sprungbett
*divorced* geschieden
*DIY* das Basteln
*do* tun; *how do you do?* guten Tag; (on being introduced) freut mich
*doctor* der Arzt
*document* das Dokument
*dog* der Hund
*doll* die Puppe
*dollar* der Dollar
*door* die Tür
*double room* das Doppelzimmer
*doughnut* der Berliner
*down* herunter; (position) unten; *down here* hier unten
*drawer* die Schublade
*drawing pin* die Heftzwecke, der Reißnagel
*dress* das Kleid
*drink* das Getränk; (verb) trinken; *would you like a drink?* möchten Sie etwas trinken?
*drinking water* das Trinkwasser
*drive* (verb) fahren
*driver* der/die Fahrer(in)
*driveway* die Einfahrt
*driving licence* der Führerschein
*drops* die Tropfen
*drunk* betrunken
*dry* trocken
*dry cleaner* die Reinigung
*dummy* (for baby) der Schnuller
*during* während

*dustbin* die Mülltonne
*duster* das Staubtuch
*Dutch* (adj) holländisch
*Dutchman/woman* der/die Holländer(in)
*duty-free* zollfrei
*duvet* die Steppdecke

# E

*each* (every) jeder, alle; *five euros each* fünf Euro das Stück
*ear* das Ohr; *ears* die Ohren (nt pl)
*early* früh
*earrings* die Ohrringe (m pl)
*east* der Osten
*easy* leicht
*eat* essen
*egg* das Ei
*eight* acht
*eighteen* achtzehn
*eighty* achtzig
*either: either of them* einer von beiden; *either... or...* entweder... oder...
*elastic* elastisch; *elastic band* das Gummiband
*elbow* der Ellbogen
*electric* elektrisch
*electrical hook-up* der Stromanschluss
*electrician* der/die Elektriker(in)
*electricity* der Strom
*eleven* elf
*else: something else* etwas anderes; *someone else* jemand anders; *somewhere else* woanders
*e-mail* die Mail
*e-mail address* die Mail Adresse
*embarrassing* peinlich
*embassy* die Botschaft
*emerald* der Smaragd
*emergency* der Notfall
*emergency brake* die Notbremse
*emergency department* die Unfallstation
*emergency exit* der Notausgang
*empty* leer
*end* das Ende
*engaged* (couple) verlobt; (occupied) besetzt
*engine* (motor) der Motor
*engineering* die Technik
*England* England
*English* (adj) englisch; (language) Englisch

*Englishman/woman* der/die Engländer(in)

*enlargement* die Vergrößerung

*enough* genug

*entertainment* die Unterhaltung

*entrance* der Eingang; *entrance ticket* die Eintrittskarte

*envelope* der (Brief)umschlag

*epileptic* der/die Epilektiker(in)

*escalator* die Rolltreppe

*especially* besonders

*estimate* der Kostenvoranschlag

*evening* der Abend

*every* jeder

*everyone* jeder

*everything* alles

*everywhere* überall

*example* das Beispiel; *for example* zum Beispiel

*excellent* ausgezeichnet

*excess baggage* das Mehrgepäck

*exchange* (verb) (um)tauschen

*exchange rate* der Wechselkurs

*excursion* der Ausflug

*excuse me!* Entschuldigung!

*executive* der/die Manager(in)

*exhaust* der Auspuff

*exhibition* die Ausstellung

*exit* der Ausgang

*expensive* teuer

*extension lead* die Verlängerungsschnur

*eye* das Auge; *eyes* die Augen

*eyebrow* das Augenbraue

# F

*face* das Gesicht

*faint* (unclear) blass; (verb) ohnmächtig werden

*fair* (funfair) der Jahrmarkt, die Kirmes; (just) gerecht, fair

*false teeth* die Prothese, das Gebiss

*family* die Familie

*fan* (ventilator) der Ventilator; (enthusiast) der Fan

*fan belt* der Keilriemen

*fantastic* fantastisch

*far* weit; *how far is it?* wie weit ist es?

*fare* der Fahrpreis

*farm* der Bauernhof

*farmer* der Bauer

*fashion* die Mode

*fast* schnell

*fat* das Fett; (person) dick

*father* der Vater

*fax* das Fax; (verb) faxen;

*fax machine* das Faxgerät

*February* Februar

*feel* (touch) fühlen; *I feel hot* mir ist heiß; *I feel like...* ich möchte gern...; *I don't feel well* mir ist nicht gut

*feet* die Füße (m pl)

*fence* der Zaun

*ferry* die Fähre

*fever* das Fieber

*fiancé* der Verlobte

*fiancée* die Verlobte

*field* das Feld; (of work) das Gebiet

*fifteen* fünfzehn

*fifty* fünfzig

*fig* die Feige

*filling* (in tooth, cake) die Füllung; (in sandwich) der Belag

*film* der Film

*filter* der Filter

*filter papers* das Filterpapier

*finger* der Finger

*fire* das Feuer

*fire extinguisher* der Feuerlöscher

*fireworks* das Feuerwerk

*first* erster; *first class* erster Klasse

*first aid* die Erste Hilfe

*first floor* der erste Stock

*first name* der Vorname

*fish* der Fisch

*fishing* das Angeln; *to go fishing* Angeln gehen

*fishmonger's* das Fischgeschäft

*five* fünf

*fizzy* sprudelnd

*fizzy water* Wasser mit Kohlensäure, das Sprudelwasser

*flag* die Fahne

*flash* (camera) der Blitz

*flat* (level) flach; (apartment) die Wohnung

*flat tyre* der Platten

*flavour* der Geschmack

*flea* der Floh

*flea spray* das Flohspray

*flight* der Flug; *flight number* die Flugnummer

*flippers* die (Schwimm)flossen (f pl)

*floor* (ground) der Fußboden, der Boden; (storey) der Stock

*florist* der Blumenladen

*flour* das Mehl

*flower* die Blume; *flower-arranging* das Blumenstecken;

*flowerbed* das Blumenbeet

*flute* die Flöte

*fly* (insect) die Fliege; (verb) fliegen

*flyover* die Überführung

*fly sheet* das Überzelt

*fog* der Nebel

*folk music* die Volksmusik

*food* das Essen

*food poisoning* die Lebensmittelvergiftung

*foot* der Fuß

*football* der Fußball

*for* für; *for me* für mich; *what for?* wofür?; *for a week* für eine Woche

*foreigner* der/die Ausländer(in)

*forest* der Wald

*forget* vergessen

*fork* die Gabel

*fortnight* zwei Wochen

*forty* vierzig

*fountain* der Brunnen

*four* vier

*fourteen* vierzehn

*fourth* vierter

*France* Frankreich

*free* frei; (no charge) kostenlos, gratis

*freezer* der Gefrierschrank

*French* französisch

*Frenchman* der Franzose

*Frenchwoman* die Französin

*Friday* Freitag

*fridge* der Kühlschrank

*fried* gebraten

*friend* der/die Freund(in)

*friendly* freundlich

*front: in front of...* vor...

*frost* der Frost

*frozen foods* die Tiefkühlkost

*fruit* das Obst, die Frucht

*fruit juice* der Fruchtsaft

*fry* braten

*frying pan* die (Brat)pfanne

*full* voll; *I'm full (up)* ich bin satt

*full board* Vollpension

*funny* komisch

*furniture* die Möbel

# G

*garage* die Garage; (for repairs) die Werkstatt

*garden* der Garten

*garden centre* das Gartencenter

*gardener* der/die Gärtner(in)

*gardening* die Gartenarbeit

*garlic* der Knoblauch

*gate* **das Tor**; (garden gate) **die Pforte**; (at airport) **der Flugsteig**

*gay* (homosexual) **schwul**

*gear* **der Gang**

*gearbox* **das Getriebe**

*gear stick* **der Schaltknüppel**

*gel* (hair) **das Gel**

*German* **der/die Deutsche**; (adj) **deutsch**; (language) **Deutsch**

*Germany* **Deutschland**

*get* (fetch) **holen**; *have you got...?* **haben Sie...?**; *to get the train* **den Zug nehmen**

*get back: we get back tomorrow* **wir kommen morgen zurück**; *to get something back* **etwas zurückbekommen**

*get in* **hereinkommen**; (arrive) **ankommen**

*get off* (bus, etc.) **aussteigen**

*get on* (bus, etc.) **einsteigen**

*get out* **herauskommen**; (bring out) **herausholen**

*get up* (rise) **aufstehen**

*gift* **das Geschenk**

*gin* **der Gin**

*ginger* (spice) **der Ingwer**

*girl* **das Mädchen**

*girlfriend* **die Freundin**

*give* **geben**

*glad* **froh**

*glass* **das Glas**

*glasses* **die Brille**

*gloves* **die Handschuhe**

*glue* **der Leim, der Klebstoff**

*go* **gehen**; (travel) **fahren**; (by plane) **fliegen**

*gold* **das Gold**

*good* **gut**

*goodbye* **Auf Wiedersehen**

*good night* **Guten Abend**

*government* **die Regierung**

*granddaughter* **die Enkelin**

*grandfather* **der Großvater**

*grandmother* **die Großmutter**

*grandparents* **die Großeltern** (m pl)

*grandson* **der Enkel**

*grapes* **die Trauben** (f pl)

*grass* **das Gras**

*Great Britain* **Großbritannien**

*great: great!* **prima!**

*green* **grün**

*grey* **grau**

*grill* **der Grill**

*grilled* **gegrillt**

*grocer's* **das Lebensmittelgeschäft**

*ground floor* **das Erdgeschoss**

*groundsheet* **der Zeltboden, die Bodenplane**

*guarantee* **die Garantie**; (verb) **garantieren**

*guard* **der Wächter**

*guest* **der Gast**

*guide* **der Führer**

*guide book* **der (Reise)führer**

*guided tour* **die Führung**

*guitar* **die Gitarre**

*gun* (rifle) **das Gewehr**; (pistol) **die Pistole**

*gutter* **die Dachrinne**

# H

*hair* **das Haar**

*haircut* **der Haarschnitt**

*hairdresser's* **der Friseur**; (ladies') **der Friseursalon**

*hair dryer* **der Fön**

*hair spray* **das Haarspray**

*half* **halb**; *half an hour* **eine halbe Stunde**

*half board* **Halbpension**

*half-brother* **der Halbbruder**

*half-sister* **die Halbschwester**

*ham* **der gekochte Schinken**

*hamburger* **der Hamburger**

*hammer* **der Hammer**

*hamster* **der Hamster**

*hand* **die Hand**

*handbag* **die Handtasche**

*handbrake* **die Handbremse**

*handle* (door) **die Klinke**

*hand luggage* **das Handgepäck**

*handshake* **der Händedruck**

*handsome* **gut aussehend**

*hangover* **der Kater**

*happy* **glücklich**

*harbour* **der Hafen**

*hard* **hart**; (difficult) **schwer**

*hardware shop* **der Eisenwarenhändler**

*hat* **der Hut**

*have* (verb) **haben**: *I have* **ich habe**; *you have* (singular informal) **du hast**; (plural informal) **ihr habt**; (singular formal; plural formal) **Sie haben**; *we have* **wir haben**; *they have* **sie haben**; *do you have ...?* **haben Sie ...?**; *I have to go* **ich muss gehen**

*hay fever* **der Heuschnupfen**

*he* **er**

*head* **der Kopf**

*headache* **die Kopfschmerzen**; *headache pill* **die Kopfschmerztablette**

*headlights* **die Scheinwerfer**

*head office* **die Zentrale**

*headphones* **der Kopfhörer**

*hear* **hören**

*hearing aid* **das Hörgerät**

*heart* **das Herz**

*heart condition: I have a heart condition* **Ich bin herzkrank**

*hearts* (cards) **Herz**

*heater* **das Heizgerät**

*heating* **die Heizung**

*heavy* **schwer**

*hedge* **die Hecke**

*heel* (shoe) **der Absatz**; (foot) **die Ferse**

*hello* **guten Tag**; (on phone) **hallo**

*help* **die Hilfe**; (verb) **helfen**

*her: it's her* **sie ist es**; *it's for her* **es ist für sie**; *give it to her* **geben sie es ihr**; *her book* **ihr Buch**; *her shoes* **ihre Schuhe**; *it's hers* **es gehört ihr**

*hi* **hallo**

*high* **hoch**

*hiking* **das Wandern**

*hill* **der Berg**

*him: it's him* **er ist es**; *it's for him* **es ist für ihn**; *give it to him* **geben sie es ihm**

*hire* **leihen, mieten**

*his: his book* **sein Buch**; *his shoes* **seine Schuhe**; *it's his* **es gehört ihm**

*history* **die Geschichte**

*hitchhike* **trampen**

*HIV positive* **HIV positiv**

*hobby* **das Hobby**

*holiday* **die Ferien, der Urlaub**

*Holland* **Holland**

*home: at home* **zu Hause**

*homeopathy* **die Homöopathie**

*honest* **ehrlich**

*honey* **der Honig**

*honeymoon* **die Hochzeitsreise**

*horn* (car) **die Hupe**; (animal) **das Horn**

*horrible* **schrecklich**

*hospital* **das Krankenhaus**

*host* **der/die Gastgeber(in)**

*hour* **die Stunde**

*house* **das Haus**

*household products* **die Haushaltswaren** (f pl)

*how?* **wie?**

*humanities* **die Geisteswissenschaften** (f pl)

*hundred* **hundert**

*hungry: I'm hungry*
   **ich habe Hunger**
*hurry: I'm in a hurry*
   **ich bin in Eile**
*husband* **der (Ehe)mann**

## I

*I* **ich**
*ice* **das Eis**
*ice cream* **die Eiscreme**
*ice lolly* **das Eis am Stiel**
*ice skates* **die Schlittschuhe**
*ice-skating: to go ice-skating*
   **Schlittschuh laufen gehen**
*if* **wenn**
*ignition* **die Zündung**
*ill* **krank**
*immediately* **sofort**
*impossible* **unmöglich**
*in* **in**; *in English* **auf Englisch**;
   *in the hotel* **im Hotel**
*indicator* **der Blinker**
*indigestion* **die**
   **Magenverstimmung**
*infection* **die Infektion,**
   **die Entzündung**
*information* **die Information**
*injection* **die Spritze**
*injury* **die Verletzung**
*ink* **die Tinte**
*inn* **das Gasthaus**
*inner tube* **der Schlauch**
*insect* **das Insekt**
*insect repellent* **das**
   **Insektenmittel**
*insomnia* **die Schlaflosigkeit**
*instant coffee* **der Pulverkaffee**
*insurance* **die Versicherung**
*interesting* **interessant**
*internet* **das Internet**
*interpret* **dolmetschen**
*interpreter* **der/die**
   **Dolmetscher(in)**
*intravenous drip* **die**
   **intravenöse Infusion**
*invitation* **die Einladung**
*invoice* **die Rechnung**
*Ireland* **Irland**
*Irish* **irisch**
*Irishman* **der Ire**
*Irishwoman* **die Irin**
*iron (material)* **das Eisen**;
   *(for clothes)* **das Bügeleisen**;
   *(verb)* **bügeln**
*is: he/she/it is...* **er/sie/es ist...**
*island* **die Insel**
*it* **es**
*Italian* **der/die Italiener(in)**;
   *(adj)* **italienisch**
*Italy* **Italien**

## J

*jacket* **die Jacke**
*jam* **die Marmelade,**
   **die Konfitüre**
*January* **Januar**
*jazz* **der Jazz**
*jeans* **die Jeans**
*jellyfish* **die Qualle**
*jeweller's* **das Juweliergeschäft**
*jewellery* **der Schmuck**
*job* **die Arbeit**
*jog (verb)* **joggen**; *to go for*
   *a jog* **joggen gehen**
*joke* **der Witz**
*journey* **die Fahrt, die Reise**
*July* **Juli**
*jumper* **der Pullover**
*June* **Juni**
*just (only)* **nur**; *it's just arrived*
   **es ist gerade angekommen**

## K

*kettle* **der Wasserkessel**
*key* **der Schlüssel**
*keyboard* **die Tastatur**
*kidney* **die Niere**
*kilo* **das Kilo**
*kilometre* **der Kilometer**
*kitchen* **die Küche**
*knee* **das Knie**
*knife* **das Messer**
*knit* **stricken**
*knitwear* **die Strickwaren (f pl)**
*know* **wissen**; *(be acquainted*
   *with)* **kennen**; *I don't know*
   **ich weiß nicht**

## L

*label* **das Etikett**
*lace* **die Spitze**
*laces (shoe)* **die Schnürsenkel**
   **(m pl)**
*lady* **die Dame**
*lake* **der See**
*lamb (animal)* **das Lamm**; *(meat)*
   **das Lammfleisch**
*lamp* **die Lampe**
*lampshade* **der Lampenschirm**
*land* **das Land**; *(verb)* **landen**
*language* **die Sprache**
*laptop* **der Laptop**
*large* **groß**
*last (final)* **letzter**;
   *last week* **letzte Woche**;
   *at last!* **endlich!**
*late* **spät**; *the bus is late*
   **der Bus hat Verspätung**
*later* **später**

*laugh* **lachen**
*launderette* **der Waschsalon**
*laundry (place)* **die Wäscherei**;
   *(dirty clothes)* **die Wäsche**
*lawn* **der Rasen**
*lawnmower* **der Rasenmäher**
*lawyer* **der Rechtsanwalt/**
   **die Rechtsanwältin**
*laxative* **das Abführmittel**
*lazy* **faul**
*lead* **die Leine**
*lead-free* **bleifrei**
*leaf* **das Blatt**
*leaflet* **die Broschüre,**
   **der Flyer**
*learn* **lernen**
*leather* **das Leder**
*lecture theatre* **der**
   **Vorlesungssaal**
*leeks* **das Breitlauch,**
   **der Porrée**
*left (not right)* **links**;
   *there's nothing left*
   **es ist nichts mehr übrig**
*left luggage locker* **das**
   **Gepäckschließfach**
*left side* **die linke Seite**
*leg* **das Bein**
*lemon* **die Zitrone**
*lemonade* **die Limonade**
*length* **die Länge**
*lens* **die Linse**
*less* **weniger**
*lesson* **die Stunde**
*letter (post)* **der Brief**; *(alphabet)*
   **der Buchstabe**
*letter box* **der Briefkasten**
*lettuce* **der Kopfsalat**
*library* **die Bibliothek,**
   **die Bücherei**
*licence* **die Genehmigung**;
   *(driving)* **der Führerschein**
*life* **das Leben**
*lift (in building)* **der Fahrstuhl**;
   *could you give me a lift?* **können**
   **Sie mich mitnehmen?**
*light* **das Licht**; *(adj)* **leicht**;
   *(not dark)* **hell**
*light bulb* **die (Glüh)birne**
*lighter* **das Feuerzeug**; *lighter fuel*
   **das Feuerzeugbenzin**
*light meter* **der**
   **Belichtungsmesser**
*like: I like you* **ich mag Sie**;
   *I like swimming* **ich**
   **schwimme gern**; *it's like...*
   **es ist wie...**; *like this* **so**
*lime (fruit)* **die Limette**
*lip salve* **der Lippen-Fettstift**
*lipstick* **der Lippenstift**
*liqueur* **der Likör**

*list* **die Liste**
*litre* **der Liter**
*litter* **der Abfall**
*litter bin* **die Mülleimer**
*little (small)* **klein**; *it's a little big*
 **es ist ein bisschen zu groß**;
 *just a little* **nur ein bisschen**
*liver* **die Leber**
*lobster* **der Hummer**
*lollipop* **der Lutscher**
*long* **lang**
*lorry* **der Lastwagen**
*lost property* **das Fundbüro**
*lot: a lot* **viel**
*loud* **laut**; *(colour)* **grell**
*lounge* **das Wohnzimmer**;
 *(in hotel)* **die Lounge**
*love* **die Liebe**; *(verb)* **lieben**
*low* **niedrig**; *(voice)* **tief**
*luck* **das Glück**; *good luck!*
 **viel Glück!**
*luggage* **der Koffer, das**
 **Gepäck**; *luggage rack*
 **die Gepäckablage**
*lunch* **das Mittagessen**
*Luxembourg* **Luxemburg**

## M

*mad* **verrückt**
*magazine* **die Zeitschrift**
*maid* **das Zimmermädchen**
*mail* **die Post**
*main courses* **die Hauptgerichte**
*main road* **die Hauptstraße**
*make* **machen**
*make-up* **das Make-up**
*man* **der Mann**
*manager* **der Geschäftsführer**
*many: not many* **nicht viele**
*map (of country)*
 **die Landkarte**;
 *(of town)* **der Stadtplan**
*marble* **der Marmor**
*March* **März**
*margarine* **die Margarine**
*market* **der Markt**
*marmalade* **die**
 **Orangenmarmelade**
*married* **verheiratet**
*mascara* **das Maskara,**
 **die Wimperntusche**
*mass (church)* **die Messe**
*match (light)* **das Streichholz**;
 *(sport)* **das Spiel**
*material (fabric)* **der Stoff**
*matter: it doesn't matter*
 **das macht nichts**
*mattress* **die Matratze**
*maybe* **vielleicht**
*me: it's me* **ich bin's**;

*it's for me* **es ist für mich**;
 *give it to me* **geben Sie es mir**
*meal* **das Essen**
*mean: what does this mean?*
 **was bedeutet das?**
*meat* **das Fleisch**
*mechanic* **der/die**
 **Mechaniker(in)**
*medication* **die Medikamente**
*medicine* **die Medizin**
*meeting* **die Besprechung,**
 **das Treffen**
*melon* **die Melone**
*men's toilets* **die Herrentoilette**
*menu* **die Speisekarte**
*message* **die Nachricht**
*metro station* **die U-Bahnstation**
*microwave* **die Mikrowelle**
*midday* **der Mittag**
*middle: in the middle*
 **in der Mitte**
*midnight* **Mitternacht**
*milk* **die Milch**
*mine: it's mine* **es gehört mir**
*mineral water* **das mineralwasser**
*minute* **die Minute**
*mirror* **der Spiegel**
*Miss* **Fräulein**
*mistake* **der Fehler**
*mobile phone* **das Handy,**
 **das Mobiltelefon**
*modem* **das Modem**
*modern architecture* **die moderne**
 **Architektur**
*Monday* **Montag**
*money* **das Geld**
*monitor* **der Monitor,**
 **der Bildschirm**
*month* **der Monat**
*monument* **das Denkmal**
*moon* **der Mond**
*moped* **das Moped**
*more* **mehr**
*morning* **der Morgen**; *in the*
 *morning* **am Morgen**
*mother* **die Mutter**
*motorbike* **das Motorrad**
*motorboat* **das Motorboot**
*motorway* **die Autobahn**
*mountain* **der Berg**
*mountain bike*
 **das Mountain-Bike**
*mouse* **die Maus**
*mousse (for hair)*
 **der Schaumfestiger**
*moustache* **der Schnurrbart**
*mouth* **der Mund**
*move (verb)* **bewegen**;
 *(house)* **umziehen**;
 *don't move!* **stillhalten!**
*movie* **der Film**

*Mr* **Herr**
*Mrs* **Frau**
*Ms* **Frau**
*much* **viel**
*mum* **die Mama**
*Munich* **München**
*museum* **das Museum**
*mushroom* **der Pilz**
*music* **die Musik**
*musical instrument* **das**
 **Musikinstrument**
*musician* **der/die Musiker(in)**
*music system* **die Musikanlange**
*mussels* **die Muscheln** *(f pl)*
*must: I must...* **ich muss...**
*mustard* **der Senf**
*my: my book* **mein Buch**;
 *my keys* **meine Schlüssel**

## N

*nail (metal, finger)* **der Nagel**
*nail clippers* **der Nagelzwicker**
*nailfile* **die Nagelfeile**
*nail polish* **der Nagellack**
*name* **der Name**; *what's your*
 *name?* **wie heißen Sie?**
*napkin* **die Serviette**
*nappy* **die Windel**
*narrow* **eng**
*near* **nah**; *near the door* **nahe der**
 **Tür**; *near London* **in der Nähe**
 **von London**
*necessary* **notwendig**
*neck* **der Hals**
*necklace* **die Halskette**
*need (verb)* **brauchen**; *I need...*
 **ich brauche...**; *there's no need*
 **das ist nicht nötig**
*needle* **die Nadel**
*negative (photo)* **das Negativ**
*nephew* **der Neffe**
*Netherlands* **die Niederlande**
*never* **nie**
*new* **neu**
*news* **die Nachrichten**
*newsagent's* **der Zeitungsladen**
*newspaper* **die Zeitung**
*New Zealand* **Neuseeland**
*New Zealander* **der/die**
 **Neuseeländer(in)**
*next* **nächster**;
 *next week* **nächste Woche**
*nice (attractive)* **hübsch**;
 *(pleasant)* **angenehm**;
 *(to eat)* **lecker**
*niece* **die Nichte**
*night* **die Nacht**
*nightclub* **der Nachtklub**
*nightdress* **das Nachthemd**
*night porter* **der Nachtportier**

nine **neun**
nineteen **neunzehn**
ninety **neunzig**
no (response) **nein;**
    I have no money
    **ich habe kein Geld**
noisy **laut**
north **der Norden**
Northern Ireland **Nordirland**
North Sea **die Nordsee**
nose **die Nase**
not **nicht**
notebook **das Notizbuch**
notepad **der Notizblock**
notes **die Banknoten (f pl)**
nothing **nichts**
novel **der Roman**
November **November**
now **jetzt**
nowhere **nirgendwo**
number **die Zahl;**
    (telephone) **die Nummer**
number plate **das**
    **Nummernschild**
nurse (man) **der**
    **Krankenpfleger;** (woman)
    **die Krankenschwester**
nut (fruit) **die Nuss;**
    (for bolt) **die Mutter**

## O

occasionally **gelegentlich**
October **Oktober**
of **von;** the name of the hotel
    **der Name des Hotels**
office **das Büro**
often **oft**
oil **das Öl**
ointment **die Salbe**
OK **okay**
old **alt;** how old are you?
    **wie alt sind Sie?**
olive **die Olive**
omelette **das Omelette**
on... **auf...**
one (number) **eins;**
    one beer/sausage
    **ein Bier/eine Wurst**
one million **eine Million**
onion **die Zwiebel**
only **nur**
open (verb) **öffnen;**
    (adj) **offen**
opening times
    **die Öffnungszeiten**
opera **die Oper**
operating theatre
    **der Operationssaal**
operation **die Operation**
operator **die Vermittlung**

opposite: opposite the hotel
    **gegenüber dem Hotel**
optician **Augenarzt/**
    **Augenärztin**
or **oder**
orange (colour) **orange;**
    (fruit) **die Orange**
orange juice **der Orangensaft**
orchestra **das Orchester**
ordinary **gewöhnlich**
other: the other...
    **der/die/das andere...**
our **unser;** it's ours **es gehört uns**
out **aus;** he's out
    **er ist nicht da**
outside **außerhalb**
oven **der Backofen**
over (more than) **über;** (finished)
    **vorbei;** (across) **über;**
    over there **dort drüben**
overtake **überholen**
oyster **die Auster**

## P

package (parcel) **das Paket**
packet **das Paket;**
    (cigarettes) **die Schachtel**
pack of cards **das Kartenspiel**
padlock **das Vorhängeschloss**
page **die Seite**
pain **der Schmerz**
painkiller (medicine)
    **die Schmerztablette**
paint **die Farbe**
pair **das Paar**
palace **der Palast**
pale **blass**
pancake **der Pfannkuchen**
paper **das Papier;** (newspaper)
    **die Zeitung**
paraffin **das Paraffin**
parcel **das Paket**
pardon? **wie bitte?**
parents **die Eltern (m pl)**
park **der Park;** (verb) **parken;**
    no parking **Parken verboten**
parsley **die Petersilie**
parting (hair) **der Scheitel**
party (celebration) **die Party;**
    (group) **die Gruppe;**
    (political) **die Partei**
passenger **der Fahrgast,**
    **der Passagier**
passport **der Pass, der Ausweis;**
    passport control
    **die Passkontrolle**
password **das Passwort**
pasta **die Nudeln**
pastry **das Gebäck**
path **der Weg**

pavement **der Bürgersteig**
pay **bezahlen**
payment **die Bezahlung**
peach **der Pfirsich**
peanuts **die Erdnüsse (f pl)**
pear **die Birne**
pearl **die Perle**
peas **die Erbsen (f pl)**
pedestrian **der Fußgänger**
pedestrian zone
    **die Fußgängerzone**
peg (clothes) **die**
    **Wäscheklammer;**
    (tent) **der Hering**
pen **der Stift**
pencil **der Bleistift;**
    pencil sharpener **der**
    **Bleistiftspitzer**
penfriend **der/die**
    **Brieffreund(in)**
penicillin **das Penizillin**
penknife **das**
    **Taschenmesser**
people **die Leute (m pl)**
pepper **der Pfeffer;** (red/green)
    **der Paprika**
peppermints **die**
    **Pfefferminzbonbons**
per: per night **pro Nacht**
perfect **perfekt**
perfume **das Parfüm**
perhaps **vielleicht**
perm **die Dauerwelle**
pet passport **der Tierpass**
petrol **das Benzin**
petrol station **die Tankstelle**
pets **die Haustiere (nt pl)**
pharmacy **die Apotheke**
phonecard **die Telefonkarte**
photocopier **der Fotokopierer**
photograph **das Foto;**
    (verb) **fotografieren**
photographer **der Fotograf**
phrase book **der Sprachführer**
piano **das Klavier**
pickpocket **der Taschendieb**
picnic **das Picknick**
piece **das Stück**
pill **die Tablette**
pillow **das Kopfkissen**
pilot **der/die Pilot(in)**
pin **die Stecknadel**
PIN (number) **die Geheimzahl**
pineapple **die Ananas**
pink **rosa**
pipe (for smoking) **die Pfeife;** (for
    water) **die Pumpe, das Rohr**
piston **der Kolben**
place **der Platz;** (town, etc.) **der**
    **Ort;** at your place **bei Ihnen**
plant **die Pflanze**

plaster (for cut) das Pflaster
plastic das Plastik
plastic bag die Tragetasche,
  die Plastiktüte
plate der Teller
platform das Gleis,
  der Bahnsteig
play (theatre) das Stück;
  (verb) spielen
please bitte
plug (electrical) der Stecker;
  (sink) der Stöpsel
plumber der/die Klempner(in)
pocket die Tasche
poison das Gift
Poland Polen
Pole (man) der Pole;
  (woman) die Polin
police die Polizei
police officer der/die Polizist(in)
police report der Polizeibericht
police station das Polizeirevier
Polish polnisch
politics die Politik
poor arm; (bad quality) schlecht
pop music die Popmusik
pork das Schweinefleisch
port (harbour) der Hafen
porter (hotel) der Portier
possible möglich
post die Post; (verb) aufgeben
postbox der Briefkasten
postcard die Postkarte
postcode die Postleitzahl
poster das Poster
postman/woman
  der/die Briefträger(in)
post office das Postamt
potato die Kartoffel
pottery die Töpferei
poultry das Geflügel
pound (money, weight)
  das Pfund
pram der Kinderwagen
prawns die Krabben (f pl)
prefer: I prefer... ich
  mag lieber...
pregnant schwager
prescription das Rezept
presentation der Vortrag
pretty (beautiful) schön;
  (quite) ziemlich;
  pretty good recht gut
price der Preis
priest Geistliche
printer der Drucker
private privat
problem das Problem
professor der/die Professor(in)
profits der Gewinn
public öffentlich

public holiday der Feiertag
pull ziehen
puncture die Reifenpanne
purple lila
purse das Portemonnaie
push drücken
pushchair der Sportwagen
put legen, stellen, setzen
pyjamas der Schlafanzug

## Q

quality die Qualität
quarter das Viertel
quay der Kai
question die Frage
queue die Schlange;
  (verb) anstehen
quick schnell
quiet still, ruhig
quite (fairly) ziemlich; (fully) ganz

## R

rabbit das Kaninchen
radiator der Heizkörper;
  (car) der Kühler
radio das Radio
radish der Rettich; (small red)
  das Radieschen
railway die Bahn
rain der Regen
raincoat der Regenmantel
raisins die Rosinen (f pl)
rake der Rechen
rare (uncommon) selten;
  (steak) blutig
raspberries die Himbeeren (f pl)
rat die Ratte
razor blades die Rasierklingen
  (f pl)
read lesen
reading lamp die Leselampe
ready fertig
ready meals die Fertiggerichte
  (nt pl)
rear lights die Rücklichter (f pl)
receipt die Quittung
reception der Empfang
receptionist die
  Empfangsperson
record (music) die Schallplatte;
  (sporting, etc.) der Rekord
record shop das
  Schallplattengeschäft
red rot
refreshments die
  Erfrischungen (f pl)
registered post das Einschreiben
relative der Verwandte
relax sich entspannen

religion die Religion
remember sich erinnern;
  I don't remember
  ich erinnere mich nicht
rent (verb) mieten
report der Bericht
research die Forschungen
reservation die
  Reservierung
rest (remainder) der Rest;
  (verb) sich ausruhen
restaurant das Restaurant
return (come back)
  zurückkommen;
  (give back) zurückgeben
return ticket die Rückfahrkarte
rhubarb der Rhabarber
rice der Reis
rich reich
right (correct) richtig;
  (direction) rechts
right side die rechte Seite
ring (jewellery) der Ring;
  (verb: to call) anrufen
ripe reif
river der Fluss
road die Straße
roasted geröstet
robbery der Diebstahl
rock (stone) der Stein;
  (music) der Rock
roll (bread) das Brötchen
roof das Dach
room das Zimmer;
  (space) der Raum
room service der Zimmerservice
rope das Seil
rose die Rose
round (circular) rund
rubber (eraser) der
  Radiergummi;
  (material) der Gummi
rubbish der Abfall
ruby (stone) der Rubin
rucksack der Rucksack
rug (mat) der Läufer;
  (blanket) die Wolldecke
ruins die Ruinen (f pl)
ruler (for drawing) das Lineal
rum der Rum
run (verb) laufen
runway die Start-und
  Landebahn

## S

sad traurig
safe sicher
safety pin die Sicherheitsnadel
sailing das Segeln
sailing boat das Segelboot

*salad* der Salat

*salami* die Salami

*sale* (at lower prices)
der Schlussverkauf

*sales* der Absatz

*salmon* der Lachs

*salt* das Salz

*same: the same dress* das gleiche
Kleid; *same again please*
nochmal dasselbe, bitte

*sand* der Sand

*sandals* die Sandalen (f pl)

*sandwich* das Sandwich,
das Butterbrot

*sanitary towels* die
Damenbinden (f pl)

*Saturday* Samstag

*sauce* die Soße

*saucepan* der Kochtopf

*saucer* die Untertasse

*sauna* die Sauna

*sausage* die Wurst

*say* sagen; *what did you say?* was
haben Sie gesagt?; *how do
you say...?* wie sagt man...?

*Scandinavia* Skandinavien

*scarf* der Schal; (head)
das Kopftuch

*schedule* der Zeitplan

*school* die Schule

*scissors* die Schere

*Scotland* Schottland

*Scotsman* der Schotte

*Scotswoman* die Schottin

*Scottish* schottisch

*screen* der Bildschirm

*screw* die Schraube

*screwdriver* der
Schraubenzieher

*sea* das Meer

*seafood* die
Meeresfrüchte (f pl)

*seat* der Sitz

*seat belt* der Sicherheitsgurt

*second* (time) die Sekunde;
(in series) zweiter;
*second class* zweiter Klasse

*secretary* der/die Sekratär(in)

*see* sehen; *I can't see* ich kann
nichts sehen; *I see* ich
verstehe; *see you soon*
bis bald; *see you tomorrow*
bis Morgen

*self-employed* selbständig

*sell* verkaufen

*seminar* das Seminar

*separate* getrennt

*separated: we are separated*
wir leben getrennt

*separately* getrennt

*September* September

*serious* ernst

*serviette* die Serviette

*seven* sieben

*seventeen* siebzehn

*seventy* siebzig

*several* mehrere

*sew* nähen

*shampoo* das Shampoo

*shave: to have a shave*
sich rasieren

*shaving foam* die Rasiercreme

*shawl* das Umhängetuch

*she* sie

*sheet* das (Bett)laken

*shell* die Muschel

*shellfish* (as food) die
Meeresfrüchte (f pl)

*sherry* der Sherry

*ship* das Schiff

*shirt* das Hemd

*shoelaces* die Schnürsenkel
(m pl)

*shoe polish* die Schuhcreme

*shoe shop* das Schuhgeschäft

*shoes* die Schuhe (m pl)

*shop* das Geschäft

*shopkeeper* der/die
Verkäufer(in)

*shopping* das Einkaufen;
(items bought) die
Einkäufe; *to go shopping*
einkaufen gehen

*short* kurz

*shorts* die Shorts

*shoulder* die Schulter

*shower* (bath) die Dusche;
(rain) der Schauer

*shower gel* das Duschgel

*shutter* (camera)
der Verschluss; (window)
der Fensterladen

*sick* (ill) krank; *I feel sick* mir ist
übel; *to be sick* (vomit)
sich übergeben

*side* die Seite; (edge)
die Kante

*sidelights* das Standlicht

*sightseeing* die Besichtigungen

*sign* das Schild

*silk* die Seide

*silver* (metal) das Silber;
(colour) silber

*simple* einfach

*sing* singen

*singing* das Singen

*single* (one) einziger; (unmarried)
ledig, single

*single room* das Einzelzimmer

*single ticket* die einfache
Fahrkarte

*sister* die Schwester

*sister-in-law* die Schwägerin

*six* sechs

*sixteen* sechzehn

*sixty* sechzig

*ski* (verb) Ski fahren

*ski binding* die Skibindung

*ski boots* die Skistiefel (m pl)

*skid* (verb) schleudern

*skiing: to go skiing*
Skifahren gehen

*ski lift* der Skilift

*skin cleanser* der Hautreiniger

*ski resort* der Skiurlaubsort

*skirt* der Rock

*skis* die Skier (m pl)

*ski sticks* die Skistöcke
(m pl)

*sky* der Himmel

*sledge* der Schlitten

*sleep* der Schlaf;
(verb) schlafen

*sleeping bag* der Schlafsack

*sleeping pill* die Schlaftablette

*sleeve* der Ärmel

*slice of...* das Stück...

*slippers* die Pantoffeln (m pl)

*slow* langsam

*small* klein

*smell* der Geruch;
(verb) riechen

*smile* das Lächeln;
(verb) lächeln

*smoke* der Rauch;
(verb) rauchen

*snack* der Imbiss

*snow* der Schnee

*so* so; *not so much* nicht so viel

*soaking solution*
(for contact lenses) die
Aufbewahrungslösung

*soap* die Seife

*socks* die Socken (f pl)

*soda water* das Sodawasser

*sofa* die Couch, das Sofa

*soft* weich

*soil* die Erde

*somebody* jemand

*somehow* irgendwie

*something* etwas

*sometimes* manchmal

*somewhere* irgendwo

*son* der Sohn

*song* das Lied

*sorry!* (apology) Verzeihung!,
Entschuldigung!; *I'm sorry*
es tut mir Leid; *sorry?*
(pardon) wie bitte?

*soup* die Suppe

*south* der Süden

*South Africa* Südafrika

*souvenir* das Souvenir

spa **der Kurort**

spade (shovel) **der Spaten**

spades (cards) **Pik**

spanner **der Schraubenschlüssel**

spares **die Ersatzteile** (nt pl)

spark(ing) plug **die Zündkerze**

speak **sprechen**; do you speak English? **sprechen Sie Englisch?**; I don't speak German **ich spreche kein Deutsch**

speed **die Geschwindigkeit**

spider **die Spinne**

spinach **der Spinat**

spoon **der Löffel**

sport **der Sport**; sports centre **das Sportzentrum**

spring (mechanical) **die Feder**; (season) **der Frühling**

square (shape) **das Quadrat**; (in town) **der Platz**

stadium **das Stadion**

staircase **die Treppe**

stairs **die Treppe**

stamp **die Briefmarke**

stand **der Stand**

stapler **der Hefter**

star **der Stern**; (film) **der Star**

start **der Start, der Anfang**; (verb) **anfangen**

starters **die Vorspeisen** (f pl)

statement **die Aussage**

station **der Bahnhof**; (underground) **die Station**

statue **die Statue**

steak **das Steak**

steal **stehlen**; it's been stolen **es ist gestohlen worden**

steamed **gedämpft**

steamer (boat) **der Dampfer**; (cooking) **der Dampfkochtopf**

steering wheel **das Lenkrad**

stepdaughter **der Stieftochter**

stepfather **der Stiefvater**

stepmother **der Stiefmutter**

stepson **der Stiefsohn**

still water **Wasser ohne Kohlensäure, das Tafelwasser**

sting **der Stich**; (verb) **stechen**

stockings **die Strümpfe** (m pl)

stomach **der Magen**

stomachache **die Magenschmerzen**

stop (bus stop) **die Haltestelle**; (verb) **anhalten**; stop! **halt!**

storm **der Sturm**

strawberries **die Erdbeeren** (f pl)

stream (**water**) **der Bach**

street **die Straße**

string (cord) **der Faden**; (guitar, etc.) **die Saite**

strong (person, drink) **stark**; (material) **stabil**; (taste) **streng**

student **der/die Student(in)**

stupid **dumm**

suburbs **der Stadtrand**

sugar **der Zucker**

suit **der Anzug**; it suits you **es steht Ihnen**

suitcase **der Koffer**

sun **die Sonne**

sunbathe **sonnenbaden**

sunburn **der Sonnenbrand**

Sunday **Sonntag**

sunglasses **die Sonnenbrille**

sunny: it's sunny **es ist sonnig**

sunshade **der Sonnenschirm**

suntan: to get a suntan **braun werden**

suntan lotion **das Sonnenöl**

suntanned **braungebrannt**

superior **Vorgesetzte**

supermarket **der Supermarkt**

supper **das Abendessen**

supplement **der Zuschlag**

suppository **das Zäpfchen**

sure **sicher**

surname **der Nachname**

sweat **der Schweiß**; (verb) **schwitzen**

sweatshirt **das Sweatshirt**

sweet (not sour) **süß**; (confectionery) **die Süßigkeit, der Bonbon**

swim (verb) **schwimmen**

swimming **das Schwimmen**

swimming costume **der Badeanzug**

swimming pool **das Schwimmbad**

swimming trunks **die Badehose**

Swiss **der/die Schweizer(in)**; (adj) **schweizerisch**

switch **der Schalter**

Switzerland **die Schweiz**

swivel chair **der Drehstuhl**

synagogue **die Synagoge**

syringe **die Spritze**

syrup **der Sirup**

## T

table **der Tisch**

tablet **die Tablette**

take **nehmen**

take-away **der Schnellimbiss**

take-off **der Abflug**

talcum powder **der Puder**

talk **das Gespräch**; (verb) **reden**

tall **groß**

tampons **die Tampons** (m pl)

tangerine **die Mandarine**

tap **der Hahn**

tapestry **der Wandteppich**

taxi **das Taxi**

taxi rank **der Taxistand**

tea **der Tee**; black tea **der schwarze Tee**; tea with milk **der Tee mit Milch**

teacher **der/die Lehrer(in)**

tea towel **das Geschirrtuch**

telephone **das Telefon**; (verb) **telefonieren**

telephone box **die Telefonzelle**

television **das Fernsehen**; to watch television **fernsehen**

temperature **die Temperatur**; (fever) **das Fieber**

ten **zehn**

tennis **das Tennis**

tent **das Zelt**

ten thousand **zehntausend**

tent peg **der Hering**

tent pole **die Zeltstange**

terminal **das Terminal**

terrace **die Terrasse**

than: bigger than **größer als**

thank (verb) **danken**; thanks **danke**; thank you **danke schön**

that: that man **dieser Mann**; that woman **diese Frau**; what's that? **was ist das?**; I think that... **ich denke, dass...**

the **der** (masculine singular); **die** (feminine singular); **das** (neuter singular); **die** (plural)

theatre **das Theater**

their: their room **ihr Zimmer**; their books **ihre Bücher**; it's theirs **es gehört ihnen**

them: it's them **sie sind es**; it's for them **es ist für sie**; give it to them **geben Sie es ihnen**

then **dann**

there **da**; there is/are... **es gibt...**; is/are there...? **gibt es...?**

these **diese**

they **sie**

thick **dick**

thief **der Dieb**

thin **dünn**

think **denken**;

*I think so* **ich glaube ja;**
*I'll think about it* **ich überlege**
**es mir**
*third* **dritter**
*thirsty* **durstig;** *I'm thirsty*
**ich habe Durst**
*thirteen* **dreizehn**
*thirty* **Dreißig**
*this: this man* **dieser Mann;** *this*
*woman* **diese Frau;** *what's this?*
**was ist das?;** *this is Mr...*
**das ist Herr...**
*those* **diese da;** *those things*
**die Dinge dort**
*thousand* **tausend**
*three* **drei**
*three hundred* **dreihundert**
*throat* **die Kehle**
*throat pastilles* **die**
**Halstabletten (f pl)**
*through* **durch**
*thunderstorm* **das Gewitter**
*Thursday* **Donnerstag**
*ticket* **die Karte;** *ticket kiosk*
**der Schalter**
*tide: high tide* **die Flut;**
*low tide* **die Ebbe**
*tie* **die Krawatte;**
*(verb)* **festmachen**
*tight* **eng**
*tights* **die Strumpfhose**
*tiles* **die Kacheln (f pl)**
*time* **die Zeit;** *what's the time?*
**wie spät ist es?**
*timetable* (train, bus)
**der Fahrplan**
*tin* **die Dose**
*tin opener* **der Dosenöffner**
*tip* (money) **das Trinkgeld;**
(end) **die Spitze**
*tired* **müde**
*tissues* **die Taschentücher**
*to: to England* **nach England;**
*to the station* **zum Bahnhof;**
*to the doctor* **zum Arzt**
*toast* **der Toast**
*tobacco* **der Tabak**
*toboggan* **der Schlitten**
*today* **heute**
*together* **zusammen**
*toilet* **die Toilette**
*toilet paper* **das Toilettenpapier**
*tomato* **die Tomate**
*tomato juice* **der Tomatensaft**
*tomorrow* **morgen**
*tongue* **die Zunge**
*tonic* **das Tonic**
*tonight* **heute abend**
*too* (also) **auch;** (excessively) **zu**
*tooth* **der Zahn**
*toothache* **die Zahnschmerzen**

*toothbrush* **die Zahnbürste**
*toothpaste* **die Zahnpasta**
*torch* **die Taschenlampe**
*tour* **die Rundreise**
*tour guide* **der/die**
**Reiseleiter(in)**
*tourist* **der/die Tourist(in)**
*tourist office* **das**
**Verkehrsbüro, das**
**Fremdenverkehrsbüro**
*towel* **das Handtuch**
*tower* **der Turm**
*town* **die Stadt**
*town hall* **das Rathaus**
*toy* **das Spielzeug**
*track suit* **der Trainingsanzug**
*tractor* **der Traktor**
*trade fair* **die Handelsmesse**
*tradition* **die Tradition**
*traffic* **der Verkehr**
*traffic jam* **der Stau**
*traffic lights* **die Ampel**
*trailer* **der Anhänger**
*train* **der Zug**
*trainee* **der/die Auszubildende**
*trainers* **die Turnschuhe**
*tram* **die Straßenbahn**
*translate* **übersetzen**
*translator* **der/die Übersetzer(in)**
*travel agency* **das Reisebüro**
*traveller's cheque* **der**
**Reisescheck**
*tray* **das Tablett**
*tree* **der Baum**
*trolley* **der Kofferkuli**
*trousers* **die Hose**
*true* **wahr**
*try* **versuchen**
*Tuesday* **Dienstag**
*tunnel* **der Tunnel**
*Turk* (man) **der Türke;**
(woman) **die Türkin**
*Turkey* **die Türkei**
*Turkish* **türkisch**
*tweezers* **die Pinzette**
*twelve* **zwölf**
*twenty* **zwanzig**
*twin beds* **die zwei Einzelbetten**
*two* **zwei**
*typewriter* **die Schreibmaschine**
*tyre* **der Reifen**

# U

*ugly* **hässlich**
*umbrella* **der (Regen)schirm**
*uncle* **der Onkel**
*under...* **unter...**
*underground* **die U-Bahn**
*underpants* **die Unterhose**
*underskirt* **der Unterrock**

*understand* **verstehen;**
*I don't understand*
**ich verstehe nicht**
*underwear* **die Unterwäsche**
*university* **die Universität**
*unleaded* **bleifrei**
*until* **bis**
*unusual* **ungewöhnlich**
*up* **oben;** *up there* **da oben**
*upwards* **nach oben**
*urgent* **dringend**
*us: it's us* **wir sind es;** *it's for us*
**es ist für uns;** *give it to us*
**geben sie es uns**
*use* **der Gebrauch;**
*(verb)* **gebrauchen;** *it's no use*
**es hat keinen Zweck**
*useful* **hilfreich**
*usual* **gewöhnlich**
*usually* **gewöhnlich**

# V

*vacancy* (room) **ein**
**freies Zimmer**
*vaccination* **die Impfung**
*vacuum cleaner* **der Staubsauger**
*valley* **das Tal**
*valuables* **die Wertsachen (f pl)**
*valve* **das Ventil**
*vanilla* **die Vanille**
*vase* **die Vase**
*veal* **das Kalbfleisch**
*vegetable* **das Gemüse**
*vegetarian* **der/die**
**Vegetarier(in);**
(adj) **vegetarisch**
*vehicle* **das Fahrzeug**
*very* **sehr**
*vest* **das (Unter)hemd**
*vet* **der Tierarzt**
*video* (tape, film) **das Video;**
*video recorder*
**der Videorecorder;**
*video tape* **die Videocassette**
*Vienna* **Wien**
*view* **der Blick**
*viewfinder* **der Sucher**
*villa* **die Villa**
*village* **das Dorf**
*vinegar* **der Essig**
*violin* **die Geige**
*visit* **der Besuch;**
*(verb)* **besuchen**
*visiting hours* **die Besuchszeit**
*visitor* **der/die Besucher(in)**
*vitamin tablet* **die**
**Vitamintablette**
*vodka* **der Wodka**
*voice* **die Stimme**
*voicemail* **die Voice-mail**

# W

wait **warten**;
wait! **warten Sie!**
waiter **der Ober**;
waiter! **Herr Ober!**
waiting room **das Wartezimmer**; (station) **der Wartesaal**
waitress **die Kellnerin**;
waitress! **Fräulein!**
Wales **Wales**
walk **der Spaziergang**; (verb) **gehen**; to go for a walk **spazieren gehen**
wall (inside) **die Wand**; (outside) **die Mauer**
wallet **die Brieftasche**
war **der Krieg**
wardrobe **der Kleiderschrank**
warm **warm**
was: I was **ich war**;
he/she/it was **er/sie/es war**
wash basin **das Waschbecken**
washing powder **das Waschpulver**
washing-up liquid **das Spülmittel**
wasp **die Wespe**
watch **die (Armband)uhr**; (verb) **ansehen**
water **das Wasser**
waterfall **der Wasserfall**
water heater **das Heißwassergerät**
wave **die Welle**; (verb: with hand) **winken**
wavy (hair) **wellig**
we **wir**
weather **das Wetter**
web site **die Webseite**
wedding **die Hochzeit**
Wednesday **Mittwoch**
weeds **das Unkraut**
week **die Woche**
welcome **willkommen**;
you're welcome **keine Ursache**
well-done (steak) **durchgebraten**
wellingtons **die Gummistiefel**
Welsh **walisisch**
Welshman/woman **der/die Waliser(in)**
were: you were (singular informal) **du warst**; (singular formal; plural) **Sie waren**; we/they were **wir/sie waren**
west **der Westen**
wet **naß**
what? **was?**
wheel **das Rad**

wheelchair **der Rollstuhl**;
wheelchair access **der Rollstuhlfahrer**
when? **wann?**
where? **wo?**
whether **ob**
which? **welcher?**
whisky **der Whisky**
white **weiß**
who? **wer?**
why? **warum?**
wide **breit**
wife **die (Ehe)frau**
wind **der Wind**
window **das Fenster**;
window box **der Blumenkasten**
windscreen **die Windschutzscheibe**
wine **der Wein**
wine list **die Weinkarte**
wing **der Flügel**
with **mit**
without **ohne**
witness **der/die Zeuge(in)**
woman **die Frau**
women's toilets **die Damentoilette**
wood (material) **das Holz**
wool **die Wolle**
word **das Wort**
work **die Arbeit**; (verb) **arbeiten**; (machine, etc.) **funktionieren**
worktop **die Arbeitsfläche**
worse **schlechter**
worst **schlechtester**
wrapping paper **das Packpapier**; (for presents) **das Geschenkpapier**
wrist **das Handgelenk**
writing paper **das Schreibpapier**
wrong **falsch**

# X, Y, Z

x-ray **die Röntgenaufnahme**
x-ray department **die Röntgenabteilung**
year **das Jahr**
yellow **gelb**
yes **ja**
yesterday **gestern**
yet: is it ready yet? **ist es schon fertig?**; not yet **noch nicht**
yoghurt **der Jogurt**
you (singular informal) **du**; (singular formal; plural) **Sie**; for you **für dich/Sie**; with you **mit dir/Ihnen**

your (singular informal) **dein**; (singular formal; plural) **Ihr**; your shoes **deine/Ihre Schuhe**
yours: is this yours? (singular informal) **gehört das dir?** (singular formal; plural) **gehört das Ihnen?**
youth hostel **die Jugendherberge**
zip **der Reißverschluß**
zoo **der Zoo**

# DICTIONARY
## German to English

The gender of German nouns listed here is indicated by the abbreviations *m* for masculine, *f* for feminine, and *nt* for neuter. Plural nouns are followed by the abbreviations *m pl*, *f pl*, and *nt pl*. The feminine form of most occupations and personal attributes is made by adding **-in** to the masculine form: **Buchhalter(in)** *accountant*, for example. Exceptions to this rule are listed separately. Where necessary, adjectives are denoted by the abbreviation *adj*.

### A

**Abend** (m) *evening*
**Abendessen** (nt) *dinner, supper*
**aber** *but*
**Abfahrt** (f) *departure*
**Abfall** (m) *litter, rubbish*
**Abfertigungsschalter** (m) *check-in* (desk)
**Abflug** (m) *departures, take-off;* **Abflughalle** (f) *departure lounge*
**Abführmittel** (nt) *laxative*
**Absatz** (m) *heel* (shoe); *sales* (figures)
**absichtlich** *deliberately*
**Abteil** (nt) *compartment*
**Abteilung** (f) *department*
**acht** *eight*
**achtzehn** *eighteen*
**achtzig** *eighty*
**Adapter** (m) *adaptor*
**Adresse** (f) *address*
**Aids** *Aids*
**Aktentasche** (f) *briefcase*
**Alkohol** (m) *alcohol*
**alle(s)** *all, every;* **alle Straßen** *all the streets;* **das ist alles** *that's all;* **alles** *everything*
**allein** *alone*
**allergisch** *allergic*
**alt** *old;* **wie alt sind Sie?** *how old are you?*
**am** *at, next to;* **am Bahnhof** *at the station;* **am Fenster** *next to the window*
**Amerika** *America*
**Amerikaner(in)** (m/f) *American* (person)
**amerikanisch** *American* (adj)
**Ampel** (f) *traffic lights*
**Ananas** (f) *pineapple*
**andere** *another* (different); **der/die/das andere...** *the other...;* **ein anderes Zimmer** *another room;* **das ist etwas**
**anderes!** *that's different!;* **etwas anderes** *something else;* **jemand anders** *someone else;* **woanders** *somewhere else;* **ein andermal** *another time*
**Anfang** (m) *start*
**anfangen** *to start*
**Anfänger** (m) *beginner*
**Angeln** (nt) *fishing;* **Angeln gehen** *to go fishing*
**angenehm** *nice, pleasant*
**anhalten** *to stop*
**Anhänger** (m) *trailer*
**ankommen** *to arrive*
**Ankunft** (f) *arrivals*
**Anrufbeantworter** (m) *answering machine*
**anrufen** *to ring, call*
**ansehen** *to watch*
**anstehen** *to queue*
**Antiquitätengeschäft** (nt) *antique shop*
**Antiseptikum** (nt) *antiseptic*
**Antragsformular** (nt) *application form*
**Anzug** (m) *suit*
**Aperitif** (m) *aperitif*
**Apfel** (m) *apple*
**Apotheke** (f) *pharmacy*
**Appetit** (m) *appetite*
**Aprikose** (f) *apricot*
**Arbeit** (f) *job, work*
**arbeiten** *to work*
**Arbeitsfläche** (f) *worktop*
**arm** *poor* (not rich)
**Arm** (m) *arm*
**Armband** (nt) *bracelet*
**Armbanduhr** (f) *watch*
**Ärmel** (m) *sleeve*
**Arzt** (m) *doctor*
**Aschenbecher** (m) *ashtray*
**Asthma** (nt) *asthma*
**atmen** *to breathe*
**attraktiv** *attractive*
**auch** *too* (also)
**auf...** *on/at/in...;* **auf der Post** *at the post office;* **auf Englisch** *in English*

**Aufbewahrungslösung** (f) *soaking solution* (for contact lenses)
**aufgeben** *to post*
**aufstehen** *to get up* (rise)
**Auf Wiedersehen** *goodbye*
**Auge** (nt) *eye;* **die Augen** *eyes*
**Augenarzt/Augenärztin** (m/f) *optician*
**Augenbraue** (nt) *eyebrow*
**August** *August*
**aus** *out*
**Ausflug** (m) *excursion*
**Ausgang** (m) *exit*
**ausgezeichnet** *excellent*
**Ausländer(in)** *foreigner*
**Auspuff** (m) *exhaust*
**ausruhen: sich ausruhen** *to rest*
**Aussage** (f) *statement*
**außerhalb** *outside*
**aussteigen** *to get off* (bus, etc.)
**Ausstellung** (f) *exhibition*
**Auster** (f) *oyster*
**Australien** *Australia*
**Australier(in)** (m/f) *Australian* (person)
**australisch** *Australian* (adj)
**Ausweis** (m) *passport*
**Auszubildende** (m/f) *trainee*
**Auto** (nt) *car*
**Autobahn** (f) *motorway*
**automatisch** *automatic*

### B

**Baby** (nt) *baby*
**Bach** (m) *stream*
**backen** *to bake*
**Bäcker** (m) *baker*
**Bäckerei** (f) *bakery*
**Backofen** (m) *oven*
**Bad** (nt) *bath;* **ein Bad nehmen** *to have a bath*
**Badeanzug** (m) *swimming costume*
**Badehose** (f) *swimming trunks*

**Badewanne** (f) bathtub
**Badezimmer** (nt) bathroom
**Bahn** (f) railway
**Bahnhof** (m) station
**Bahnsteig** (m) platform
**Balkon** (m) balcony
**Ball** (m) ball
**Ballett** (nt) ballet
**Banane** (f) banana
**Band** (f) band (musicians)
**Bank** (f) bank
**Banknoten** (f pl) (bank)notes
**Bar** (f) bar (drinks)
**Bargeld** (nt) cash; **bar bezahlen**
   to pay cash
**Bart** (m) beard
**Batterie** (f) battery
**Bauarbeiter(in)** builder
**Bauer** (m) farmer
**Bauernhof** (m) farm
**Baum** (m) tree
**Baumwolle** (f) cotton
**Bayern** Bavaria
**Becken** (nt) basin (sink)
**bedeutet: was bedeutet das?**
   what does this mean?
**behindert** disabled
**beide** both; **wir beide**
   both of us
**beige** beige
**bei Ihnen** at your place
**Bein** (nt) leg; **Beinbruch** (m)
   broken leg
**Beispiel** (nt) example; **zum**
   **Beispiel** for example
**beißen** to bite
**Belag** (m) filling (in sandwich)
**Belgien** Belgium
**Belgier(in)** (m/f)
   Belgian (person)
**belgisch** Belgian (adj)
**Belichtungsmesser** (m)
   light meter
**Benzin** (nt) petrol
**Berater(in)** consultant
**Berg** (m) hill, mountain
**Bericht** (m) report
**Berliner** (m) doughnut
**beschäftigt** busy (occupied)
**Bescheinigung** (f) certificate
**besetzt** engaged (occupied)
**Besichtigungen** (f) sightseeing
**besonders** especially
**Besprechung** (f) meeting
**besser** better
**Basteln** (nt) DIY
**bester** best
**bestreiten** to deny
**Besuch** (m) visit
**besuchen** to visit
**Besucher(in)** (m/f) visitor

**Besuchszeit** (f) visiting hours
**betrunken** drunk
**Bett** (nt) bed
**Bettlaken** (nt) sheet
**Bettwäsche** (f) bed linen
**bewegen** to move
**bezahlen** to pay
**Bezahlung** (f) payment
**BH** (m) bra
**Bibliothek** (f) library
**Bier** (nt) beer
**Bikini** (m) bikini
**Bildschirm** (m) screen, monitor
**billig** cheap
**bin: ich bin** I am
**Biochemie** (f) biochemistry
**Birne** (f) pear
**bis** until; **bis Freitag**
   by Friday; **bis Morgen**
   see you tomorrow;
   **bis bald** see you soon
**Biss** (m) bite (by dog, etc.)
**bißchen** a little; **es ist**
   **ein bisschen zu groß**
   it's a little big; **nur ein**
   **bisschen** just a little
**bist: du bist** you are (informal)
**bitte** please; **wie bitte?** pardon?
**bitter** bitter
**Blase** (f) blister
**blass** faint (unclear), pale
**Blatt** (nt) leaf
**blau** blue
**blaue Fleck** (m) bruise
**bleichen** to bleach (hair)
**Bleichmittel** (nt) bleach
**bleifrei** unleaded
**Bleistift** (m) pencil
**Bleistiftspitzer** (m)
   pencil sharpener
**Blick** (m) view
**blind** blind (cannot see)
**Blinker** (m) indicator
**Blitz** (m) flash (camera)
**blond** blond (adj)
**Blume** (f) flower
**Blumenbeet** (nt) flowerbed
**Blumenkasten** (m)
   window box
**Blumenkohl** (m) cauliflower
**Blumenladen** (m) florist
**Blumenstecken** (nt)
   flower-arranging
**Bluse** (f) blouse
**Blut** (nt) blood
**blutig** rare (steak)
**Blutprobe** (f) blood test
**Boden** (m) bottom, floor, ground;
   **Bodenplane** (f) groundsheet
**Bohnen** (f pl) beans
**Boiler** (m) boiler

**Bonbon** (m) sweet (candy)
**Boot** (nt) boat (small)
**Bordkarte** (f) boarding pass
**Botschaft** (f) embassy
**Boxen** (nt) boxing
**braten** fry
**Bratpfanne** (f) frying pan
**brauchen** to need; **ich**
   **brauche...** I need...
**braun** brown; **braun werden**
   to get a suntan
**braungebrannt** suntanned
**breit** wide
**Breitlauch** (nt) leeks
**Bremse** (f) brake
**bremsen** to brake
**brennen** to burn
**Bridge** (nt) bridge (game)
**Brief** (m) letter (post)
**Brieffreund(in)** (m/f)
   penfriend
**Briefkasten** (m) letter box,
   postbox
**Briefmarke** (f) stamp
**Brieftasche** (f) wallet
**Briefträger(in)** (m/f)
   postman(woman)
**Briefumschlag** (m) envelope
**Brille** (f) glasses
**britisch** British
**Brombeere** (f) blackberry
**Brosche** (f) brooch
**Broschüre** (f) brochure, leaflet
**Brot** (nt) bread
**Brötchen** (nt) bread roll
**Brücke** (f) bridge
**Bruder** (m) brother
**Brunnen** (m) fountain
**Brüssel** Brussels
**Brust** (f) chest (part of body)
**Buch** (nt) book
**buchen** to book
**Bücherei** (f) library
**Buchhalter(in)** (m/f)
   accountant
**Buchhandlung** (f) bookshop
**Buchstabe** (m) letter (alphabet)
**Budget** (nt) budget
**Bügeleisen** (nt) iron (for clothes)
**bügeln** to iron
**Burg** (f) castle
**Bürgersteig** (m) pavement
**Büro** (nt) office
**Bürste** (f) brush
**bürsten** to brush (hair)
**Bus** (m) bus
**Busbahnhof** (m)
   bus/coach station
**Büstenhalter** (m) bra
**Butter** (f) butter
**Butterbrot** (nt) sandwich

# C

**Café** (nt) *café*
**Campinggas** (nt)
 *camping gas*
**Campingplatz** (m) *campsite*
**Campingplatzverwaltung** (f)
 *campsite office*
**Chips** (f) *crisps*
**Compact-Disc** (f)
 *compact disc*
**Computer** (m) *computer*
**Computerspiele** (nt pl)
 *computer games*
**Couch** (f) *sofa*
**Creme** (f) *cream* (lotion)
**Curry** (nt) *curry*

# D

**da** *there*
**Dach** (nt) *roof*
**Dachboden** (m) *attic*
**Dachrinne** (f) *gutter*
**Dame** (f) *lady, woman*
**Damenbinden** (f pl)
 *sanitary towels*
**Damentoilette** (f)
 *women's toilets*
**Dampfer** (m) *steamer* (boat)
**Dampfkochtopf** (m)
 *steamer* (cooking)
**Däne** *Dane* (man)
**Dänemark** *Denmark*
**Dänin** *Dane* (woman)
**dänisch** *Danish*
**danken** *to thank;*
 **danke** *thanks;*
 **danke schön** *thank you*
**dann** *then*
**das** (nt) *the;*
 **das ist Herr...** *this is Mr...*
**Dauerwelle** (f) *perm*
**Decke** (f) *blanket; ceiling*
**dein(e)** *your* (sing, informal)
**Delegierte(r)** *delegate*
**denken** *to think*
**Denkmal** (nt) *monument*
**Deodorant** (nt) *deodorant*
**der** *the* (masculine)
**deutsch** *German* (adj); **Deutsch**
 *German* (language)
**Deutsche** (m/f) *German* (person)
**Deutschland** *Germany*
**Dezember** *December*
**Diabetiker(in)** *diabetic*
**Diamant** (m) *diamond* (gem)
**dick** *fat* (adj: person); *thick*
**die** *the* (feminine and plural)
**Dieb** (m) *thief*
**Diebstahl** (m) *robbery*

**Dienstag** *Tuesday*
**diese: diese Frau**
 *that/this woman*
**Diesel** (m) *diesel*
**dieser: dieser Mann**
 *that/this man*
**Dirigent** (m) *conductor*
 (orchestra)
**Dokument** (nt) *document*
**Dollar** (m) *dollar*
**dolmetschen** *to interpret*
**Dolmetscher(in)** (m/f)
 *interpreter*
**Dom** (m) *cathedral*
**Donau: die Donau** *Danube*
**Donnerstag** *Thursday*
**Doppelzimmer** (nt)
 *double room*
**Dorf** (nt) *village*
**dort drüben** *over there*
**Dose** (f) *can, tin;* **Dosenöffner**
 (m) *tin opener*
**Drahtseilbahn** (f) *cable car*
**Drehstuhl** (m) *swivel chair*
**drei** *three*
**dreihundert** *three hundred*
**Dreißig** *thirty*
**dreizehn** *thirteen*
**dringend** *urgent*
**dritter** *third*
**drücken** *to push*
**Drucker** (m) *printer*
**du** *you* (singular informal)
**dumm** *stupid*
**dunkel** *dark*
**dünn** *thin*
**durch** *through*
**Durchfall** (m) *diarrhoea*
**durchgebraten** *well-done* (meat)
**Durst** (m) *thirst;* **ich habe Durst**
 *I'm thirsty*
**durstig** *thirsty*
**Dusche** (f) *shower*
**Duschgel** (nt) *shower gel*

# E

**Ebbe** (f) *low tide*
**Ecke** (f) *corner*
**Ehefrau** (f) *wife*
**Ehemann** (m) *husband*
**ehrlich** *honest*
**Ei** (nt) *egg*
**Eile: ich bin in Eile**
 *I'm in a hurry*
**Eimer** (m) *bucket*
**Einbrecher** (m) *burglar*
**einchecken** *to check in*
**einer von beiden** *either*
 *of them*
**einfach** *simple;* **einfache**

**Fahrkarte** (f) *single ticket*
**Einfahrt** (f) *driveway*
**Eingang** (m) *entrance*
**Einkäufe** (f) *shopping*
 (items bought)
**Einkaufen** (nt) *shopping* (activity);
 **einkaufen gehen**
 *to go shopping*
**Einladung** (f) *invitation*
**einlösen** *to cash*
**eins** *one* (number);
 **ein Bier/eine Wurst**
 *one beer/one sausage*
**Einschreiben** (nt)
 *registered post*
**einsteigen** *to get on* (bus, etc.)
**Eintrittskarte** (f)
 *entrance ticket*
**Eintrittspreis** (m)
 *admission charge*
**Einwegwindeln** (f pl)
 *disposable nappies*
**Einzelzimmer** (nt) *single room*
**einziger** *single* (one)
**Eis** (nt) *ice, ice cream;*
 **Eiscreme** (f) *ice cream;*
 **Eis am Stiel** (nt) *ice lolly*
**Eisen** (nt) *iron* (metal)
**Eisenwarenhändler** (m)
 *hardware shop*
**elastisch** *elastic*
**Elektriker(in)** (m/f) *electrician*
**elektrisch** *electric*
**elf** *eleven*
**Ellbogen** (m) *elbow*
**Eltern** (m pl) *parents*
**Empfang** (m) *reception*
**Empfangsperson** (m/f)
 *receptionist*
**Ende** (nt) *end*
**endlich!** *at last!*
**eng** *narrow, tight*
**England** *England*
**Engländer(in)** (m/f)
 *Englishman(woman)*
**englisch** *English* (adj); **Englisch**
 *English* (language)
**Enkel** (m) *grandson*
**Enkelin** (f) *granddaughter*
**Entschuldigung!** *excuse me!,*
 *sorry!*
**entweder... oder...**
 *either... or...*
**entwickeln** *to develop* (film)
**Entzündung** (f) *infection*
**Epilektiker(in)** (m/f) *epileptic*
**er** *he*
**Erbsen** (f pl) *peas*
**Erdbeeren** (f pl) *strawberries*
**Erde** (f) *soil*
**Erdgeschoss** (nt) *ground floor*

**Erdnüsse** (f pl) *peanuts*
**Erfrischungen** (f pl) *refreshments*
**erinnern: sich erinnern**
  *to remember;* **ich erinnere**
  **mich nicht** *I don't remember*
**Erkältung** (f) *cold (illness);* **ich**
  **bin erkältet** *I have a cold*
**Ermäßigungen** (f) *discounts*
**ernst** *serious*
**Ersatzteile** (nt pl) *spares*
**Erste Hilfe** (f) *first aid*
**erster** *first;* **erster Klasse** *first*
  *class;* **erste Stock** (m) *first floor*
**es** *it*
**Essen** (nt) *food, meal;*
  **essen** *to eat*
**Essig** (m) *vinegar*
**Etikett** (nt) *label*
**etwa: etwa 16** *about 16*
**etwas** *something*

# F

**Faden** (m) *string (cord)*
**Fahne** (f) *flag*
**Fähre** (f) *ferry*
**fahren** *to drive, go (travel)*
**Fahrer(in)** (m/f) *driver*
**Fahrgast** (m) *passenger*
**Fahrplan** (m) *timetable*
  *(train, bus)*
**Fahrpreis** (m) *fare*
**Fahrrad** (nt) *bicycle*
**Fahrstuhl** (m) *lift (in building)*
**Fahrt** (f) *journey*
**Fahrzeug** (nt) *vehicle*
**fair** *fair (just)*
**falsch** *wrong*
**Familie** (f) *family*
**Fan** (m) *fan (enthusiast)*
**fantastisch** *fantastic*
**Farbe** (f) *colour, paint*
**Farbfilm** (m) *colour film*
**fast** *almost*
**faul** *lazy*
**Fax** (nt) *fax (document)*
**faxen** *to fax*
**Faxgerät** (nt) *fax machine*
**Februar** *February*
**Feder** (f) *spring (mechanical)*
**Fehler** (m) *mistake*
**Feiertag** (m) *public holiday*
**Feige** (f) *fig*
**Feinkostgeschäft** (nt)
  *delicatessen*
**Feld** (nt) *field*
**Fenster** (nt) *window*
**Fensterladen** (m) *shutter*
**Ferien** (f) *holiday*
**Fernsehen** (nt) *television;*
  **fernsehen** *to watch television*

**Ferse** (f) *heel (foot)*
**fertig** *ready;* **Fertiggerichte**
  (nt pl) *ready meals*
**festmachen** *to tie*
**Fett** (nt) *fat*
**feucht** *damp*
**Feuer** (nt) *fire*
**Feuerlöscher** (m)
  *fire extinguisher*
**Feuerwerk** (nt) *fireworks*
**Feuerzeug** (nt) *lighter*
**Feuerzeugbenzin** (nt)
  *lighter fuel*
**Fieber** (nt) *temperature, fever*
**Film** (m) *film, movie*
**Filter** (m) *filter*
**Filterpapier** (nt) *filter papers*
**Finger** (m) *finger*
**Fisch** (m) *fish*
**Fischgeschäft** (nt) *fishmonger's*
**flach** *flat (level)*
**Flasche** (f) *bottle*
**Flaschenöffner** (m)
  *bottle opener*
**Fleisch** (nt) *meat*
**Fliege** (f) *fly (insect)*
**fliegen** *to fly*
**Floh** (m) *flea*
**Flohspray** (nt) *flea spray*
**Flöte** (f) *flute*
**Flug** (m) *flight*
**Flügel** (m) *wing*
**Flughafen** (m) *airport*
**Flughafenbus** (m) *airport bus*
**Fluglinie** (f) *airline*
**Flugnummer** (f)
  *flight number*
**Flugsteig** (m) *gate*
  *(at airport)*
**Flugzeug** (nt) *aircraft*
**Fluss** (m) *river*
**Flut** (f) *high tide*
**Flyer** (m) *leaflet, flyer*
**Fön** (m) *hair dryer*
**Forschungen** (f) *research*
**Foto** (nt) *photograph*
**Fotograf** (m) *photographer*
**fotografieren** *to photograph*
**Fotokopierer** (m) *photocopier*
**Frage** (f) *question*
**Frankreich** *France*
**Franzose** (m) *Frenchman*
**Französin** (f) *Frenchwoman*
**französisch** *French*
**Frau** *Mrs*
**Frau** *Ms*
**Frau** (f) *woman, wife*
**Fräulein** *Miss;*
  **Fräulein!** *waitress!*
**frei** *free*
**Freitag** *Friday*

**Fremdenverkehrsbüro** (nt)
  *tourist office*
**Freund(in)** (m/f) *friend*
**freundlich** *friendly*
**freut mich** *pleased to meet you*
**Friedhof** (m) *cemetery*
**Friseur** (m) *hairdresser's*
**Friseursalon** (m)
  *ladies' hairdresser's*
**Fritten** (m pl) *chips*
**froh** *glad*
**Frost** (m) *frost;*
**Frucht** (f) *fruit;* **Fruchtsaft** (m)
  *fruit juice*
**früh** *early*
**Frühling** (m) *spring (season)*
**Frühstück** (nt) *breakfast*
**fühlen** *to feel (touch)*
**Führer** (m) *guide*
**Führerschein** (m)
  *driving licence*
**Führung** (f) *guided tour*
**Füllung** (f) *filling (in tooth, cake)*
**Fundbüro** (nt) *lost property*
**fünf** *five*
**fünfzehn** *fifteen*
**fünfzig** *fifty*
**funktionieren** *to work*
  *(machine, etc.)*
**für** *for;* **für mich** *for me;*
  **wofür?** *what for?;*
  **für eine Woche**
  *for a week*
**furchtbar** *awful*
**Fuß** (m) *foot;* **Füße**
  (m pl) *feet*
**Fußball** (m) *football*
**Fußboden** (m) *floor (ground)*
**Fußgänger** (m) *pedestrian;*
  **Fußgängerzone** (f)
  *pedestrian zone*

# G

**Gabel** (f) *fork*
**Gang** (m) *aisle*
**ganz** *quite (fully)*
**Garage** (f) *garage (for parking)*
**Garantie** (f) *guarantee*
**garantieren** *to guarantee*
**Garten** (m) *garden*
**Gartenarbeit** (f) *gardening*
**Gartencenter** (nt)
  *garden centre*
**Gärtner(in)** (m/f) *gardener*
**Gaspedal** (nt) *accelerator*
**Gast** (m) *guest*
**Gastgeber(in)** (m/f) *host*
**Gasthaus** (nt) *inn*
**Gebäck** (nt) *pastry*
**Gebäude** (nt) *building*

**geben** to give
**Gebiet** (nt) field of work
**Gebiss** (m) dentures,
  false teeth
**geboren** to be born:
  **ich bin in... geboren**
  I was born in...
**gebraten** fried
**Gebrauch** (m) use
**gebrauchen** to use
**gebrochen** broken (arm, etc.)
**Geburtstag** (m) birthday;
  **Herzlichen Glückwunsch!**
  happy birthday!
**Geburtstagsgeschenk** (nt)
  birthday present
**Geburtstagskarte** (f)
  birthday card
**gedämpft** steamed
**gefährlich** dangerous
**Geflügel** (nt) poultry
**Gefrierschrank** (m) freezer
**gegen** against
**gegenüber** opposite
**gegrillt** grilled
**Geheimzahl** (f) PIN (number)
**gehen** to go, walk;
  **gehen Sie weg!** go away!
**Geige** (f) violin
**Geisteswissenschaften**
  (f pl) humanities
**Geistliche** (m/f) priest
**gekocht** boiled
**gekochte Schinken** (m) ham
**Gel** (nt) gel (hair)
**gelb** yellow
**Geld** (nt) money
**Geldautomat** (m)
  cash machine (ATM)
**Geldschein** (m) banknote
**gelegentlich** occasionally
**Gemüse** (nt) vegetable
**Genehmigung** (f) licence
**genug** enough
**Gepäck** (nt) luggage
**Gepäckablage** (f) luggage rack
**Gepäckausgabe** (f)
  baggage claim
**Gepäckschließfach** (nt)
  left luggage locker
**gerade** just; **es ist gerade**
  **angekommen** it's just arrived
**gerecht** fair (just)
**gern: ich schwimme gern**
  I like swimming
**geröstet** roasted
**Geruch** (m) smell
**Geschäft** (nt) business, shop
**Geschäftsführer**
  (m) manager
**Geschenk** (nt) gift;

**Geschenkpapier** (nt)
  wrapping paper
**Geschichte** (f) history
**geschieden** divorced
**Geschirrspülmaschine** (f)
  dishwasher
**Geschirrtuch** (nt)
  tea towel
**geschlossen** closed
**Geschmack** (m) flavour
**Geschwindigkeit** (f) speed
**Gesicht** (nt) face
**Gespräch** (nt) talk
**gestern** yesterday
**Getränk** (nt) drink
**getrennt** separate(ly);
  **wir leben getrennt**
  we are separated
**Getriebe** (nt) gearbox
**Gewehr** (nt) gun (rifle)
**Gewinn** (m) profits
**Gewitter** (nt) thunderstorm
**gewöhnlich** ordinary,
  usual, usually
**gibt: es gibt...** there is/are...;
  **gibt es...?** is/are there...?
**Gift** (nt) poison
**Gin** (m) gin
**Gitarre** (f) guitar
**Glas** (nt) glass
**glaube: ich glaube ja**
  I think so
**gleiche:** the same; **gleiche**
  **Kleid** the same dress
**Gleis** (nt) platform
**Glocke** (f) bell (church)
**Glück** (nt) luck; **viel Glück!**
  good luck!
**glücklich** happy
**Glühbirne** (f) light bulb
**Gold** (nt) gold
**Grafiker(in)** (m/f) designer
**Gras** (nt) grass
**gratis** free (no charge)
**grau** grey
**grell** loud (colour)
**Grenze** (f) border
**Grill** (m) barbecue, grill
**groß** big, large, tall;
  **größer als** bigger than
**Großbritannien** Great Britain
**Großeltern** (m pl) grandparents
**Großmutter** (f) grandmother
**Großstadt** (f) city
**Großvater** (m) grandfather
**grün** green
**Grund** (m) bottom (sea)
**Gruppe** (f) party (group)
**Gummi** (m) rubber (material)
**Gummiband** (nt) elastic band
**Gummistiefel** (f) wellingtons

**Gurke** (f) cucumber
**Gürtel** (m) belt
**gut** good; **mir ist nicht gut**
  I don't feel well
**gut aussehend** handsome
**Guten Abend** good night
**guten Tag** hello, good day

# H

**Haar** (nt) hair
**Haarschnitt** (m) haircut
**Haarspray** (nt) hair spray
**Haarspülung** (f) conditioner
**haben** have; **ich habe...** I have...;
  **haben Sie...?** do you have...?
**Hafen** (m) harbour, port
**Hahn** (m) tap
**Hähnchen** (nt) chicken (cooked)
**halb** half; **eine halbe Stunde**
  half an hour
**Halbbruder** (m) half-brother
**Halbpension** half board
**Halbschwester** (f) half-sister
**hallo** hello (on phone); hi
**Hals** (m) neck
**Halsband** (nt) collar
**Halskette** (f) necklace
**Halstabletten** (f pl)
  throat pastilles
**halt!** stop!
**Haltestelle** (f) stop (bus stop)
**Hamburger** (m) hamburger
**Hammer** (m) hammer
**Hamster** (m) hamster
**Hand** (f) hand
**Handbremse** (f) handbrake
**Händedruck** (m) handshake
**Handelsmesse** (f) trade fair
**Handgelenk** (nt) wrist
**Handgepäck** (nt) hand luggage
**Handschuhe** (m) gloves
**Handtasche** (f) handbag
**Handtuch** (nt) towel
**Handy** (nt) mobile phone
**hart** hard
**hässlich** ugly
**Hauptgericht** (nt) main course
**Hauptstraße** (f) main road
**Haus** (nt) house;
  **zu Hause** at home
**Haushaltswaren** (f pl)
  household products
**Hausmeister(in)** caretaker
**Haustiere** (nt pl) pets
**Hautreiniger** (m) skin cleanser
**Hecke** (f) hedge
**Hefter** (m) stapler
**Heftzwecke** (f) drawing pin
**heiß** hot; **mir ist heiß**
  I feel hot

**heißen** to be called;
**wie heißt das?** what's it
called?; **wie heißen Sie?**
what's your name?
**Heißwassergerät** (nt)
water heater
**Heizgerät** (nt) heater
**Heizkörper** (m) radiator
**Heizung** (f) heating
**helfen** to help
**hell** light (not dark)
**Hemd** (nt) shirt
**herauskommen** to get out
**Herd** (m) cooker
**hereinkommen** to come in
**Hering** (m) tent peg
**Herr** Mr
**Herrenfriseur** (m) barber's
**Herrentoilette** (f)
men's toilets
**herunter** down
**Herz** (nt) heart, hearts (cards);
**ich bin herzkrank** I have
a heart condition
**herzlichen Glückwunsch!**
congratulations!
**Heuschnupfen** (m) hay fever
**heute** today; **heute**
**abend** tonight
**Hilfe** (f) help
**hilfreich** useful
**Himbeeren** (f pl) raspberries
**Himmel** (m) sky
**hinter...** behind...
**HIV positiv** HIV positive
**Hobby** (nt) hobby
**hoch** high
**Hochzeit** (f) wedding
**Hochzeitsreise** (f) honeymoon
**Höhle** (f) cave
**holen** to get (fetch)
**Holland** Holland
**Holländer(in)** (m/f)
Dutchman(woman)
**holländisch** Dutch (adj)
**Holz** (nt) wood (material)
**Homöopathie** (f) homeopathy
**Honig** (m) honey
**hören** hear
**Hörgerät** (nt) hearing aid
**Horn** (nt) horn (animal)
**Hose** (f) trousers
**Hosenträger** (nt pl) braces
**hübsch** nice (attractive)
**Huhn** (nt) chicken (animal)
**Hummer** (m) lobster
**Hund** (m) dog
**hundert** hundred
**Hunger** (m) hunger; **ich habe**
**Hunger** I'm hungry
**Hupe** (f) horn (car)

**husten** to cough;
**Husten** (m) cough
**Hut** (m) hat

# I

**ich** I; **ich bin** I am
**ihr(e)** their/her; your
(singular formal)
**im: im Hotel** in the hotel
**Imbiss** (m) snack
**immer** always
**Impfung** (f) vaccination
**in** in; **in der Nacht** at night
**Infektion** (f) infection
**Information** (f) information
**Ingwer** (m) ginger (spice)
**Insekt** (nt) insect
**Insektenmittel** (nt)
insect repellent
**Insel** (f) island
**interessant** interesting
**Internet** (nt) internet
**intravenöse Infusion** (f)
intravenous drip
**Ire** (m) Irishman
**irgendwie** somehow
**irgendwo** somewhere
**Irin** (f) Irishwoman
**irisch** Irish
**Irland** Ireland
**ist** is; **er/sie/es ist...**
he/she/it is...
**Italien** Italy
**Italiener(in)** (m/f) Italian
**italienisch** Italian (adj)

# J

**ja** yes
**Jacke** (f) jacket
**Jahr** (nt) year
**Jahrmarkt** (m) fair, funfair
**Jalousie** (f) blinds
**Januar** January
**Jazz** (m) jazz
**Jeans** (f) jeans
**jeder** each, every, everyone
**jemand** somebody
**jetzt** now
**joggen** to jog;
**joggen gehen**
to go for a jog
**Jogurt** (m) yoghurt
**Jucken** (nt) itch
**Jugendherberge** (f)
youth hostel
**Juli** July
**Junge** (m) boy
**Juni** June
**Juweliergeschäft** (nt) jeweller's

# K

**Kabelfernsehen** (nt)
cable TV
**Kacheln** (f pl) tiles
**Kaffee** (m) coffee;
**Kaffee ohne Milch**
black coffee
**Käfig** (m) cage
**Kai** (m) quay
**Kalbfleisch** (nt) veal
**kalt** cold (adj);
**mir ist kalt** I am cold
**Kamera** (f) camera
**Kamm** (m) comb
**Kanada** Canada
**Kanadier(in)** (m/f)
Canadian (person)
**kanadisch** Canadian (adj)
**Kanal** (m) canal (m)
English Channel
**Kanaltunnel** (m)
Channel Tunnel
**Kaninchen** (nt) rabbit
**kann ich... haben?**
can I have...?
**Kante** (f) side (edge)
**Kanu** (nt) canoe
**kaputt** broken (machine, etc.)
**Karo** diamonds (cards)
**Karotte** (f) carrot
**Karte** (f) card, ticket;
**Kartenspiel** (nt)
pack of cards
**Kartoffel** (f) potato
**Käse** (m) cheese
**Kasse** (f) box office, checkout
**Kassette** (f) cassette
**Kassettenrecorder** (m)
cassette player
**Kassierer(in)** cashier
**Kater** (m) hangover
**Katze** (f) cat
**kaufen** to buy
**Kaufhaus** (nt)
department store
**Kaugummi** (m) chewing gum
**Kaution** (f) deposit
**Kehle** (f) throat
**kehren** to sweep
**Keilriemen** (m) fan belt
**kein** not any;
**ich habe kein Geld**
I don't have any money
**keine Ursache** you're welcome
**Keller** (m) cellar
**Kellnerin** (f) waitress
**kennen** to know (to be
acquainted with)
**Kerze** (f) candle
**Kilo** (nt) kilo

**Kilometer** (m) *kilometre*
**Kind** (nt) *child*
**Kinder** *children*
**Kinderbett** (nt) *cot*
**Kindersitz** (m) *car seat*
**Kinderstation** (f)
    *children's ward*
**Kinderwagen** (m) *pram*
**Kino** (nt) *cinema*
**Kirche** (f) *church*
**Kirmes** (f) *fair, funfair*
**Kirsche** (f) *cherry*
**Kissen** (nt) *cushion*
**klar** *clear*
**Klasse** (f) *class*
**klassische Musik** (f)
    *classical music*
**Klavier** (nt) *piano*
**Kleid** (nt) *dress*
**Kleider** (nt pl) *clothes*
**Kleiderbügel** (m) *coat hanger*
**Kleiderschrank** (m) *wardrobe*
**klein** *little, small*
**Kleingeld** (nt) *change (money)*
**kleinschneiden** *to chop, cut*
**Klempner(in)** (m/f) *plumber*
**Klimaanlage** (f) *air conditioning*
**Klingel** (f) *(door) bell*
**Klinke** (f) *handle (door)*
**Klub** (m) *club*
**klug** *clever*
**Knie** (nt) *knee*
**Knoblauch** (m) *garlic*
**Knöchel** (m) *ankle*
**Knochen** (m) *bone*
**Knopf** (m) *button*
**Koch** (m) *cook*
**kochen** *to boil, cook*
**Kochtopf** (m) *saucepan*
**Köder** (m) *bait*
**Koffer** (m) *suitcase;*
    **Kofferkuli** (m) *luggage trolley*
**Kofferraum** (m) *boot (car)*
**Kohl** (m) *cabbage*
**Kolben** (m) *piston*
**Köln** *Cologne*
**komisch** *funny*
**kommen** *to come;* **ich komme
    aus...** *I come from...;* **kommen
    Sie her!** *come here!*
**Kommode** (f) *chest of drawers*
**kompliziert** *complicated*
**Konditorei** (f) *cake shop*
**Kondom** (nt) *condom*
**Konferenz** (f) *conference*
**Konferenzzimmer** (nt)
    *conference room*
**Konfitüre** (f) *jam*
**können Sie...?** *can you...?*
**Konsulat** (nt) *consulate*
**Kontaktlinsen** (f) *contact lenses*

**Konzert** (nt) *concert*
**Kopf** (m) *head*
**Kopfhörer** (m) *headphones*
**Kopfkissen** (nt) *pillow*
**Kopfsalat** (m) *lettuce*
**Kopfschmerzen** (f) *headache*
**Kopftuch** (nt) *headscarf*
**Korb** (m) *basket*
**Korken** (m) *cork*
**Korkenzieher** (m) *corkscrew*
**Körper** (m) *body*
**Korridor** (m) *corridor*
**Kosmetika** (f) *cosmetics*
**kosten** *to cost;* **was kostet das?**
    *what does it cost?*
**kostenlos** *free (no charge)*
**Kostenvoranschlag** (m) *estimate*
**Kotelett** (nt) *chop (food)*
**Krabbe** (f) *crab*
**Krabben** (f pl) *prawns*
**Kragen** (m) *collar*
**Krampf** (m) *cramp*
**krank** *ill, sick*
**Krankenhaus** (nt) *hospital*
**Krankenpfleger** (m) *nurse (man)*
**Krankenschwester** (f)
    *nurse (woman)*
**Krankenwagen** (m) *ambulance*
**Krawatte** (f) *tie*
**Krebs** (m) *crayfish*
**Kreditkarte** (f) *credit card*
**Kreuz** (nt) *clubs (cards)*
**Kreuzfahrt** (f) *cruise*
**Krieg** (m) *war*
**Krücken** (f pl) *crutches*
**Küche** (f) *kitchen*
**Kuchen** (m) *cake*
**kühl** *cool*
**Kühler** (m) *radiator (car)*
**Kühlschrank** (m) *fridge*
**Kunde** (m) *client*
**Kunst** (f) *art*
**Kunstgalerie** (f) *art gallery*
**Künstler(in)** (m/f) *artist*
**Kupplung** (f) *clutch*
**Kurort** (m) *spa*
**kurz** *short*
**Kusine** (f) *cousin (female)*

## L

**Lächeln** (nt) *smile;*
    **lächeln** *to smile*
**lachen** *to laugh*
**Lachs** (m) *salmon*
**Ladegerät** (nt) *charger*
**Lagerfeuer** (nt) *campfire*
**Lamm** (nt) *lamb (animal)*
**Lammfleisch** (nt) *lamb (meat)*
**Lampe** (f) *lamp*
**Lampenschirm** (m) *lampshade*

**Land** (nt) *country, land*
**landen** *to land*
**Landkarte** (f) *map (of country)*
**lang** *long*
**Länge** (f) *length*
**langsam** *slow*
**langweilig** *boring*
**Laptop** (m) *laptop (computer)*
**Lastwagen** (m) *lorry*
**laufen** *to run*
**Läufer** (m) *rug (mat)*
**laut** *loud, noisy*
**Leben** (nt) *life*
**Lebensmittelgeschäft** (nt)
    *grocer's*
**Lebensmittelvergiftung** (f)
    *food poisoning*
**Leber** (f) *liver*
**lecker** *nice (to eat)*
**Leder** (nt) *leather*
**ledig** *single (unmarried)*
**leer** *empty*
**Leerung** (f) *collection (postal)*
**legen** *to put*
**Lehrer(in)** *teacher*
**Leiche** (f) *body (corpse)*
**leicht** *easy, light (not heavy)*
**Leid: es tut mir Leid** *I'm sorry*
**leihen** *to hire*
**Leim** (m) *glue*
**Leine** (f) *lead*
**Lenkrad** (nt) *steering wheel*
**lernen** *to learn*
**Leselampe** (f) *reading lamp*
**lesen** *to read*
**letzter** *last (final);*
    **letzte Woche** *last week*
**Leute** (m pl) *people*
**Licht** (nt) *light*
**lieb** *dear (person)*
**Liebe** (f) *love*
**lieben** *to love;* **ich mag lieber...**
    *I prefer...*
**Lied** (nt) *song*
**Lieferung** (f) *delivery*
**Liegestuhl** (m) *deck chair*
**Likör** (m) *liqueur*
**lila** *purple*
**Limette** (f) *lime (fruit)*
**Limonade** (f) *lemonade*
**Lineal** (nt) *ruler*
    *(for drawing)*
**links** *left (not right);*
    **linke Seite** *left side*
**Linse** (f) *lens*
**Lippen-Fettstift** (m) *lip salve*
**Lippenstift** (m) *lipstick*
**Liste** (f) *list*
**Liter** (m) *litre*
**Locken** (f pl) *curls*
**Löffel** (m) *spoon*

**Lounge** (f) *lounge (in hotel)*
**Luft** (f) *air*
**Luftmatratze** (f) *air mattress*
**Luftpost** (f) *airmail*
**Lutscher** (m) *lollipop*
**Luxemburg** *Luxembourg*

# M

**machen** *to make;* **macht nichts**
*it doesn't matter*
**Mädchen** (nt) *girl*
**Magen** (m) *stomach;*
**Magenschmerzen** (f)
*stomachache;*
**Magenverstimmung** (f)
*indigestion*
**Mail** (f) *e-mail;* **Mail Adresse** (f)
*e-mail address*
**Make-up** (nt) *make-up*
**Maler(in)** *decorator*
**Manager(in)** *executive*
**manchmal** *sometimes*
**Mandarine** (f) *tangerine*
**Mann** (m) *man, husband*
**Manschettenknöpfe** (m pl)
*cufflinks*
**Mantel** (m) *coat*
**Margarine** (f) *margarine*
**Markt** (m) *market*
**Marmelade** (f) *jam*
**Marmor** (m) *marble*
**März** *March*
**Maskara** (nt) *mascara*
**Matratze** (f) *mattress*
**Mauer** (f) *wall (outside)*
**Maus** (f) *mouse*
**Mechaniker(in)** *mechanic*
**Medikamente** (f) *medication*
**Medizin** (f) *medicine*
**Meer** (nt) *sea;* **Meeresfrüchte**
(f pl) *seafood, shellfish*
**Mehl** (nt) *flour*
**mehr** *more;* **Mehrgepäck** (nt)
*excess baggage*
**mehrere** *several*
**mein(e)** *my*
**Melone** (f) *melon*
**Messe** (f) *mass (church)*
**Messer** (nt) *knife*
**Metzgerei** (f) *butcher's*
**mieten** *to rent*
**Mikrowelle** (f) *microwave*
**Milch** (f) *milk*
**Million** *million*
**eine Million** *one million*
**Mineralwasser** (nt)
*mineral water*
**Minute** (f) *minute*
**mir: es gehört mir** *it's mine*
**mit** *with*

**Mittag** (m) *midday;*
**Mittagessen** (nt) *lunch*
**Mitte** (f) *centre, middle;*
**in der Mitte** *in the middle*
**Mitternacht** *midnight*
**Mittwoch** *Wednesday*
**Möbel** (f) *furniture*
**Mobiltelefon** (nt) *mobile phone*
**möchten Sie...?**
*would you like...?*
**Mode** (f) *fashion*
**Modem** (nt) *modem*
**moderne Architektur** (f)
*modern architecture*
**möglich** *possible;*
**so bald wie möglich**
*as soon as possible*
**Möhre** (f) *carrot*
**Molkereiprodukte**
(nt pl) *dairy products*
**Monat** (m) *month*
**Mond** (m) *moon*
**Monitor** (m) *monitor*
**Montag** *Monday*
**Moped** (nt) *moped*
**Morgen** (m) *morning;* **am
Morgen** *in the morning;*
**morgen** *tomorrow*
**Motor** (m) *engine (motor)*
**Motorboot** (nt) *motorboat*
**Motorhaube** (f) *bonnet (car)*
**Motorrad** (nt) *motorbike*
**Mountain-Bike** (nt)
*mountain bike*
**müde** *tired*
**Mülleimer** (f) *litter bin*
**Müllsack** (m) *bin liner*
**Mülltonne** (f) *dustbin*
**München** *Munich*
**Mund** (m) *mouth*
**Münze** (f) *coin*
**Muschel** (f) *shell*
**Muscheln** (f pl) *mussels*
**Museum** (nt) *museum*
**Musik** (f) *music;*
**Musikanlange** (f) *music
system;* **Musikinstrument** (nt)
*musical instrument*
**Musiker(in)** (f) *musician*
**mussen** *to have to (must);*
**ich muss...** *I must...*
**Mutter** (f) *mother; nut (for bolt)*
**Mütze** (f) *cap (hat)*

# N

**nach** *after, towards;* **nach
England** *to England*
**Nachname** (m) *surname*
**Nachricht** (f) *message*
**Nachrichten** *news*

**nächster** *next;*
**nächste Woche** *next week*
**Nacht** (f) *night*
**Nachthemd** (nt) *nightdress*
**Nachtisch** (m) *desserts*
**Nachtklub** (m) *nightclub*
**Nachtportier** (m) *night porter*
**Nachttisch** (m) *bedside table*
**Nadel** (f) *needle*
**Nagel** (m) *nail (metal, finger);*
**Nagelfeile** (f) *nailfile;*
**Nagellack** (m) *nail polish;*
**Nagelzwicker** (m)
*nail clippers*
**nah** *close, near;* **nahe der Tür**
*near the door;* **in der
Nähe von London**
*near London*
**nähen** *to sew*
**Name** (m) *name*
**Nase** (f) *nose*
**naß** *wet*
**Nebel** (m) *fog*
**neben** *beside*
**Neffe** (m) *nephew*
**Negativ** (nt) *negative (photo)*
**nehmen** *take*
**nein** *no (response)*
**neu** *new*
**neun** *nine*
**neunzehn** *nineteen*
**neunzig** *ninety*
**Neuseeland** *New Zealand*
**Neuseeländer(in)** (m/f)
*New Zealander*
**nicht** *not;*
**nicht so viel** *not so much;*
**nicht viele** *not many*
**Nichte** (f) *niece*
**nichts** *nothing*
**nie** *never*
**Niederlande: die Niederlande**
*the Netherlands*
**niedrig** *low*
**Niere** (f) *kidney*
**nirgendwo** *nowhere*
**noch ein** *another one;*
**noch einen Kaffee,
bitte** *another coffee, please*
**nochmal** *again;*
**nochmal dasselbe, bitte**
*same again, please*
**noch nicht** *not yet*
**Nockenwelle** (f) *camshaft*
**Norden** (m) *north*
**Nordirland** *Northern Ireland*
**Nordsee: die Nordsee**
*North Sea*
**Notausgang** (m) *emergency exit*
**Notbremse** (f) *emergency brake*
**Notfall** (m) *emergency*

**nötig: das ist nicht nötig**
*there's no need*
**Notizblock** (m) *notepad*
**Notizbuch** (nt) *notebook*
**notwendig** *necessary*
**November** *November*
**Nudeln** (f) *pasta*
**Nummer** (f) *number;*
**Nummernschild** (nt)
*number plate*
**nur** *just, only*
**Nuss** (f) *nut* (fruit)

# O

**ob** *whether*
**oben** *up;*
**nach oben** *upwards;*
**da oben** *up there*
**Ober** (m) *waiter;*
**Herr Ober!** *waiter!*
**Obst** (nt) *fruit*
**oder** *or*
**offen** *open* (adj)
**öffentlich** *public*
**öffnen** *to open*
**Öffnungszeiten**
*opening times*
**oft** *often*
**ohne** *without*
**ohnmächtig werden**
*to faint*
**Ohr** (nt) *ear;*
**Ohren** (nt pl) *ears*
**Ohrringe** (m pl) *earrings*
**okay** *OK*
**Oktober** *October*
**Öl** (nt) *oil*
**Olive** (f) *olive*
**Omelette** (nt) *omelette*
**Onkel** (m) *uncle*
**Oper** (f) *opera*
**Operation** (f) *operation*
**Operationssaal** (m)
*operating theatre*
**Orange** (f) *orange* (fruit);
**orange** *orange* (colour)
**Orangenmarmelade** (f)
*marmalade*
**Orangensaft** (m)
*orange juice*
**Orchester** (nt) *orchestra*
**Ort** (m) *place*
(town, etc.)
**Osten** (m) *east*
**Österreich** *Austria*
**Österreicher(in)** (m/f)
*Austrian* (person);
**österreichisch**
*Austrian* (adj)
**Ostsee** (f) *Baltic Sea*

# P

**Paar** (nt) *pair*
**Packpapier** (m) *wrapping paper*
**Paket** (nt) *package, packet, parcel*
**Palast** (m) *palace*
**Panne** (f) *breakdown* (car)
**Pantoffeln** (m pl) *slippers*
**Papier** (nt) *paper*
**Paprika** (m) *pepper*
(red/green)
**Paraffin** (nt) *paraffin*
**Parfüm** (nt) *perfume*
**Park** (m) *park*
**parken** *to park;* **Parken
verboten** *no parking*
**Parkplatz** (m) *car park*
**Partei** (f) *party* (political,
celebration)
**Pass** (m) *passport*
**Passagier** (m) *passenger*
**passen Sie auf!** *be careful!*
**Passkontrolle** (f)
*passport control*
**Passwort** (nt) *password*
**peinlich** *embarrassing*
**Penizillin** (nt) *penicillin*
**perfekt** *perfect*
**Perle** (f) *pearl*
**Petersilie** (f) *parsley*
**Pfannkuchen** (m) *pancake*
**Pfeffer** (m) *pepper* (spice)
**Pfefferminzbonbons**
(f) *peppermints*
**Pfeife** (f) *pipe* (for smoking)
**Pfirsich** (m) *peach*
**Pflanze** (f) *plant*
**Pflaster** (nt) *plaster* (for cut)
**Pforte** (f) *gate* (garden gate)
**Pfund** (nt) *pound*
(money, weight)
**Picknick** (nt) *picnic*
**Pik** *spades* (cards)
**Pilot(in)** (m/f) *pilot*
**Pilz** (m) *mushroom*
**Pinsel** (m) *paint brush*
**Pinzette** (f) *tweezers*
**Pistole** (f) *gun* (pistol)
**Plastik** (nt) *plastic*
**Plastiktüte** (f) *plastic bag*
**Platten** (m) *flat tyre*
**Platz** (m) *place, square*
(in town)
**Plätzchen** (nt) *biscuit*
**Pole** (m) *Pole* (man)
**Polen** *Poland*
**Polin** (f) *Pole* (woman)
**Politik** (f) *politics*
**Polizei** (f) *police*
**Polizeibericht** (m)
*police report*

**Polizeirevier** (nt)
*police station*
**Polizist(in)** (m/f)
*police officer*
**polnisch** *Polish*
**Pommes** (m pl) *chips*
**Popmusik** (f) *pop music*
**Porrée** (m) *leeks*
**Portemonnaie** (nt) *purse*
**Portier** (m) *porter* (hotel)
**Portwein** (m) *port* (drink)
**Porzellan** (nt) *china*
**Post** (f) *mail, post*
**Postamt** (nt) *post office*
**Poster** (nt) *poster*
**Postkarte** (f) *postcard*
**Postleitzahl** (f) *postcode*
**Preis** (m) *price*
**prima!** *great!*
**privat** *private*
**pro** *per;* **pro Nacht** *per night*
**Problem** (nt) *problem*
**Professor(in)** (m/f) *professor*
**prost!** *cheers!*
**Prothese** (f) *dentures,*
*false teeth*
**Puder** (m) *powder* (cosmetics),
*talcum powder*
**Pullover** (m) *jumper*
**Pulver** (nt) *powder*
**Pulverkaffee** (m) *instant coffee*
**Pumpe** (f) *pipe* (for water)
**Puppe** (f) *doll*
**Putzfrau** (f) *cleaner*

# Q, R

**Quadrat** (nt) *square* (shape)
**Qualität** (f) *quality*
**Qualle** (f) *jellyfish*
**Quittung** (f) *receipt*
**Rad** (nt) *wheel*
**radfahren** *to cycle*
**Radiergummi** (m)
*rubber* (eraser)
**Radieschen** (nt) *radish*
**Radio** (nt) *radio*
**Rang** (m) *circle*
**Rasen** (m) *lawn*
**Rasenmäher** (m) *lawnmower*
**Rasiercreme** (f) *shaving foam*
**rasieren: sich rasieren**
*to shave*
**Rasierklingen** (f pl)
*razor blades*
**Rasierwasser** (nt) *aftershave*
**Rathaus** (nt) *town hall*
**Ratte** (f) *rat*
**Rauch** (m) *smoke*
**rauchen** *to smoke*
**Raum** (m) *room* (space)

**Rechen** (m) *rake*
**Rechner** (m) *calculator*
**Rechnung** (f) *bill, invoice*
**recht (gut)** *fairly (good)*
**rechts** *right* (direction); **rechte Seite** (f) *right side*
**Rechtsanwalt/ Rechtsanwältin** (m/f) *lawyer*
**reden** *to talk*
**Regen** (m) *rain*
**Regenmantel** (m) *raincoat*
**Regenschirm** (m) *umbrella*
**Regierung** (f) *government*
**reich** *rich*
**reif** *ripe*
**Reifen** (m) *tyre*
**Reifenpanne** (f) *puncture*
**Reinigung** (f) *dry cleaner*
**Reis** (m) *rice*
**Reise** (f) *journey*
**Reisebüro** (nt) *travel agency*
**Reiseführer** (m) *guidebook*
**Reiseleiter(in)** (m/f) *tour guide*
**Reisescheck** (m) *traveller's cheque*
**Reißnagel** (m) *drawing pin*
**Reißverschluß** (m) *zip*
**Rekord** (m) *record* (sporting, etc.)
**Religion** (f) *religion*
**Reservierung** (f) *reservation*
**Rest** (m) *rest* (remainder)
**Restaurant** (nt) *restaurant*
**Rettich** (m) *radish*
**Rezept** (nt) *prescription*
**Rhabarber** (m) *rhubarb*
**richtig** *right (correct)*
**riechen** *to smell*;
  **Das riecht gut** *that smells good*
**Riegel** (m) *bolt (on door)*
**Rindfleisch** (nt) *beef*
**Ring** (m) *ring* (jewellery)
**Rock** (m) *skirt; rock (music)*
**Rohr** (nt) *pipe (for water)*
**Rollstuhl** (m) *wheelchair*
**Rollstuhlfahrer** (m) *wheelchair access*
**Rolltreppe** (f) *escalator*
**Roman** (m) *novel*
**Röntgenabteilung** (f) *x-ray department*
**Röntgenaufnahme** (f) *x-ray*
**rosa** *pink*
**Rose** (f) *rose*
**Rosinen** (f pl) *raisins*
**rot** *red*
**Rubin** (m) *ruby (gem)*
**Rücken** (m) *back (body)*
**Rückfahrkarte** (f) *return ticket*

**Rücklichter** (f pl) *rear lights*
**Rucksack** (m) *rucksack*
**Rückseite** (f) *back (not front)*
**rufen** *to shout*
**ruhig** *quiet*
**Ruinen** (f pl) *ruins*
**Rum** (m) *rum*
**rund** *round (circular)*
**Rundreise** (f) *tour*

## S

**sagen** *to say*;
  **was haben Sie gesagt?** *what did you say?*;
  **wie sagt man...?** *how do you say...?*
**Sahne** (f) *cream (for cake, etc.)*
**Saite** (f) *string (guitar, etc.)*
**Salami** (f) *salami*
**Salat** (m) *salad*
**Salbe** (f) *ointment*
**Salz** (nt) *salt*
**Sammlung** (f) *collection (stamps, etc.)*
**Samstag** *Saturday*
**Sand** (m) *sand*
**Sandalen** (f pl) *sandals*
**Sandwich** (nt) *sandwich*
**Satellitenfernsehen** (nt) *satellite TV*
**satt: ich bin satt** *I'm full (up)*
**sauber** *clean*
**Sauna** (f) *sauna*
**Schach** *chess*
**Schachtel** (f) *box, packet*;
  **Schachtel Pralinen** (f) *box of chocolates*
**Schaffner** (m) *conductor (bus)*
**Schal** (m) *scarf*
**Schallplatte** (f) *record (music)*
**Schallplattengeschäft** (nt) *record shop*
**Schalter** (m) *switch; ticket kiosk*
**Schaltknüppel** (m) *gear lever*
**Schauer** (m) *shower (rain)*
**Schaumfestiger** (m) *mousse (for hair)*
**Scheck** (m) *cheque*
**Scheckheft** (nt) *chequebook*
**Scheckkarte** (f) *cheque card*
**Scheinwerfer** (m pl) *headlights*
**Scheitel** (m) *parting (hair)*
**Schere** (f) *scissors*
**Schiff** (nt) *boat, ship*
**Schild** (nt) *sign*
**Schlaf** (m) *sleep*
**Schlafanzug** (m) *pyjamas*
**schlafen** *to sleep*
**Schlaflosigkeit** (f) *insomnia*

**Schlafsack** (m) *sleeping bag*
**Schlaftablette** (f) *sleeping pill*
**Schlafzimmer** (nt) *bedroom*
**Schlange** (f) *queue*
**Schlauch** (m) *inner tube*
**schlecht** *bad, poor (quality)*
**schlechter** *worse*
**schlechtester** *worst*
**schleudern** *to skid*
**schließen** *to close*
**Schlitten** (m) *sledge, toboggan*
**Schlittschuhe** *ice skates*;
  **Schlittschuh laufen gehen** *to go ice-skating*
**Schloss** (nt) *castle*
**Schlüssel** (m) *key*
**Schlussverkauf** (m) *sale (at reduced prices)*
**Schmerz** (m) *ache, pain*
**Schmerztablette** (f) *painkiller*
**Schmuck** (m) *jewellery*
**schmutzig** *dirty*
**Schnee** (m) *snow*
**schneiden** *to cut*
**schnell** *fast, quick*
**Schnellimbiss** (m) *take-away*
**Schnitt** (m) *cut*
**Schnuller** (m) *dummy (for baby)*
**Schnurrbart** (m) *moustache*
**Schnürsenkel** (m pl) *shoelaces*
**Schokolade** (f) *chocolate*
**schon** *already, yet*;
  **ist es schon fertig?** *is it ready yet?*
**schön** *beautiful, pretty*
**Schornstein** (m) *chimney*
**Schotte** (m) *Scotsman*
**Schottin** (f) *Scotswoman*
**schottisch** *Scottish*
**Schottland** *Scotland*
**Schrank** (m) *cupboard*
**Schraube** (f) *screw*
**Schraubenschlüssel** (m) *spanner*
**Schraubenzieher** (m) *screwdriver*
**schrecklich** *horrible*
**Schreibmaschine** (f) *typewriter*
**Schreibpapier** (nt) *writing paper*
**Schreiner(in)** *carpenter*
**Schublade** (f) *drawer*
**Schuhcreme** (f) *shoe polish*
**Schuhe** (m pl) *shoes*
**Schuhgeschäft** (nt) *shoe shop*
**Schule** (f) *school*
**Schulter** (f) *shoulder*
**Schüssel** (f) *bowl*
**schwager** *pregnant*
**Schwager** (m) *brother-in-law*

**Schwägerin** (f) *sister-in-law*
**schwarz** *black*
**schwarze Johannisbeere** (f) *blackcurrant*
**Schwarzwald** (m) *Black Forest*
**Schweinefleisch** (nt) *pork*
**Schweiß** (m) *sweat*
**Schweiz: die Schweiz** *Switzerland*
**Schweizer(in)** (m/f) *Swiss (person)*
**schweizerisch** *Swiss* (adj)
**schwer** *heavy, hard* (difficult)
**Schwester** (f) *sister*
**schwierig** *difficult*
**Schwimmbad** (nt) *swimming pool*
**Schwimmen** (nt) *swimming*; **schwimmen** *to swim*
**Schwimmflossen** (f pl) *flippers*
**schwitzen** *to sweat*
**schwul** *gay* (homosexual)
**sechs** *six*
**sechzehn** *sixteen*
**sechzig** *sixty*
**See** (m) *lake*
**Segelboot** (nt) *sailing boat*
**Segeln** (nt) *sailing*
**sehen** *to see*; **ich kann nichts sehen** *I can't see*
**sehr** *very*
**Seide** (f) *silk*
**Seife** (f) *soap*
**Seil** (nt) *rope*
**sein(e)** *his*
**Seite** (f) *page, side*
**Sekratär(in)** (m/f) *secretary*
**Sekunde** (f) *second* (time)
**selbständig** *self-employed*
**selten** *rare* (uncommon)
**Seminar** (nt) *seminar*
**Senf** (m) *mustard*
**September** *September*
**Serviette** (f) *napkin, serviette*
**Sessel** (m) *armchair*
**setzen** *put*
**Shampoo** (nt) *shampoo*
**Sherry** (m) *sherry*
**Shorts** (f) *shorts*
**sicher** *safe, sure*; **Sicherheitsgurt** (m) *seat belt*; **Sicherheitsnadel** (f) *safety pin*
**Sie** *you* (singular, formal); **sie** *she/they*
**sieben** *seven*
**siebzehn** *seventeen*
**siebzig** *seventy*
**Silber** (nt) *silver* (metal); **silber** *silver* (colour)

**sind: wir/sie/Sie sind;** *we/they/you* (formal) *are*
**Singen** (nt) *singing*; **singen** *to sing*
**Sirup** (m) *syrup*
**Sitz** (m) *seat*
**Skandinawien** *Scandinavia*
**Skibindung** (f) *ski binding*
**Skier** (m pl) *skis*
**Ski fahren** *to ski*; **Skifahren gehen** *to go skiing*
**Skilift** (m) *ski lift*
**Skistiefel** (m pl) *ski boots*
**Skistöcke** (m pl) *ski sticks*
**Skiurlaubsort** (m) *ski resort*
**Smaragd** (m) *emerald*
**so** *like this, so*
**Socken** (f pl) *socks*
**Sodawasser** (nt) *soda water*
**Sofa** (nt) *sofa*
**sofort** *immediately*
**Sohn** (m) *son*
**Sonderangebot** (nt) *bargain*
**Sonne** (f) *sun*
**sonnenbaden** *to sunbathe*
**Sonnenbrand** (m) *sunburn*
**Sonnenbrille** *sunglasses*
**Sonnenöl** (nt) *suntan lotion*
**Sonnenschirm** (m) *sunshade*
**sonnig** *sunny*
**Sonntag** *Sunday*
**sorgfältig** *careful*
**Soße** (f) *sauce*
**Souvenir** (nt) *souvenir*
**sowohl... als auch...** *both... and...*
**spät** *late*
**Spaten** (m) *spade* (shovel)
**später** *later*
**spazieren gehen** *to go for a walk*
**Spaziergang** (m) *walk* (stroll)
**Speck** (m) *bacon*
**Speisekarte** (f) *menu*
**Speiseraum** (m) *dining room*
**Spiegel** (m) *mirror*
**Spiel** (nt) *match* (sport)
**spielen** *to play*
**Spielzeug** (nt) *toy*
**Spinat** (m) *spinach*
**Spinne** (f) *spider*
**Spitze** (f) *lace; tip* (end)
**Sport** (m) *sport*; **Sportzentrum** (nt) *sports centre*
**Sportwagen** (m) *pushchair*
**Sprache** (f) *language*
**Sprachführer** (m) *phrase book*
**sprechen** *to speak*; **sprechen Sie Englisch?** *do you speak English?*;

**ich spreche kein Deutsch** *I don't speak German*
**Spritze** (f) *injection, syringe*
**sprudelnd** *fizzy*
**Sprung** (m) *dive*
**Sprungbett** (nt) *diving board*
**Spülmittel** (nt) *washing-up liquid*
**stabil** *strong, stable* (material)
**Stadion** (nt) *stadium*
**Stadt** (f) *town, city*
**Stadtplan** (m) *town plan, map*
**Stadtrand** (m) *suburbs*
**Stadtzentrum** (nt) *city/city centre*
**Stand** (m) *stand*
**Standlicht** (nt) *sidelights*
**Star** (m) *star* (film)
**stark** *strong* (person, drink)
**Start** (m) *start*
**Start-und Landebahn** (f) *runway*
**Station** *station* (underground)
**Statue** (f) *statue*
**Stau** (m) *traffic jam*
**Staubsauger** (m) *vacuum cleaner*
**Staubtuch** (nt) *duster*
**Steak** (nt) *steak*
**stechen** *to bite, sting* (insect)
**Stecker** (m) *plug* (electrical)
**Stecknadel** (f) *pin*
**stehlen** *to steal*; **es ist gestohlen worden** *it's been stolen*
**steht: es steht Ihnen** *it suits you*
**Stein** (m) *rock* (stone)
**stellen** *to put*
**Steppdecke** (f) *duvet*
**sterben** *to die*
**Stern** (m) *star*
**Stich** (m) *bite, sting* (by insect)
**stickig** *close* (stuffy)
**Stiefel** (m) *boot* (footwear)
**Stiefmutter** (m) *stepmother*
**Stiefsohn** (m) *stepson*
**Stieftochter** (m) *stepdaughter*
**Stiefvater** (m) *stepfather*
**Stift** (m) *pen*
**still** *quiet*
**stillhalten!** *don't move!*
**Stimme** (f) *voice*
**Stock** (m) *floor* (storey)
**Stoff** (m) *material* (fabric)
**Stöpsel** (m) *plug* (sink)
**Stoßstange** (f) *bumper*
**Strand** (m) *beach*
**Straße** (f) *road, street*
**Straßenbahn** (f) *tram*
**Streichholz** (nt) *match* (light)
**streng** *strong* (taste)
**stricken** *to knit*
**Strickwaren** (f pl) *knitwear*
**Strom** (m) *electricity*

**Stromanschluss** (m) *electrical hook-up*
**Strümpfe** (m pl) *stockings*
**Strumpfhose** (f) *tights*
**Stück** (nt) *piece, slice, play (theatre);* **fünf Euro das Stück** *five euros each*
**Student(in)** (m/f) *student*
**Stuhl** (m) *chair*
**Stunde** (f) *hour, lesson*
**Sturm** (m) *storm*
**Sucher** (m) *viewfinder*
**Südafrika** *South Africa*
**Süden** (m) *south*
**Supermarkt** (m) *supermarket*
**Suppe** (f) *soup*
**süß** *sweet (not sour)*
**Süßigkeit** (f) *sweet (candy)*
**Sweatshirt** (nt) *sweatshirt*
**Synagoge** (f) *synagogue*

# T

**Tabak** (m) *tobacco*
**Tablett** (nt) *tray*
**Tablette** (f) *pill, tablet*
**Tafel Schokolade** (f) *bar of chocolate*
**Tafelwasser** (nt) *still water*
**Tag** (m) *day*
**Tagebuch** (nt) *diary*
**Tagesdecke** (f) *bedspread*
**Tagesordnung** (f) *agenda*
**Tal** (nt) *valley*
**Tampons** (m pl) *tampons*
**Tankstelle** (f) *petrol station*
**Tante** (f) *aunt*
**Tanz** (m) *dance*
**tanzen** *to dance*
**Tasche** (f) *pocket, bag*
**Taschendieb** (m) *pickpocket*
**Taschenlampe** (f) *torch*
**Taschenmesser** (nt) *penknife*
**Taschentücher** (f) *tissues*
**Tasse** (f) *cup*
**Tastatur** (f) *keyboard*
**taub** *deaf*
**tauchen** *to dive*
**tauschen, umtauschen** *to exchange*
**tausend** *thousand*
**Taxi** (nt) *taxi*
**Taxistand** (m) *taxi rank*
**Technik** (f) *engineering*
**Tee** (m) *tea;* **schwarze Tee** *black tea;* **Tee mit Milch** *tea with milk*
**Teilchen** (nt) *danish pastry*
**Telefon** (nt) *telephone*
**Telefonbuch** (nt) *directory*
**telefonieren** *to telephone*

**Telefonkarte** (f) *phonecard*
**Telefonzelle** (f) *telephone box*
**Teller** (m) *plate*
**Temperatur** (f) *temperature*
**Tennis** (nt) *tennis*
**Teppich** (m) *carpet*
**Termin** (m) *appointment*
**Terminal** (nt) *terminal*
**Terrasse** (f) *terrace*
**Tesafilm** (m) *sellotape*
**teuer** *expensive, dear*
**Theater** (nt) *theatre*
**tief** *deep, low (voice)*
**Tiefkühlkost** (f) *frozen foods*
**Tierarzt** (m) *vet*
**Tierpass** (m) *pet passport*
**Tinte** (f) *ink*
**Tisch** (m) *table*
**Toast** (m) *toast*
**Tochter** (f) *daughter*
**Toilette** (f) *toilet*
**Toilettenpapier** (nt) *toilet paper*
**Tomate** (f) *tomato*
**Tomatensaft** (m) *tomato juice*
**Tonic** (nt) *tonic*
**Töpferei** (f) *pottery*
**Tor** (nt) *gate*
**tot** *dead*
**Tourist(in)** *tourist*
**Tradition** (f) *tradition*
**Tragetasche** (f) *plastic bag*
**Trainingsanzug** (m) *track suit*
**Traktor** (m) *tractor*
**trampen** *to hitchhike*
**Trauben** (f pl) *grapes*
**traurig** *sad*
**Treffen** (nt) *meeting*
**Treppe** (f) *stairs, staircase*
**trinken** *to drink*
**Trinkgeld** (nt) *tip (money)*
**Trinkwasser** (nt) *drinking water*
**trocken** *dry*
**Tropfen** (m) *drops*
**Truhe** (f) *chest (furniture)*
**tun** *to do*
**Tunnel** (m) *tunnel*
**Tür** (f) *door*
**Türke** *Turk (man)*
**Türkin** *Turk (woman)*
**Türkei: die Türkei** *Turkey*
**türkisch** *Turkish*
**Turm** (m) *tower*
**Turnschuhe** *trainers*

# U

**U-Bahn** (f) *underground, metro*
**U-Bahnstation** (f) *metro station*
**übel: mir ist übel** *I feel sick*

**über** *over, across, more than*
**überall** *everywhere*
**Überführung** (f) *flyover*
**überfüllt** *crowded*
**übergeben: sich übergeben** *to be sick (vomit)*
**überholen** *to overtake*
**Überlandbus** (m) *coach*
**übersetzen** *to translate*
**Übersetzer(in)** (m/f) *translator*
**Überzelt** (nt) *fly sheet*
**Uhr** (f) *clock, watch*
**um 3 Uhr** *at 3 o'clock*
**Umhängetuch** (nt) *shawl*
**umziehen** *to move (house)*
**umziehen: sich umziehen** *to change (clothes)*
**und** *and*
**Unfall** (m) *accident*
**Unfallstation** (f) *emergency department*
**ungewöhnlich** *unusual*
**Universität** (f) *university*
**Unkraut** (nt) *weeds*
**unmöglich** *impossible*
**unten** *down;* **hier unten** *down here*
**unter...** *below..., under...*
**Untergeschoss** (nt) *basement*
**Unterhaltung** (f) *entertainment*
**Unterhemd** (nt) *vest*
**Unterhose** (f) *underpants*
**Unterkunft** (f) *accommodation*
**Unterrock** (m) *underskirt*
**Untertasse** (f) *saucer*
**Unterwäsche** (f) *underwear*
**Urlaub** (m) *holiday*

# V

**Vanille** (f) *vanilla*
**Vase** (f) *vase*
**Vater** (m) *father*
**Vegetarier(in)** (m/f) *vegetarian (person)*
**vegetarisch** *vegetarian (adj)*
**Ventil** (nt) *valve*
**Ventilator** (m) *fan (ventilator)*
**Verband** (m) *bandage*
**Verbrennung** (f) *burn*
**Vergaser** (m) *carburettor*
**vergessen** *to forget*
**Vergrößerung** (f) *enlargement*
**verheiratet** *married*
**Verhütungsmittel** (nt) *contraceptive*
**verkaufen** *to sell*
**Verkäufer(in)** (m/f) *shopkeeper*
**Verkehr** (m) *traffic*

**Verkehrsbüro** (nt) *tourist office*
**Verlängerungsschnur** (f) *extension lead*
**Verletzung** (f) *injury*
**verlobt** *engaged (couple)*
**Verlobte** (m/f) *fiancé(e)*
**Vermittlung** (f) *operator*
**verriegeln** *to bolt*
**verrückt** *mad*
**verschieden** *different*
**Verschluss** (m) *cap (bottle), shutter (camera)*
**Versicherung** (f) *insurance*
**verspätet** *delayed*
**Verspätung: der Bus hat Verspätung** *the bus is late*
**verstehen** *understand;* **ich verstehe** *I see/I understand;* **ich verstehe nicht** *I don't understand*
**versuchen** *to try*
**Vertrag** (m) *contract*
**Vertreter** (m) *agent*
**Verwandte** (m) *relative*
**Verzeihung!** *sorry! (apology)*
**Vetter** (m) *cousin (male)*
**Video** (nt) *video*
**Videocassette** (f) *video tape*
**Videorecorder** (m) *video recorder*
**viel** *a lot, much*
**vielleicht** *maybe, perhaps*
**vier** *four*
**Viertel** (nt) *quarter*
**vierter** *fourth*
**vierzehn** *fourteen*
**vierzig** *forty*
**Villa** (f) *villa*
**Visitenkarte** (f) *business card*
**Vitamintablette** (f) *vitamin tablet*
**Vogel** (m) *bird*
**Voice-mail** (f) *voicemail*
**Volksmusik** (f) *folk music*
**voll** *busy (bar, etc.), full*
**Vollpension** *full board*
**von** *of*
**vor...** *before..., in front of...*
**vorbei** *over (finished)*
**Vorgesetzte** (m/f) *superior*
**Vorhang** (m) *curtain*
**Vorhängeschloss** (nt) *padlock*
**Vorlesungssaal** (m) *lecture theatre*
**Vorname** (m) *first name*
**Vorspeisen** (f pl) *starters*
**Vortrag** (m) *presentation*

# W

**Wächter** (m) *guard*
**Wagen** (m) *carriage (train)*
**wahr** *true*
**während** *during*
**Wald** (m) *forest*
**Wales** *Wales*
**Waliser(in)** (m) *Welshman/Welshwoman*
**walisisch** *Welsh*
**Wand** (f) *wall (inside)*
**Wandern** (nt) *hiking*
**Wandteppich** (m) *tapestry*
**wann?** *when?*
**war** *was;* **ich war** *I was;* **er/sie/es war** *he/she/it was*
**waren** *were;* **wir/sie waren** *we/they were;* **Sie waren** *you (formal) were*
**warm** *warm*
**warst** *were;* **du warst** *you (informal) were*
**warten** *wait;* **warten Sie!** *wait!*
**Wartesaal** (m) *waiting room (station)*
**Wartezimmer** (nt) *waiting room*
**warum?** *why?*
**was?** *what?;* **was ist das?** *what's that/this?*
**Waschbecken** (nt) *wash basin*
**Wäsche** (f) *laundry (dirty clothes)*
**Wäscheklammer** (f) *clothes peg*
**Wäscherei** (f) *laundry (place)*
**Waschpulver** (nt) *washing powder*
**Waschsalon** (m) *launderette*
**Wasser** (nt) *water;* **Wasser mit Kohlensäure, das Sprudelwasser** *fizzy water;* **Wasser ohne Kohlensäure** *still water*
**Wasserfall** (m) *waterfall*
**Wasserkessel** (m) *kettle*
**Watte** (f) *cotton wool*
**Webseite** (f) *website*
**Wechselkurs** (m) *exchange rate*
**wechseln** *to change (money)*
**Wecker** (m) *alarm clock*
**weder... noch...** *neither... nor...*
**Weg** (m) *path*
**weich** *soft*
**Weihnachten** (nt) *Christmas*
**weil** *because*
**Wein** (m) *wine;* **Weinkarte** (f) *wine list*
**Weinbrand** (m) *brandy*

**weinen** *to cry (weep)*
**weiß** *white*
**weit** *far;* **wie weit ist es?** *how far is it?;* **ist es weit von hier?** *is it far away?*
**welcher?** *which?*
**Welle** (f) *wave*
**wellig** *wavy (hair)*
**weniger** *less*
**wenn** *if*
**wer?** *who?*
**Werkstatt** (f) *car repairs, garage*
**Wertsachen** (f pl) *valuables*
**Wespe** (f) *wasp*
**Westen** (m) *west*
**Wetter** (nt) *weather*
**Whisky** (m) *whisky*
**wie?** *how?;* **wie heißen Sie?** *what's your name?;* **wie spät ist es?** *what's the time?*
**Wien** *Vienna*
**willkommen** *welcome*
**Wimperntusche** (f) *mascara*
**Wind** (m) *wind*
**Windel** (f) *nappy*
**Windschutzscheibe** (f) *windscreen*
**winken** *to wave*
**wir** *we*
**wissen** *to know (a fact);* **ich weiß nicht** *I don't know*
**Witz** (m) *joke*
**wo?** *where?*
**Woche** (f) *week*
**Wodka** (m) *vodka*
**Wohnmobil** (nt) *camper van*
**Wohnung** (f) *apartment, flat*
**Wohnwagen** (m) *caravan*
**Wohnzimmer** (nt) *lounge (in house)*
**Wolldecke** (f) *rug (blanket)*
**Wolle** (f) *wool*
**Wort** (nt) *word*
**Wörterbuch** (nt) *dictionary*
**Wurst** (f) *sausage*

# Z

**Zahl** (f) *number*
**Zahn** (m) *tooth*
**Zahnarzt** (m) *dentist*
**Zahnbürste** (f) *toothbrush*
**Zahnpasta** (f) *toothpaste*
**Zahnschmerzen** (f) *toothache*
**Zäpfchen** (nt) *suppository*
**Zaun** (m) *fence*
**zehn** *ten*
**zehntausend** *ten thousand*
**Zeit** (f) *time*
**Zeitplan** (m) *schedule*
**Zeitschrift** (f) *magazine*

**Zeitung** (f) *newspaper*

**Zeitungsladen** (m)
*newsagent's (shop)*

**Zelt** (nt) *tent*

**Zeltboden** (m) *groundsheet*

**Zeltstange** (f) *tent pole*

**Zentrale** (f) *head office*

**Zentralheizung** (f)
*central heating*

**zerbrochen** *broken* (vase, etc.)

**Zeuge(in)** (m/f) *witness*

**ziehen** *pull*

**ziemlich** *fairly, quite*

**Zigarette** (f) *cigarette*

**Zigarre** (f) *cigar*

**Zimmer** (nt) *room*

**Zimmermädchen** (nt) *maid*

**Zimmerservice** (m)
*room service*

**Zitrone** (f) *lemon*

**Zoll** (m) *Customs*

**zollfrei** *duty-free*

**Zoo** (m) *zoo*

**zu** *too* (excessively)

**Zucker** (m) *sugar*

**Zug** (m) *train*

**zum** *to*; **zum Bahnhof**
*to the station*

**Zündkerze** (f) *spark plug*

**Zündung** (f) *ignition*

**Zunge** (f) *tongue*

**zurückgeben** *to return*
(give back)

**zurückkommen** *to return*
(come back)

**zusammen** *together*

**Zusammenbruch** (m)
*nervous breakdown*

**Zuschlag** (m) *supplement*

**zwanzig** *twenty*

**Zweck** (m) *purpose*; **es hat
keinen Zweck** *it's no use*

**zwei** *two*;
**zwei Einzelbetten** *twin beds*;
**zwei Wochen** *fortnight*

**Zweigstelle** (f) *branch*

**zweiter** *second* (in series);
**zweiter Klasse** *second class*

**Zwiebel** (f) *onion*

**zwischen...** *between...*

**zwölf** *twelve*

# Acknowledgments

The publisher would like to thank the following for their help in the preparation of this book: Edith and Dieter Gollnow for the organization of location photography in Germany; Die Bahn DB, Deutsche Bahn AG, Hannover; Üstra Hannoversche Verkehrsbetriebe AG, Hannover; Raustaurant: Der Gartensaal im Neuen Rathaus, Hannover; Sprengel-Museum Hannover; Polizei-Direktion Hannover; Café An der Martkirche, Hannover; Teestübchen Am Ballhof; Europa-Apotheke, Hannover; Wochenmarkt Gretchenstraße; Magnet Showroom, Enfield; MyHotel, London; Kathy Gammon; Juliette Meeus and Harry.

*Language content for Dorling Kindersley by* **g-and-w publishing**
*Managed by* **Jane Wightwick**
*Editing and additional input:* **Sam Fletcher, Christopher Wightwick**

*Additional design assistance:* **Lee Riches, Fehmi Cömert, Sally Geeve**
*Additional editorial assistance:* **Paul Docherty, Mary Lindsay, Lynn Bresler**
*Picture research:* **Louise Thomas**

## Picture credits

**Key:** *t=top; b=bottom; l=left, r=right; c=centre; A=above; B=below*

p2 **Alamy RF:** Chris Warham; p4/5 **Alamy RF:** Goodshoot tr; p6/7 **Laura Knox:** cl; p10/11 **Alamy RF:** BananaStock cAr, bl; RubberBall cBl; p12/13 **Alamy RF:** John Foxx cAr; RubberBall br; **DK Images:** cl; Steve Shott cBr; **Ingram Image Library:** tr, cr; p14/15 **Alamy RF:** Comstock Images tcr; **Ingram Image Library:** cAl, cl, cBl, cAr, cBr, bcr; p16/17 **Alamy RF:** RubberBall bcr; **Ingram Image Library:** tr; p18/19 **Alamy:** Foodfolio cr; **DK Images:** David Murray tr; Ian O'Leary clB; p22/23 **Alamy RF:** Image Source crA; Think Stock bcl; **DK Images:** cl, Susanna Price br; Magnus Rew tcrB; **Ingram Image Library:** tcr; p24/25 **Alamy:** Archivberlin Fotoagentur GmbH clA, Dave King tcr; p26/27 **Ingram Image Library:** cl; p28/29 **DK Images:** Dave King cr; Stephen Oliver tcr; Matthew Ward bclA; **Ingram Image Library:** bcrA, bcr; p30/31 **Alamy RF:** Comstock Images bcl; **DK Images:** cl, bclA; Andy Crawford crA; p34/35 **Ingram Image Library:** tcr; p36/37 **DK Images:** bcl, bcr; Magnus Rew cl; **Ingram Image Library:** bl; p38/39 **Alamy RF:** Imageshop / Zefa Visual Media cl; p40/41 **Alamy:** Archiv Fotoagentur GmbH bcr; **DK Images:** Dorota and Mariusz Jarymowicz cl; p42/43 **Alamy:** Michael Klinec tcrB; **Alamy RF:** Comstock Images cAr; Goodshoot tcr; Nigel Schermuly: cr; p44/45 Courtesy of **Audi UK** c; p46/47 **Alamy RF:** Imageshop / Zefa Visual Media br; Courtesy of **Audi UK:** tcr; **DK Images:** Dorota and Mariusz Jarymowicz bcl, bcr; **Ingram Image Library:** tclB; Nigel Schermuly: cr; p48/49 **Alamy:** Chris Warham c; **DK Images:** Dorota and Mariusz Jarymowicz bcl; p50/51 **Alamy:** Andre Jenny c; p52/53 **Alamy:** Pat Behnke tcrB; **Alamy RF:** Image Farm Inc cAr; **DK Images:** cl; p54/55 **Alamy:** Jackson Smith bclA; **Alamy RF:** BananaStock bcl; John Foxx c; Image Source cAr; ThinkStock tcr; **DK Images:** Andy Crawford bcl; p56/57 **Alamy RF:** Goodshoot clA; Chris Warham cl; Courtesy of **Audi UK:** bc; **DK Images:** Dorota and Mariusz Jarymowicz tl, clAA; p58/59 **Alamy:** Michael Juno tcr; **Alamy RF:** Brand XPictures cBl, cBBl; Image Source cAAl; **DK Images:** cAl; p60/61 **Alamy:** Robert Harding Picture Library bcr; **Alamy RF:** imagebroker bl; Image Source cAr; **DK Images:** Steve Gorton tcrB; Pia Tryde cAAr; **Ingram Image Library:** cr; p62/63 **DK Images:** Stephen Whitehorn c; p64/65 **Alamy:** Arcaid bcrA; Dennis Hallinan c; **Alamy RF:** GKPhotography cBr; Goodshoot cAAr; Justin Kase tcrB; **DK Images:** Steve Tanner cAr; **Ingram Image Library:** br; p66/67 **Alamy:** Arcaid tl; **Alamy RF:** Image Source cAr; **DK Images:** tr; Stephen Whitehorn bl; **Ingram Image Library:** br; p68/69 **Alamy:** Balearic Pictures cr; **Alamy RF:** Celestial Panoramas cAl; p70/71 **Ingram Image Library:** cr; p72/73 **Alamy RF:** imagebroker tcrB; Image Source cAr; Comstock Images tcr; Elizabeth Whiting & Associates bl; p74/75 **Alamy RF:** Doug Norman bl; **Ingram Image Library:** c; p76/77 **Alamy:** Balearic Pictures cBl; **Alamy RF:** Celestial Panoramas Ltd bcl; p80/81 **Getty:** Taxi / Rob Melnychuk bc; **Ingram Image Library:** cr; **Xerox UK Ltd:** tcr; p82/83 **Alamy:** wildphotos.com tcr; **Alamy RF:** FogStock cAAl; Momentum Creative Group cAl; Shoosh / Up the Res cBl; **Ingram Image Library:** cl; p84/85 **Alamy:** Brand XPictures cr; f1 Online c; **Alamy RF:** image100 bl; SuperStock tr; **Ingram Image Library:** crB; p86/87 **Getty:** Taxi / Rob Melnychuk tc; p90/91 **Alamy RF:** Brand X Pictures tcr; **DK Images:** cl; David Jordan cAr; Stephen Oliver cr; **Ingram Image Library:** cBr; p82/93 **Alamy RF:** Pixland cr; **DK Images:** cl; Guy Ryecart cr; p94/95 **Alamy:** David Kamm cl; Phototake Inc bcl; **Alamy RF:** Comstock Images cr; ImageState Royalty Free bcr; **DK Images:** Stephen Oliver tcr; **Alamy RF:** Pixland br; **DK Images:** tl; **Ingram Image Library:** cr; p98/99 **Alamy:** Bildarchiv Monheim GmbH / Jochen Helle c; **Alamy RF:** ThinkStock br; **DK Images:** Jake Fitzjones bl; Peter Kindersley cr; p100/101 **DK Images:** Steve Gorton tcr; p102/103 **Alamy:** The Garden Picture Library tcr, cAAr; Hortus b; D Hurst tcrB; **Ingram Image Library:** cAr; p104/105 **DK Images:** Paul Bricknell cl(6); Jane Burton bcl; Geoff Dann cl(2); Max Gibbs cl(4); Frank Greenaway cl(3); Dave King cl(1), cAr; Tracy Morgan c(5); p106/107 **Alamy:** The Garden Picture Library br; **DK Images:** Peter Kindersley cr; p108/109 **Alamy RF:** John Foxx tcr; p110/111 **Alamy RF:** RubberBall cr; **DK Images:** Andy Crawford cl; p112/113 **Alamy RF:** Image Source cl; **DK Images:** Dave King bcl; Steve Shott bl; **Ingram Image Library:** bcrA; p114/115 **Alamy:** FogStock tcr; **Alamy RF:** Image Source cAr; Index Stock cAl; p116/117 **Alamy:** The Garden Picture Library cAl; **Alamy RF:** clB; p118/119 **DK Images:** Steve Gorton tcr; **GettyNews:** Giuseppe Cacace c; p120/121 **Alamy:** ImageState / Pictor International cl; Shotfile cBl; **Alamy RF:** Sarkis Images tcr; **DK Images:** bcl; p122/123 **Alamy RF:** BananaStock cA; **Ingram Image Library:** cl; p124/125 **Alamy:** ImageState / Pictor International bclA; Shotfile cBl; **DK Images:** bcl; Paul Bricknell tc(5); Geoff Dann tc(3); Max Gibbs tc(1); Frank Greenaway tc(2); Dave King tc(4); Tracy Morgan tc(6); **Ingram Image Library:** bl; p126/127 **Alamy:** Pat Behnke blA; **Alamy RF:** Image Farm Inc bl; p128 **DK Images.**

*All other images* **Mike Good.**